The Dead Father

M000159423

This book constructs a much needed framework to allow psychoanalysts to consider the difficulties of a generation without a solid anchor in the Father. *The Dead Father: A Psychoanalytic Inquiry* provides a necessary addition to decades of work on the role of the mother in development. The editors bring together world renowned scholars to discuss current observations in their fields, in terms of the Father's changing but essential functions, both in the lives of the individual and collective. Divided into four parts, chapters focus on:

- The Lost Father
- The Father Embodied
- The Father in Theory
- Father Culture.

Exploring the role of the father in individual psychology, everyday interpersonal and social experience and cultural phenomena writ large, this book will be essential reading for psychoanalysts, as well as psychologists, social workers and scholars in the humanities.

Lila J. Kalinich is a Training and Supervising Analyst at the Columbia University Center for Psychoanalytic Training and Research, where she has included Lacan and contemporary philosophy in her teaching for many years. She is also Clinical Professor of Psychiatry at Columbia University College of Physicians and Surgeons, and is in private practice.

Stuart W. Taylor is a member of the faculty of the Columbia University Center for Psychoanalytic Training and Research and is Assistant Clinical Professor of Psychiatry at Columbia University College of Physicians and Surgeons. He is on the faculty of the Department of English and Comparative Literature at Columbia College, where he teaches Freud to undergraduates. He is also in private practice.

The Dead Father

A psychoanalytic inquiry

Edited by Lila J. Kalinich and
Stuart W. Taylor

Routledge
Taylor & Francis Group

LONDON AND NEW YORK

First published 2009
by Routledge
27 Church Road, Hove, East Sussex BN3 2FA

Simultaneously published in the USA and Canada
by Routledge
270 Madison Avenue, New York NY 10016

Routledge is an imprint of the Taylor & Francis Group, an Informa business

© 2009 Selection and editorial matter, Lila J. Kalinich and
Stuart W. Taylor; individual chapters, the contributors

Typeset in Times by
RefineCatch Limited, Bungay, Suffolk
Printed and bound in Great Britain by
TJ International Ltd, Padstow, Cornwall

Paperback cover design by Gerald Myers
Paperback cover image: Sigmund Freud fishing with his son Ernst
near Bad Reichenhall, 1901. Reproduced with permission of the
Estate of A. W. Freud et al., by arrangement with Paterson Marsh Ltd.,
London.

This publication has been produced with paper manufactured to
strict environmental standards and with pulp derived from
sustainable forests.

All rights reserved. No part of this book may be reprinted or
reproduced or utilized in any form or by any electronic,
mechanical, or other means, now known or hereafter
invented, including photocopying and recording, or in any
information storage or retrieval system, without permission in
writing from the publishers.

British Library Cataloguing in Publication Data
A catalogue record for this book is available from the British Library

Library of Congress Cataloging-in-Publication Data
The dead father : a psychoanalytic inquiry / edited by Lila J. Kalinich
and Stuart W. Taylor.
       p. cm.
   Proceedings of a conference held in Apr. 2006.
   Includes bibliographical references.
   ISBN 978–0–415–44994–6 (hardback) – ISBN: 978–0–415–
   44995–3 (pbk.)   1. Father and child – Congresses.   2.
   Psychoanalysis – Congresses.   I. Kalinich, Lila J., 1944–
   II. Taylor, Stuart W., 1959–
   BF723.F35D43 2008
   155.9′24 – dc22

                                                2008014903

ISBN: 978–0–415–44994–6 (hbk)
ISBN: 978–0–415–44995–3 (pbk)

For Ramon, Jessie and David,
and Francesca and Giacomo

with love

Contents

Acknowledgements   ix
List of contributors   x

Introduction   1
LILA J. KALINICH

Prologue   9
STUART W. TAYLOR

PART I
The lost father   21

1 **The construction of the lost father**   23
   ANDRÉ GREEN

2 **Fatherhood revisited: the dead father, fraternal**
   pact and analytic filiation in the work of
   André Green   47
   FERNANDO URRIBARRI

PART II
The father embodied   59

   Introduction   59
   MARIA CRISTINA AGUIRRE

3 **The death of the dead father?**   65
   MARILIA AISENSTEIN

4   A new love for the father   75
    ERIC LAURENT

5   Unmastered remains: fathers in Freud and me   91
    THOMAS W. LAQUEUR

PART III
The father in theory   103

    Introduction   103
    ARNOLD RICHARDS

6   The dead father figure and the symbolization process   111
    CHRISTINE ANZIEU-PREMMEREUR

7   The dead father and the sacrifice of sexuality   121
    ROSINE JOZEF PERELBERG

8   Constructing and deconstructing the conglomerate: thoughts
    about the father in life, in death, and in theory   133
    JAMES M. HERZOG

PART IV
Father culture   145

    Introduction   145
    JOHN P. MULLER

9   A little pedagogy, then and now   153
    EDWARD W. TAYLER

10 The dead but living father, the living but dead father   163
    VINCENT CRAPANZANO

11 A father is beaten to death   175
    JULIA KRISTEVA

    Epilogue   189
    HELEN C. MEYERS

    Index   195

Acknowledgements

With gratitude to those who helped this project along, in ways both large and small: Graciela Abelin-Sas, Bonita D'Amil, Edith Cooper, Roberta Garruccio, Robert Glick, Jonathan House, Joan Jackson, Lawrence Jacobsberg, David Bowen Kalinich, Bonnie Kaufman, Edward Kenny, Gregorio Kohon, Andreas Kraebber, Catherine Maheux, Judy Mars, Donald Meyers, Susan Rogers, John Munder Ross, George Sagi, Jonah Schein, Paul Stepansky, Craig Tomlinson, Joel Whitebook, James Williams, Francesca Zavolta. And abundant thanks to Kate Hawes, Jane Harris, Sarah Gibson and Kate Moysen of Routledge, and Penelope Allport, freelance copy-editor, for their patience and guidance.

Permissions acknowledgements

The editors and publisher are grateful to the following for their permission to reproduce passages from copyright material as follows:

Extract from John Milton, *Areopagitica*, in Merritt Y. Hughes (ed.) *John Milton: Complete Poems and Major Prose*, © 1957, first edition: sixteenth printing, 1973, Cambridge MA, Hackett Publishing Company. All rights reserved. Extract from E. Vinavar (ed.) (1971) *The Works of Sir Thomas Malory*, Oxford, Oxford University Press. By permission of Oxford University Press. Extracts from G. B. Evans (ed.) (1974) *The Riverside Shakespeare*, Boston, Houghton Mifflin Company. Copyright © 1974 by Houghton Mifflin Company. Extract from "In Memory of Sigmund Freud" © 1940 by W. H. Auden and renewed 1968 by W. H. Auden from *Collected Poems* by W. H. Auden. Reprinted by permission of Curtis Brown, Ltd., for World excluding the US and UK. Reprinted by permission Faber and Faber Ltd., for UK and British Commonwealth and electronic rights. Used by permission of Random House, Inc., for USA. Excerpt from *A Thousand Acres* by Jane Smiley © 1991. Published New York, Ballantine Publishing Group. Reproduced by permission Random House, Inc., for World excluding UK and electronic rights and The Friedrich Agency for UK and electronic rights. Excerpt from *The Moor's Last Sigh* by Salman Rushdie © 1995. Published by Pantheon Books, New York (original work published in Great Britain, 1995, by Jonathan Cape, London). Reproduced by permission Random House, Inc., for World excluding UK and electronic rights and The Wylie Agency (UK), Ltd for UK and electronic rights.

Contributors

Maria Cristina Aguirre. PhD in psychoanalysis from the University of Paris VII; Senior Psychologist at Elmhurst Hospital in NYC; Editor of *Lacanian Compass*, an online Lacanian newsletter.

Marilia Aisenstein. Former President of both the Parisian Psychoanalytic Society (IPA) and the Psychoanalytic Institute for Psychosomatic Diseases; currently represents Europe at the IPA executive committee; active in establishing mental health public policy in France.

Christine Anzieu-Premmereur. Director of the Parent–Infant Program at the Columbia University Center for Psychoanalytic Training and Research. Trained in France. On the editorial board of *Revue Française de Psychanalyse*. Author of two books in French on work with babies, children and parents.

Vincent Crapanzano. Distinguished Professor of Comparative Literature and Anthropology at the Graduate Center of the City University of New York. Prolific author of books and articles in diverse areas.

André Green. Psychoanalytic theorist and clinician with a wide international reputation. Member of the Psychoanalytic Society of Paris. Widely published in several psychoanalytic areas. His paper "The Dead Mother" still has wide impact. Most recent work on the work of the "negative" in psychic life.

James M. Herzog. Assistant Professor of Psychiatry at Harvard Medical School. Adjunct Professor of Psychiatry at the University of Hamburg. Training and supervising analyst in adult analysis and supervising analyst in child and adolescent at the Boston Psychoanalytic Society and Institute. Supervising analyst at Sigmund Freud Institute in Zurich. Prolific author of papers and books on children, most recently *Father Hunger*.

Lila J. Kalinich. Training and supervising analyst at the Columbia University Center for Psychoanalytic Training and Research. Recent Past President of the Association for Psychoanalytic Medicine. She is a Clinical Professor of Psychiatry at Columbia University. Author of articles and book reviews in psychoanalysis and other disciplines. Long-time teacher of Lacan and other French theorists.

Julia Kristeva. Director of the Institute for the Study of Texts and Documents at the University of Paris VII. Visiting Professor at Columbia University. Practicing psychoanalyst. Recipient of France's "Chevalier de legion d'honneur" as well as the Holberg International Memorial Prize.

Thomas W. Laqueur. Helen Fawcett Distinguished Professor, Department of History, University of California at Berkeley and UCSF School of Medicine. Recipient of many awards and fellowships, among them the Guggenheim. Author of several acclaimed books, including *Making Sex: Body and Gender from the Greeks to Freud*.

Eric Laurent. Practicing Lacanian Psychoanalyst in Paris, he holds Masters Degrees in Ethnology and Psychology and a PhD in Psychoanalysis. He is President of the World Association of Psychoanalysis. His extensive publications have been translated into many languages.

Helen C. Meyers. Training and supervising analyst at the Columbia University Center for Psychoanalytic Training and Research. Clinical Professor of Psychiatry at Columbia University College of Physicians and Surgeons. Recipient of many awards. Served on the editorial boards of the *International Journal of Psychotherapy* and the *Journal of the American Psychoanalytic Association*. Renowned internationally as a leader in psychoanalytic education and as a thinker and writer.

John P. Muller. Currently Director of Training at the Austen Riggs Psychiatric Center in Stockbridge, Massachusetts. Member of the faculty of the Berkshire Psychoanalytic New Training Facility. Recipient of the Felix and Helena Deutsch Prize from the Boston Psychoanalytic Institute. On the editorial board of several publications, including *Psychoanalysis and Contemporary Thought*. Author of several highly acclaimed books.

Rosine Jozef Perelberg. PhD in social anthropology from the London School of Economics. Visiting Professor, Psychoanalysis Unit, UCL. Training analyst and supervisor and Fellow of the British Psycho-analytic Society. Former Associate Editor of the New Library of Psychoanalysis. Among other publications, she is working on two new psychoanalytic books.

Arnold Richards. Training and supervising analyst at the New York Psychoanalytic Institute. Faculty of the New York University and the Mount Sinai School of Medicine Departments of Psychiatry. Editor of *Journal of the American Psychoanalytic Association* from 1994–2003. Has edited numerous collections of psychoanalytic essays, such as *The Perverse Transference and Other Matters: Essays in Honor of Horatio Etchegoyen*. Winner of the Mary S. Sigourney Award.

Edward W. Tayler. Shakespeare and Milton scholar. Lionel Trilling Professor Emeritus in the Humanities at Columbia University. Revered teacher and recipient of many academic awards such as the University Presidential Award for Outstanding Teaching. Author of many publications, including "King Lear and Negation."

Stuart W. Taylor. A faculty member of the Columbia University Center for Psychoanalytic Training and Research, Taylor has also taught Freud in the English Department of Columbia College for many years. He is a recipient of the Sabshin Award and has presented numerous psycho-analytic articles at international meetings. He was Program Chair for the Symposium on The Dead Father.

Fernando Urribarri. Psychoanalyst of the Argentinean Psychoanalytic Society (IPA) where he chairs a research seminar on French Psycho-analysis. He is Senior Lecturer at the University of Paris X. He has co-chaired international conferences on psychoanalysis and French theory at Columbia University and at the Centre International de Cerisy-France. He is editor of the book series "Contemporary Thought". In France he co-edited the book *On André Green's Work*.

Introduction

Lila J. Kalinich

Sometime in the mid-1990s, a headmaster at an elite private secondary school in New York City instituted what he wryly called a "navel blockade" to prohibit young women students from coming to class in spare shirts and low-cut pants that exposed their bellies. Clever creatures that they were, these blooming adolescents had managed to abide by a dress code while at the same time complying with the new fashion trend. This was especially remarkable in this rather conservative establishment that cherished its early American origins. The school had lifted the uniform requirement only in its recent history.

The psychoanalyst in me was delighted by the pun in the phrase. Through its military reference, it economically captured the transgenerational culture war waged by young people challenging the limits imposed by tradition, at the same time making clear that an important field of battle was the body, the sexual body, the body of desire. I was also taken with how the phrase simultaneously reflected the rather warlike attitude of American foreign policy toward societies that differed in major ways from our own. Clinton had after all bombed four countries during his presidency, and his administration was in the run-up to the 78-day air attack on Serbia (while managing to overlook the fact that Osama Bin Laden had a Bosnian passport).

With the tragedy of September 11, the headmaster's little phrase seemed full of prescience, anticipating Huntington's "clash of civilizations."[1] Although conservative commentators such as Thomas Fleming and his colleagues at the Rockford Institute (paleoconservatives by their own lights)[2] for years had been writing about the insidious attack on Western civilization coming from our more fervent Islamic neighbors in the Middle East, few Americans took him seriously. When the twin towers went down, the attack on what the World Trade Center symbolized for this culture of free market capitalism and individualism was undeniable. The readers all know what has followed. It is of note that the dress code of the women is also a front where this clash is engaged. Is the veiling of women a threat to the way we live? Or does the insistence that women remove the veil undermine dearly held democratic principles? The sexual body is again a flashpoint.

This version of recent history is, of course, condensed and shortsighted.

Cultural conservatives long before had become a prominent presence in the United States in answer to the social unrest of the 1960s. A backlash reacted to the sex, drugs and rock and roll that swept much of the Western world. Feminism, the advances in birth control that enabled the sexual revolution, gay rights, and protests against the Vietnam War tore at the seams of a nation that had not long before embraced without question an ideal of progress. Arnold Richards in his introduction to Part III, "The Father in Theory," discusses how the year 1968 made an impact on even the practice of psychoanalysis and ultimately its theories.

Ordinary people in vast sectors of the country, challenged by the rapidity of change, called for a reassertion of "family values." Politicians invoked the "silent majority" and the "moral majority." The liberation of the sexual body from the constraints of pregnancy and even gender was too much for most. Women in the workplace altered the traditional family structure and seemed to undermine the father's authority. In an effort to find some shred of the sacred, the nation saw a resurgence of religion. God was not dead as an American magazine feared he might be only four decades earlier,[3] but alive and well and living among a growing fundamentalist movement both in religion and the law. Contributor anthropologist Vincent Crapanzano studied this group. In his *Serving the Word: Literalism in America from the Pulpit to the Bench* (2000), he notes that in an effort to stabilize meaning, "serving the word" can become "subservience" to it.[4] The symbolic, emptied of complexity, becomes rigidly fixed to one referent. In Chapter 10 Crapanzano again examines the transmutation of the word, this time among the Algerian Harki in France, where the authority of the father is undercut for vastly different reasons.

All that said, there was nothing life threatening at stake in this culture clash until the ubiquity of the terrorist threat was at the doorstep. There had always been rules of engagement that conflicting sides had more or less followed. At least there had been rules to be violated, a kind of "Geneva convention" that guaranteed that some father somewhere was refereeing the game. The enemy's terms of engagement seemed no longer intelligible or predictable. Where had that father gone? What kind of father would allow the killing of non-combatants, would seek to obliterate an entire nation in the name of God? What was the psychology of the suicide bombers, and their mothers? Despite a moralistic pretense to the contrary, the United States was itself culpable of making its own rules. Killing civilians could be justified from the distance of 35,000 feet, inflicting only "collateral damage."

Psychoanalysts in particular struggled with these questions, trying to determine whether our models of individual psychology could shed any light at all on these phenomena. Most of those models seemed inadequate to the task, failing to understand the interface at the boundary of culture, a system of transmitted meanings embodied in public symbols (Paul, 1976, p. 317).[5] Talk of "good" and "bad" objects or the "grandiose self" just wasn't sufficient.

Transformations in American culture clearly pointed to a change in the function of the father and in his representation in the psyche. The stark changes on the world scene seemed to point in that direction as well.

A group of us within the Association for Psychoanalytic Medicine, the Society affiliated with the Columbia University Center for Psychoanalytic Training and Research in New York City, took up the question of the father very seriously. Study groups lasting over a year culminated in April 2006 in an international symposium after which this book takes its title. For the most part, the contributors to the symposium are the authors of this volume. They represent multiple academic disciplines and psychoanalytic schools from all over the world, who came together despite internecine conflicts because of their recognition of the importance of expanding psychoanalytic understanding of the variables at this confusing moment in human history. Their reflections on times past are in no way a call for a return to the good old days, but rather an inquiry into them from a psychoanalytic point of view.

Freud described the organizational function of the father in his foundational myth *Totem and Taboo* (1913). (The reader will find several re-iterations of this narrative among the authors herein, so I will not add yet another.) Most rejected this work as fanciful, but Freud never abandoned the idea that a primal crime had actually occurred at some point during mankind's prehistoric development. Although he was willing to grant that the crime, the murder of the father who had prevented the sons from having sexual access to the women, might have occurred repeatedly over hundreds of years among countless hordes, he did so mostly as a nod to his many critics. Both in *Totem and Taboo* and *Moses and Monotheism* (1939), his final work, Freud related the tale as though the murder had been a single, historical event. The consequence of the killing of the father marked the origin of culture. Guilt over their crime inspired the sons to develop the rules of operation that made possible things like deviance, and therefore creativity rather than violence and chaos. The primal father, now absent, had to be represented or symbolized. All of the contributors to this volume take the murder of the father of prehistory seriously insofar as it offers a view into psychic structure contingent on the social.

Whether an actual event or not, either remembered in some deeply encoded way or simply repeated in the evolution of the individual subject, the castration threat by the father and his murder by the son have been central to psychoanalytic theory for most of its history. The Oedipus conflict and the vicissitudes of its resolution made up the lion's share of the field's focus and development. Even in France, where Jacques Lacan put his unique stamp on Freud and psychoanalysis, the father in the form of the symbolic father occupied the fulcrum of his formulation.

Although several women analysts in the early analytic movement made contributions that considered the role of the mother, particularly challenging Freud's understanding of female sexuality (see Richards in this volume), those contributions remained rather marginal. Despite the pioneering work of Melanie Klein, Donald Winnicott and other British object relations theorists on the early dyadic life of the infant, the Oedipal father remained pre-eminent in the United States until the 1970s and early 1980s when Ross, Abelin and Blos explored the role of the father in the pre-Oedipal period. Ross looked at "fathering" from the perspective of the father.[6] Their important works were largely supplanted in the late 1980s and early 1990s when the mother–child dyad took center stage. Although initially resisted by psychoanalysts of a more traditional orientation, self-psychology and attachment theory came to be enthusiastically embraced by large sectors of working analysts, especially the more recently trained (see Richards in this volume for a fuller discussion). This shift in the psychoanalytic terrain mirrored the ascendancy of the role of women in society.

It was André Green's landmark paper "The Dead Mother"[7] that really opened the door to the mother, who'd been standing there knocking for some time. Written in 1980 and published in France as "*Narcissisme de vie. Narcissisme de mort,*" it described the consequences of maternal depression for the psyche of the infant. "Thus," says Green, "the dead mother, contrary to what one might think, is a mother who remains alive, but who is, so to speak, psychically dead in the eyes of the young child in her care." Green nonetheless always kept an eye to the father, emphasizing his importance as the *third* for the structuring of the psyche, with the Oedipus complex as the "essential symbolic matrix . . . the fate of the human psyche is to have always *two* objects and never one alone, however far one goes back to try to understand the earliest psychical structure" (Green, 1986, p. 146), Green has maintained this commitment to the role of the "third" throughout his career. Green's *tour de force*, "The Construction of the Lost Father" that opens this volume, elaborates in some detail just how this third functions, particularly through the father's representation as "absence."

André Green makes clear that much of his thinking is grounded in the theoretical approach of Jacques Lacan, one of his formative influences. Fernando Urribarri, in his review in Chapter 2 of Green's work, "Fatherhood Revisited: The Dead Father, Fraternal Pact and Analytic Filiation in the Work of André Green," intended to orient the reader to Green's complex trajectory, also properly credits Lacan's influence. He charts Green's course through Lacan, describing how Green and other colleagues struggled to differentiate their thinking from that of their psychoanalytic father, particularly in the face of the political dissension that beset the French psychoanalytic scene. Masterfully guiding the reader, he makes potentially murky waters very clear.

Urribarri holds a place among Green's most dedicated disciples, and his loyalties definitely show! In a section entitled "Beyond Lacan," Urribarri takes pains to say that in the "beyond" he means that Green stops using Lacan as a point of reference with whom he either agrees or disagrees, moving on to the autonomous thought that has invigorated contemporary psychoanalysis. The reader will suspect, however, that "beyond" for Urribarri means "surpassed." And while it is certainly the case that André Green has made an immense contribution to current analytic thinking, it is also true that contemporary mainstream Lacanians have developed their intellectual legacy "beyond" the one left to them at Lacan's death. Psychoanalyst Eric Laurent, one of Lacan's most articulate proponents, demonstrates this in Chapter 4, "A New Love for the Father."

Lacanian Maria Cristina Aguirre opens Part II, "The Father Embodied," introducing the chapters that show how the Dead Father, the symbolic father, marks the lived body, both "real" and "imaginary," in distinct and observable ways. While Green embraces drive theory in order to maintain a place for the real body in the theory, Lacan dismisses it insofar as for him the physical is accessible only through its derivatives. It is the "imaginary" body that is available to the psyche. Green considers affect a signifier; Lacan does not.

In Chapter 3, Marilia Aisenstein, member of the Parisian Psychosomatic School, provides clinical material that dramatically illustrates the interaction between the actual body and its intrapsychic registers. She presents two patients with life-threatening illnesses who suffer from an insufficiency in their representational capacities. Both with fathers absent in different ways, their failure to install the symbolic father in the flesh wrote itself into the soma. In Chapter 4 Eric Laurent traces the substantial alterations in the paternal function wrought by recent advances in reproductive technology, especially as market forces have wed the capacity to father. Historian Thomas Laqueur, well known for his work on the cultural construction of the body, then helps the reader to grasp just how resoundingly culture affects how one carries oneself. In Chapter 5 he writes a moving portrait of his own father and the devastating impact of the loss of his "beloved Germany" on his father's life and on his death.

Part III, "The Father in Theory," introduced by Arnold Richards, offers three highly clinical chapters, each of which supports the importance of the actual father in the development of children and adolescents. The authors demonstrate the role of the father in the theories they practice through a rather detailed description of their clinical work. In Chapter 6, Christine Anzieu-Premmereur, a child analyst trained in France, now working in New York City, reveals how a problematic paternal representation in the parents affects the next generation. In that she utilizes the mirror in her analytic work with small children, Anzieu-Premmereur makes the mirror stage in development come alive for the reader. Her incorporation of the father, the vital third, into the work of the session helps one of her toddler patients to stand erect. In Chapter 7 Rosine Jozef Perelberg of London describes her work with violent adolescents whose fathers had no intrapsychic place. Perelberg was originally an anthropologist. She therefore brings a wealth of knowledge to bear on her treatment of Freudian concepts as advanced in *Totem and*

Taboo, Moses and Monotheism and elsewhere. James Herzog is known for his extensive work on "father hunger" among children and adolescents. Using the "actual life circumstance" of two analysands, in Chapter 8 he examines the "fate of paternal representations, both self with father and self with father and mother together, when no father has actually been present." One of the cases is a child of two lesbian mothers. What he finds in her psychological life has led him to conclusions that will not easily be embraced by alternative communities.

The Dead Father: A Psychoanalytic Inquiry turns to the theme of culture writ large in its final part, "Father Culture." John Muller, one of the first to bring the work of Lacan to an American audience, establishes that culture is the "primary domain" of the dead father in Freud's work. In the chapters that follow in Part IV, Muller notes, the verbal authority of the symbolic father, diminished, "frozen," and reinterpreted, is what is at issue in all three. Noted Shakespeare scholar and much loved professor Edward Tayler reveals in Chapter 9 just how myopic my earlier version of recent cultural history actually is. Taking the study of the paternal back to Elizabethan England, he discusses the rigors and the benefits of schooling in Latin, the Father Tongue, offered to privileged young males. English, in contrast, was the Mother Tongue. The rod was not spared to enforce discipline. Tayler recalls his own teaching experiences and the remarkable changes in the university culture over the course of his career. Vincent Crapanzano recounts his work with the Harki population living in France (Chapter 10). The Harki are the dispossessed Algerians who fought with the French in the Algerian war for independence. The Harki men, suffering torture and subjugation in Algeria and discrimination in France, became "living-dead" fathers who passed on their stories to their children in stale and repetitive ways. Underscoring the role of the "Third" in discourse, Crapanzano compassionately articulates what he calls the "frozen discourse" of these people.

Julia Kristeva, linguist, theorist, fiction writer, and critic, concludes "Father Culture" with a daring reinterpretation of the Crucifixion and Resurrection of Christ. Reflecting first on the murder of her own father by a more contemporary version of the primal horde, she examines how the Christian narrative articulates an Oedipal resolution through identification with the *Father* who is beaten to death. In his introduction, Muller appropriately critiques the version of theology that Kristeva uses to reach this conclusion. However, whether or not Kristeva gets Christian thinking quite right, she does capture the important resonance of religious faith for the individual subject despite her declared atheism. Early in the chapter she suggests that perhaps psychoanalysts, children of the enlightenment, have "rushed to proclaim the death of God too quickly."

Helen Meyers wraps up the volume with her Epilogue. As the most senior faculty member at the Columbia University Center for Psychoanalytic Training and Research, Meyers has had an impact on the training of most of our community. Though she still embraces ego psychology, she introduced the teaching of multiple psychoanalytic models decades ago. She reads the contributions of the volume's authors from that perspective and responds.

Conclusion

In his discussion of Green, Fernando Urribarri finds it an advance that Green avoids the "potential for the negative theology of a transcendent symbolic structure. . . ." I personally fail to see just how this would be an advantage. Despite the remarkable pliability of the signifying chain, the symbolic is a closed system. Yet that system has the capacity to refer to a "beyond" itself, invoking the mystery and the unknowability of the real (see Muller) into which humankind finds itself thrown. Furthermore, the aspect of the fundamentalisms, religious, judicial or psychoanalytic, that seems so problematic is their *certainty*, something upon which negative theology does not insist.

Thinking the "beyond" has been an irresistible, compulsive characteristic of the structure, pushing the limits of the knowable into the outer reaches. (Urribarri's chapter itself shows just how irresistible the pull of "beyond" is.) Absent the beyond, the vector of thought doubles back on itself, creating aspects of the self-involvement of contemporary culture. Eventually, like those young New York students, people come to have little choice but to ponder the navel, one of the few culturally available signifiers of the realm of mystery! As Aisenstein says in her conclusion, "The body seems to have become the site of frenzied and ferocious care. . . ."

Today we children of modernity know little of the marriage of "scientific rationality" and the marketplace that began in Newton's day and is still ongoing. Just as global financial interests alter the paternal function via reproductive technologies, an earlier version of those interests worked to undermine the symbolic Father through what Weber called the "disenchantment" of the world. Bilgrami points out that there is in fact a metaphysics that parades behind the ideal of scientific objectivity.[8] Psychoanalysis in practice straddles multiple metaphysical schemata. As a result we have both the capacity and the opportunity to put a bit of enchantment back into the world if we take a little care not to join the parade. The discourse of the unconscious, the operation of the word on the physical and its perception, are wondrous in and of themselves. Opening the window onto those mysteries can in fact make all things new. It is in that spirit that we offer this volume.

Notes

1 Huntington, S. (1996) *The Clash of Civilizations and the Remaking of the World Order*, New York: Simon and Schuster.
2 See www.rockfordinstitute.org
3 See cover of *Time Magazine*, April 8, 1966.

4 Crapanzano, V. (2000) *Serving the Word: Literalism in America from the Pulpit to the Bench*, New York: New Press.
5 Paul, R. (1976) "Did the Primal Crime Take Place?", *Ethos* 4(3): 311–52.
6 Ross, J.M. (1975) "The Development of Paternal Identity: A Critical Review of the Literature on Nurturance and Generativity in Boys and Men", *Journal of the American Psychoanalytic Association* 23: 783–817.
7 Green, A. (1986) "The Dead Mother", in *Private Madness*, New York: International Universities Press, pp. 140–73.
8 Bilgrami, A. (2006) "Occidentalism, the Very Idea: An Essay on Enlightenment and Enchantment", *Critical Inquiry* 32(3): 381–411.

Prologue

Stuart W. Taylor

> For out of olde feldes, as men seyth
> Cometh al this new corn from yer to yere,
> And out of old bokes, in good feyth.
> Cometh al this newe science that men lere.
> (Chaucer, 1380: 311)

The narrative of the symbolic father has organized culture for all of human history. In a sense, the Dead Father is in the word.

The foundation of psychoanalysis itself is deeply rooted in language. The generative importance of Freud's neuropsychoanalytic[1] work, especially his 1891 study *On Aphasia*, has been elaborated by Forrester (1980), Greenberg (1997) and Rizzuto (2002) among others. On the other hand, the influence of the German language and Freud's German literary heritage on his work have been richly discussed by scholars such as Anzieu (1986), Grubrich-Simitis (1986) and Ticho (1986). However, Anzieu (1986, p. 222) argues that Freud could never have founded psychoanalysis without the "polymorphously linguistic" milieu he cultivated for himself (learning English, romance and classical languages) which allowed him to transcend certain cultural limits in various ways.

One result of Freud's dual academic heritage is that Freud's own work reads like literature. Freud's own writing, full of references to poets and writers, and allusions to literary figures, earned him the Goethe Prize in literature. And although Freud (1895, p. 160) felt it "strange" that his "case histories should read like short stories" rather than science, Patrick Mahoney (1982, pp. 11–2) shows that Freud was also an aspiring novelist.

Another result, perhaps more important theoretically, is that Freud's theory is essentially a linguistic theory. Dreams, symptoms and even ordinary thought have a linguistic structure: they are communications, they are built on the ambiguity of words, they have an associative, chainlike structure, they involve condensation, displacement and retranscription or revision and require interpretation. Dreams are regarded as "Holy Writ" (Freud, 1900,

p. 514). Slips of the tongue and parapraxes, for example, illustrate the influence of the unconscious on everyday speech and activity. Even Freud's conception of aphasia was based on language. Challenging the localizing tendencies of his distinguished neurological peers, Freud (1891, p. 53) argued that the neurons contained representations the way "a poem contains the alphabet."[2] He also described a word as a "complex" of perceptual and motor impressions.

For Freud, culture too was founded on linguistic terms. His early remark (1893, p. 36) in the context of explaining that there are limits on responding to trauma – "the man who first flung a word of abuse at his enemy instead of a spear was the founder of civilization" – establishes the necessity of limits on deeds, long before *Totem and Taboo* in which "No," a verbal prohibition, becomes law, leading Freud to conclude (1913a, p. 156) that "the beginnings of religion, morals, society and art converge on the Oedipus complex."

In this context, it is easy to see why Lacan's rereading of Freud led him to claim that "the unconscious is structured like a language" (1966a, pp. 148, 234; 1966b, pp. 187–9; 1973, pp. 20–1, 203; 1975, p. 48). This particular formulation has been challenged vigorously by many including Green (1994, pp. 169–85; see also Kohon, 1999, pp. 17–26) and will not itself be taken up here. However, it seems fair to conclude that much of the recent interest in Freud's linguistic background stems from Lacan's claim.[3] Kristeva (1981, pp. 265–77) has demonstrated the value of psychoanalysis for the study of language, and has articulated (1994) Freudian models of language. Makari and Shapiro (1993) have put Freud's and Lacan's work in a broad context of developments in linguistics, while also emphasizing the relevance of language to psychoanalysis.

It is sufficient for my purpose to draw attention to Freud's own claim that " 'speech' must be understood not merely to mean the expression of thought in words but to include the speech of gesture and every other method, such, for instance, as writing, by which mental activity can be expressed" (1913b, p. 176). Freud's conception of the motivation for speech was dyadic, as seen in his description of the reflexive expression of need (Freud, 1895, p. 366), and his "intimate" references to his mother tongue (Grubrich-Simitis, 1986).

Lacan's contribution to understanding the symbolic aspects of speech includes the father and hence the triangular structure from the beginning. For the child, the parental relation is manifest in that the father is desired by the mother, a fact evident as early as the child perceives that she speaks to the father – in a language the child does not initially understand, and thus has to learn to speak in order to gain her attention. Certainly such formulations illustrate how language structures the subject. Lacan also pointed out that we have a symbolic existence before we are born, in the sense that we are imagined and spoken about. There can be little doubt about the importance of narrative, stories, in our development.

The father shares this dependence on narrative for his constitution. Because his relationship with his children is more distant, less physical than is that between mother and children, a living father must be learned about in other ways, narrative being a vital one. But even an actually dead father can have a life in the family if he is remembered and evoked in narrative form. The father, as André Green (Kohon, 1999, p. 54) has remarked, "is also the ancestors, the lost people of earlier generations which came to form the family."

Thus the function of narrative in the formation of identity is tremendous, from conveying our prenatal constitution, to knowing our parents, especially the father, to the transmission of family stories. On two occasions, attempting to explain phylogenetic inheritance, Freud (1913a, p. 158; 1938, p. 207)[4] quoted Goethe: "What thou hast inherited from thy fathers, acquire it to make it thine." In what form do we inherit anything, other than in narrative form? That which is most significant, and that which we truly can "make our own" is our verbal story, including that of our family and ancestors. There seems no sense in substituting for this a disembodied superego.

But a practical problem remains. How, specifically, are narratives transmitted from generation to generation? Fishing is an excellent example of an activity with a symbolic structure which provides for the transmission of narratives. One of the most celebrated tribal activities practiced today, fishing is primarily a male pursuit, and when practiced in groups, fishing has considerable social benefit. Fishing sublimates primitive impulses to acquire women,[5] as well as to slaughter kinfolk. Fishing also allows for fathers[6] and sons to be present together and for the intergenerational transmission of knowledge of the world,[7] family heritage and the law.

Besides oral history, the most time-honored tradition for transmitting narratives must now be writing. It is then worth recalling that in the course of analyzing his dream of the botanical monograph, Freud (1900, p. 172) tells us that his "first passion" was "collecting and owning books;" in short, Freud was "a bookworm" by his own estimation. And when asked to list ten good books, Freud (1907, p. 246) commented that good books must be books to which "one owes a part of one's knowledge of life and view of the world."

Academia relies heavily on a tradition of written discourse, and there are many explicit and implicit rules pertaining to conduct regarding books. Such rules go to the heart of the symbolic father. For example, when Professor Laqueur called me in April 2006 looking for a copy of André Green's classic paper, "The Dead Mother," while working on his own paper because the library at U.C. Berkeley could not find its volume with the paper in it (i.e. *On Private Madness*, Green, 1972), it was precisely because of an attack on the Dead Father. Professor Laqueur was being polite. The library at Berkeley is not staffed with mixed-up librarians. The books that are most in demand, that inspire intellectual collaboration like the present volume, are, if they are "missing," probably stolen. In short, the library was a crime scene. The law says don't steal the books. Breaking the law – stealing a book – is not just a misdemeanor. Psychically, it is tantamount to a capital felony offense: killing the author, the authority, the father, by preventing the circulation of his ideas. On this point, recall the *Areopagitica*:

> For books are not absolutely dead things, but do contain a potency of life in them . . . Who kills a man kills a reasonable creature, God's image; but he who destroys a good book, kills reason itself, kills the image of God, as it were in the eye. . . . a good book is the precious life-blood of a master spirit, embalmed and treasured up on purpose to a life beyond life.
>
> (Milton, 1644, p. 720, © 1957, Hackett Publishing Company)

Milton's sentiment is not an idle academic rant. In Freud's own words (1910, p. 121), "there is no doubt that the creative artist feels toward his works like a father." The theft of a work, if it is eventually returned, might count as kidnapping; if it is not returned, murder of the Dead Father is the verdict.

The trials and tribulations of the Dead Father are depicted clearly and compellingly in literature and the arts; since Freud's time film has come to play an important role in conveying knowledge about life and views of the world. The original *Star Wars* (Lucas, 1977) is a classic example. The basic plot elaboration on the battle of good versus evil (the Rebel Alliance against the Evil Empire and similarly, The Force against the Dark Side) is that the son, Luke Skywalker, and his companions seek to kill and destroy Darth Vader, who is not only evil embodied, but also, unknown to Luke, Luke's real father. This is straight out of *Oedipus*. The film also contains an explicit reference to Freud's formulation. The following exchange occurs in the scene in which Luke, Obi-Wan (Luke's adopted mentor and father figure) and company are trying to escape from Darth's spaceship and Obi-Wan is trapped by Darth Vader as Luke and the others just barely make it to safety:

Darth Vader [menacing technovoice]:   Your powers are weak old man.
Obi-Wan: You can't win Darth, if you strike me down, I shall become stronger than you can possibly imagine.

Freud's line from *Totem and Taboo* (1913a) echoes here almost verbatim: "The dead father became stronger than the living one had been." Dramatically, Darth kills Obi-Wan who then becomes the voice of The Force for Luke.

At the turn of the millennium, when Star Wars re-released with additional episodes, my just school age son asked, "Why does Luke hear Obi-Wan's voice if he [Obi-Wan] is dead?" I explained that Obi-Wan, the only father Luke has known, still exists in Luke's mind, and that Luke can remember or imagine – almost hear – what Obi-Wan would say in stressful situations. Obi-Wan may be a kinder, gentler Dead Father than many, inspiring and representing possibility, but he is always, by virtue of his death/absence, a reminder of limits and loss. The cinematic device of Obi-Wan's voice is a perfect demonstration of the alloy of the real (hallucination), imaginary (memories/stories), symbolic (identification with a personification of the superego).

Yet the Dead Father is precisely not a modern invention created by a filmmaker who has perhaps read too much Freud. Consider the genius of Sir Thomas Malory, in a time arguably more lawless than ours, who collected the English, French, Celtic, Roman sources, and wove them into a coherent narrative, largely around King Arthur's effort to institute the round table as a moral and filial principle against a bloody "might makes right" code. The knights, being human, fail in the Grail quest, and ultimately, Arthur's social dream fails, undone in part by a pair of Oedipal transgressions.[8] One might expect the defeated Arthur to adopt the wary tone of "Civilization and Its Discontents." But Malory, even after Arthur is killed by his son, is reluctant to admit the death of Arthur the leader and social innovator, writing in Christian terms:

> Yet som men say in many p[art]ys of Inglonde that kynge Arthure ys nat dede, but h[ad] by the wyll of oure lorde Jesu into another place; and men say that he shall com agayne, and he shall wynne the Holy Crosse. Yet I woll nat say that hit shall be so, but rather I wolde sey: here in thys worlde he chaunged hys lyff. And many men say that there ys written upon the tumbe thys:
> HIC IACET ARTHURUS, REX QUONDAM REXQUE FUTURUS
> (Malory, 1485, p. 717, © 1971, Oxford University Press)

Despite the prevalence of the story of the Dead Father in Western culture, Freud has been criticized for inventing a ridiculous myth and passing it off as history. Too, he has been accused of misappropriating Oedipus as a model for the story and for his theory (see Armstrong, 1998). Among those who are quickest to kill off the paradigm of the Dead Father are psychoanalysts, perhaps enacting an identification with Oedipus (Lear, 1998, p. 83).

It seems that such critics have forgotten Lévi-Strauss's (1949, p. 491) gloss of Freud: the Dead Father story must express an "ancient and lasting dream" and that psychic phenomena which structure the mind are repeated in each consciousness by virtue of "an order which transcends both historical successions and contemporary correlations." In short, it is the symbolic that structures our experience, with language being the vector par excellence.

Thus, the enigma of Freud's closing remark in *Totem and Taboo*: " 'in the beginning was the deed' "[9] might best be resolved by considering this a negation which brings to mind a repressed echo, "in the beginning was the word." As Green (Kohon, 1999) among others has noted, in French at least, the phrase is "In the beginning was the verb," further highlighting the link between language and a constitutive act.

But by invoking an event, Freud creates a paradox. In the time before the traumatic event, not only the murderous wish existed, but a prohibition must have existed, even if only implicit and unstated. Following the "deed," the prohibition is made explicit – it is stated and encoded in language. A step forward, yes, but a traumatic one in and of itself. This is perhaps more clear in Freud's later *Moses and Monotheism* (1939), a revised version of the same elemental story: the delivery of the tablets containing the written Law is traumatic. The establishment of a text, and to a different extent the spoken word, is traumatic because it requires interpretation. Early in his career, Freud (1895, p. 281ff) had become concerned with both the "mutilated manner"[10] in which his patients told their stories and the possibility for the analyst to distort meaning. In *Moses and Monotheism* (1939, p. 43) he is explicit that a text can be "mutilated ... distorted", and that doing so "resembles a murder."

Yet, it is precisely where interpretation is required that trouble ensues. On the Good Friday and Passover weekend in which we were trying to find Green's book for Professor Laqueur, most places were closed owing to the cultural sense of piety and respect for the dead, and holidays relating to Judeo-Christian traditions. Ironically, it seemed as if the Dead Father was impeding our efforts to pay tribute to Him. Even more ironically, on that same Good Friday the two soccer teams in Milan, Italy were playing a match despite bitter protests from the Vatican. This did seem duplicitous, since almost exactly a year earlier both teams had honored the death of the late Pope John Paul II, who, on the occasion of the 1984 Olympics, emphasized the importance of rules to the Italian athletes (John Paul II, 1984): "Sport risks degrading Man if it is not based on and supported by the human virtues of loyalty, generosity and respect for the rules of the game and of the players."[11] The moral of this story is that, despite our wishes, there are no absolute interpretations of rules.

Unfortunately, in other circumstances the impulse to interpret absolutely is used for actually murderous goals. Freud was mistaken when he responded to the burning of his books in Berlin with the comment (Jones, 1957, p. 182): "What progress we are making. In the Middle Ages they would have burnt me; nowadays they are content with burning my books." Terrorists and fundamentalists of any sort are not content with killing people; it is discourse, ideas, history, culture, in short the symbolic itself, that they want to destroy.

In various ways then, psychoanalysts ignore at their own peril the literature and art bequeathed to them and their role as "practitioners of the symbolic function" (Lacan, 1966a, p. 72) both in the clinic and in culture at large. Freud himself credited "the poets and philosophers before him" with discovering the unconscious (Lehrman, 1954, p. 264). And elsewhere (1907, p. 143), Freud claimed that "every man is a poet"[12] referring to processes of creativity. Apparently not satisfied with this admission, critic Harold Bloom goes so far as to claim that it was Shakespeare rather than Freud who invented Freudian psychology.[13]

Shakespeare was indeed concerned with the importance of dead fathers in psychic life. Some, such as King Hamlet's Ghost, among the most famous of all dead fathers, appear in this volume. Other examples illustrate various aspects of the Dead Father: in *The Merchant of Venice* (I.ii.24–5),[14] Portia, forced to "choose" a spouse by the three coffin game, complains poignantly, "so is the will of a living daughter/curb'd by the will of a dead father." And is not *Romeo and Juliet* (see II.ii.34–43) in crucial ways about "denying the father" and "refusing [the] name" of the father? *King Lear* (III.iv.72) considers "discarded fathers." The sense of mystery, power, and the sacred that attend the Dead Father are evident in Ariel's haunting song in *The Tempest*, (I.ii.397–405): "Full fadom five thy father lies . . .."[15]

There can hardly be any mistake that the essential aspects of the Dead Father – the themes of erotic and violent impulses, the unknown and the mysterious (unknowable), the problematic of order and repression: in short the law, the capacities of the body, the necessity of representation and disguise – all these recur through the ages. Had Freud not chosen the myth inherited by Sophocles, he could have chosen any of many well-known protagonists in this ongoing drama.

As foreseen long ago by Malory, the "once and future King" has already returned; if not as Luke Skywalker, then surely as Harry Potter. Written by a single mother, the basic story is of a boy whose parents have been murdered, who studies witchcraft and wizardry with some close pals. To oversimplify, let me just say that Harry and his friends are continually confronted with the question of what is the law, including the terrifying observation that Harry speaks parseltongue, the most perfect example I've seen yet of what Julia Kristeva (1997) has called an "other language." Straight from his unconscious, this native tongue alienates Harry from his friends and worries him about himself. And, like Oedipus, Harry must construct his identity from "vague and ancient rumors" (Sophocles, p. 289). And Harry bears a scar from the same assault in which his parents were killed, a scar through which he imagines filiation with his parents – or is it his enemies? Through all his adventures, Harry desperately seeks fatherly advice and support.[16] Seeking, forever seeking. The Dead Father is intimately connected with the Grail quest.

Readers will not find in the present volume explicit answers to all the relevant questions that may emerge regarding the Dead Father. "Knowledge is patchwork" Freud (1909, p. 100) reminds us. And even this is borrowed wisdom, from the Bible[17] if not before. Moreover, Freud always reserved a place for that which we cannot comprehend: the navel of the dream. Perhaps most to the point, as articulated by Green, a crucial function of the father as the third is to raise questions.

The reflections that follow comprise an evocative collection of contemporary perspectives on the Dead Father that help locate his place, and the place of psychoanalysis in our world. The essays also attempt to elucidate the father's tripartite constitution and changing configurations: the real or particular father, the imaginary father and the general or cultural father that structures all three, importantly through discourse.

Green (Chapter 1) and Herzog (Chapter 8) both address the constructed nature of the Dead Father. For Green and for Anzieu-Premmeurer (Chapter 6), the intervention of the father is necessary for thinking itself and for the capacity to symbolize. Perelberg (Chapter 7) shows clinically how violence and psychosis result from failed prohibition, and Tayler (Chapter 9) traces changes in educational structure through the years. A dead father's ashes, and a child's self-made scars/tattoos reflect aspects of the father in the real for Laqueur (Chapter 5) and Aisenstein (Chapter 3) respectively. Laurent (Chapter 4) recovers the particular and the real father by exploring contemporary *père-versions*. Crapanzano (Chapter 10) shows how discourse frozen by trauma can deprive a younger generation of its legacy. Kristeva (Chapter 11) offers a psychoanalytic theological account of assaults on the Father.

Indeed, more questions about the Dead Father are only just emerging as the symbolic structure of our world changes. For example, will written information come to dominate culture and render expendable the oral knowledge and memory of wise elderly members as physiologist anthropologist Jared Diamond (2001) wonders? Will the changing types and capacities of archiving written communications change the nature of discourse itself, including psychoanalytic discourse, as Derrida (1995) suggests? Will it prove true, as Lacan (1966a, p. 310) stated, that "the Oedipus Complex cannot run indefinitely in forms of society that are more and more losing the sense of tragedy?"

Regarding the future, Freud (1929, p. 43) once said: "Writing is the voice of an absent person." What the Dead Father says to us, whether we hear it or read it, will ultimately depend on the articulation of our desire. What stories will reach our children's children? And their children?

Notes

1 Freud's early work is generally referred to as his "pre-psychoanalytic" work. This conception was favored by Freud, who commented that he found it "difficult to identify himself" (his psychoanalytic work) with the earlier work, and who asked to have some of the earlier work excluded from his collected work. However, given the renewed attempts to integrate neuroscience with psychoanalysis, it seems perverse not to give Freud credit for this "new" interdisciplinary field.

2 Recent work in neuroscience (Castrén, 2005) suggests that a network theory (akin to Freud's suggestion) may explain certain cerebral functions better than the aged but persistent idea of gross anatomical localities.

3 The number of references to language in the literature before and after 1966 may be some guide. A quick study on PEPWeb showed three psychoanalytic journals in existence before 1966. Searching for the term "language" in paper titles before (and including) 1966 vs. after 1966 gave the following results for each journal:

   International Journal of Psychoanalysis, est. 1920: 2 before, 53 after; *Psychoanalytic Quarterly*, est. 1932: 9 before, 106 after; *Psychoanalytic Study of the Child*, est. 1945: 1 before, 8 after.

4 Strachey's translation of this difficult passage is a bit flat, not really conveying the activity of earning (or constructing) one's inheritance in order to own it, claim it, as Goethe's words seem to convey (see Barnstorff, 1943).

5 I am suggesting that "beautiful" elusive fish represent women. Freud might argue that fish are a totem animal, representing the father, to be both protected and eaten. However, for more on the fish as women in common experience, hear the song, "Madison Brown" about a particularly captivating piscine femme fatale at: http://prairiehome.publicradio.org/programs/2006/09/30/

   Also, who hasn't been told, when rejected in love, "There's lots of other fish in the sea"? In fact, fish may just be the ultimate embodiment of *objet petit a*: they too often get away and go elsewhere. And if you catch one, your eye immediately goes after another one.

6 The substitutability of fathers (as opposed to mothers) discussed by Green (Kohon, 1999) is evident here.

7 In fact, I had occasion to discuss the Dead Father with some pediatricians who fish and who are naturally very much concerned with the Father's health in society. I learned that a recent article from the American Academy of Pediatrics (AAP) entitled, "Fathers and Pediatricians: Enhancing Men's Roles in the Care and Development of Their Children" (Coleman *et al.*, 2004), emphasized the need for pediatricians to support and encourage fathers' involvement in families, in the face of changing socioeconomic factors and parental roles, and the difficulty of providing that support. My boat mate, John, said, "You know I see that all the time. . . . When a father comes in with the family, I find myself talking to the mother. I don't know how to engage fathers."

8 Best known is the affair of Lancelot (who is "like a son" to Arthur) with Arthur's wife, Guenyvere. The resulting disruption in Camelot is seized upon by the disenchanted Mordred (who in Malory and other medieval writers is the real son of Arthur and his own half-sister; neither of the two knew this family history at the time of the encounter). Mordred seeks to bring down Arthur and Arthur seeks to stop Mordred's traitorous ways. In the inevitable battle between them, they kill each other.

9 Freud was quoting Goethe.

10 Freud was concerned with this throughout his career and in various contexts.

11 Translated by Francesca Zavolta and Roberta Garruccio. Original: "Lo sport rischia di degradare l'uomo, se non è basato e sorretto dalle virtù umane della lealtà, della generosità e del rispetto delle leggi del gioco, oltre che del giocatore."

12 For modern twists on this idea, see Edward W. Tayler's Chapter 9 in this volume.

13 See: http://prelectur.stanford.edu/lecturers/bloom/interviews.html

14 All references to Shakespeare in this chapter are to the 1974 edition of *The Riverside Shakespeare* (see References, Shakespeare, 1623).

15 Full fadom five thy father lies . . .
   Of his bones are coral made;
   Those are pearls that were his eyes:
   Nothing of him that doth fade,
   But doth suffer a sea-change
   Into something rich and strange.
   Sea-nymphs hourly ring his knell:
       Burthen (within). Ding-dong.
   Hark! now I hear them – Ding-dong bell.

16 The similarities between the wizard-like mentors/surrogate fathers are striking: Merlin, Obi-Wan, Dumbledore.

17 St. Paul, 1 Corinthians 13.

References

Anzieu, D. (1986) "The Place of Germanic Language and Culture in Freud's Discovery of Psychoanalysis Between 1895 and 1900", *International Journal of Psychoanalysis* 67: 219–26.

Armstrong, R. (1998) "Oedipus as Evidence", *PSYART: An Online Journal for the Psychological Study of the Arts*, viewed 25 February 2008, http://www.clas.ufl.edu/ipsa/journal/1999_armstrong01.shtml

Barnstorff, H. (1943) "Translating and Interpreting Goethe's Faust, I, 682/3", *Modern Language Notes* 58(4): 288–91.

Castrén, E. (2005) "Is Mood Chemistry?", *Nature Reviews Neuroscience* 6(3): 241–46.

Chaucer, G. (1380) "The Parliament of Fowls", reprinted in F.N. Robinson (ed.) (1957) *The Works of Geoffrey Chaucer*, 2nd edn, Boston: Houghton Mifflin/Riverside Press.

Coleman, W.L. and Garfield, C. and the Committee on Psychosocial Aspects of Child and Family Health (2004) "Fathers and Pediatricians: Enhancing Men's Roles in the Care and Development of Their Children", *Pediatrics* 113(5): 1406–11.

Derrida, J. (1995) *Archive Fever*, Chicago: University of Chicago Press.

Diamond, J. (2001) "Unwritten Knowledge", *Nature* 410: 521.

Forrester, J. (1980) *Language and the Origins of Psychoanalysis*, Basingstoke: Macmillan Press.

Freud, S. (1891) *On Aphasia: A Critical Study*, trans. E. Stengel (1953), New York: International Universities Press.

—— (1893) "On the Psychical Mechanism of Hysterical Phenomena: A Lecture", trans. James Strachey (1962), *Standard Edition*, Volume 3, London: Hogarth Press.

—— (1895) "Studies On Hysteria", trans. James Strachey (1955), *Standard Edition*, Volume 2, London: Hogarth Press.

—— (1900) "The Interpretation of Dreams", trans. James Strachey (1953), *Standard Edition*, Volume 4, London: Hogarth Press.

—— (1907) "Contribution to a Questionnaire on Reading", trans. James Strachey (1959), *Standard Edition*, Volume 9, London: Hogarth Press.

—— (1908) "Creative Writers and Day-Dreaming", trans. James Strachey (1959), *Standard Edition*, Volume 9, London: Hogarth Press.

—— (1909) "Analysis of a Phobia in a Five-Year-Old Boy", trans. James Strachey (1955), *Standard Edition*, Volume 10, London: Hogarth Press.

—— (1910) "Leonardo Da Vinci and a Memory of his Childhood", trans. James Strachey (1957), *Standard Edition*, Volume 11, London: Hogarth Press.

—— (1913a) "Totem and Taboo", trans. James Strachey (1955), *Standard Edition*, Volume 13, London: Hogarth Press.

—— (1913b) "The Claims of Psycho-Analysis to Scientific Interest", trans. James Strachey (1955), *Standard Edition*, Volume 13, London: Hogarth Press.

—— (1929) "Civilization and Its Discontents", trans. James Strachey (1961), *Standard Edition*, Volume 21, London: Hogarth Press.

—— (1938) "An Outline of Psycho-Analysis", trans. James Strachey (1964), *Standard Edition*, Volume 23, London: Hogarth Press.

—— (1939) "Moses and Monotheism", trans. James Strachey (1964), *Standard Edition*, Volume 23, London: Hogarth Press.

Green, A. (1972) *On Private Madness*, London: Hogarth Press.

—— (1994) "Against Lacanism: A Conversation", trans. Gianmaria Senia (1995), *Journal of European Psychoanalysis* 2, Fall 1995–Winter 1996.

Greenberg, V. (1997) *Freud and His Aphasia Book: Language and the Sources of Psychoanalysis*, Ithaca: Cornell University Press.

Grubrich-Simitis, I. (1986) "Reflections on Sigmund Freud's Relationship to the German Language and to some German-Speaking Authors of the Enlightenment", *International Journal of Psychoanalysis* 67: 287–94.

Jones, E. (1957) *The Life and Work of Sigmund Freud: Volume 3, The Last Phase, 1919–1939*, New York: Basic Books.

Kohon, G. (1999) "The Greening of Psychoanalysis: André Green in Dialogues with Gregorio Kohon", in G. Kohon (ed.) *The Dead Mother: The Work of André Green*, London: Routledge.

Kristeva, J. (1981) *Language – The Unknown: An Initiation into Linguistics*, trans. Anne M. Menke (1989), New York: Columbia University Press.

—— (1994) "Freudian Models of Language: A Conversation", *Journal of European Psychoanalysis* 3–4, Spring 1997–Winter 1997.

—— (1997) "L'autre langue, ou traduire le sensibile", *L'Infini* 57, republished as "The Love of Another Language", trans. in J. Herman (2002), *Intimate Revolt: The Powers and Limits of Psychoanalysis*, New York: Columbia University Press.

Lacan, J. (1966a) *Ecrits: A Selection*, trans. A. Sheridan (1977), New York: Norton.

—— (1966b) "Of Structure as an Inmixing of an Otherness Prerequisite to Any Subject Whatever", in R. Macksey and E. Donato (eds) (1970) *The Structuralist Controversy: The Languages of Criticism and the Sciences of Man, 40th Anniversary Edition*, Baltimore: Johns Hopkins University Press, 2007.

—— (1973) *The Seminar of Jacques Lacan, Book XI, The Four Fundamental Concepts of Psychoanalysis*, trans. Jacques-Alain Miller (1977), Alan Sheridan (ed.), New York: Norton.

—— (1975) *The Seminar of Jacques Lacan, Book XX Encore 1972–1973, On Feminine Sexuality: The Limits of Love and Knowledge*, trans. Jacques-Alain Miller (1998), New York: Norton.

Lear, J. (1998) *Open Minded: Working Out the Logic of the Soul*, Cambridge, MA: Harvard University Press.

Lehrman, P.R. (1954) "*A History of Psychoanalysis in America*, by Clarence P. Oberndorf, M.D. (1953) New York: Grune and Stratton, Inc., 280 pp.", *Psychoanalytic Quarterly* 23: 263–65.

Lévi-Strauss, C. (1949) *Les Structures élémentaires de la Parenté* [The Elementary Structures of Kinship], trans. J.H. Hill, J.R. von Sturmer, and R. Needham (1969), R. Needham (ed.), London: Eyre and Spottiswoode.

Mahony, P. (1982) *Freud as a Writer*, New York: International Universities Press.

Makari, G. and Shapiro, T. (1993) "On Psychoanalytic Listening: Language and Unconscious Communication", *Journal of the American Psychoanalytic Association* 41: 991–1020.

Malory, T. (1485) *Le Morte Darthur*, republished as E. Vinaver (ed.) (1971) *The Works of Sir Thomas Malory*, 2nd edn, Oxford: Oxford University Press.

Milton, J. (1644) "Areopagitica", reprinted in M.Y. Hughes (ed.) (1957) *John Milton: The Complete Poetry and Major Prose*, Indianapolis: Bobbs-Merrill/Odyssey Press.

Pope John Paul II (1984) *Discorso di Giovanni Paolo II Agli Atleti Italiani Premiati Nelle Ultime Olimpiadi di Los Angeles* [Address by John Paul II to Italian athletes at the Los Angeles Olympics]. The Vatican Online, viewed 25 February 2008, http://www.vatican.va/holy_father/john_paul_ii/speeches/1984/november/documents/hf_jp-ii_spe_19841124_gruppo-olimpionici_it.html

Rizzuto, A. (2002) "Speech Events, Language Development and the Clinical Situation", *International Journal of Psychoanalysis* 83: 1325–43.

Shakespeare, W. (1623) *Mr. William Shakespeares Comedies, Histories, and Tragedies*, republished as G.B. Evans (ed.) (1974) *The Riverside Shakespeare*, Boston: Houghton Mifflin.

Sophocles. *Sophocles: Ajax Electra Oedipus Tyrannus*, trans. H. Lloyd-Jones (ed.) (1994), *Loeb Classical Library*, Volume 20, Cambridge, MA: Harvard University Press.

Star Wars (1977), Motion picture, Lucasfilm Ltd., and 20th Century Fox, California. Written, produced and directed by George Lucas.

Ticho, E. (1986) "The Influence of the German-Language Culture on Freud's Thought," *International Journal of Psychoanalysis* 67: 227–34.

Part I

The lost father

Chapter 1

The construction of the lost father[1]

André Green

To reflect on the dead father might seem like reopening an old forgotten chapter in classical Freudian psychoanalysis. Freud was preoccupied with this idea for his entire life. Is it not in the famous letter of October 1897 that he makes the first allusion to the Oedipus complex, in a reference to a play with which he was familiar: *Oedipus Rex*? And doesn't he extend his thoughts to *Hamlet*?

He presented the Oedipus complex from three angles: (1) personal self-analysis; (2) culture with universally celebrated works of art; and (3) clinically from material from patients. Freud was constantly concerned with the subject of the murder of the father. He confessed that *The Interpretation of Dreams* was "a portion of my own self analysis, my reaction to my father's death, that is to say to the most important event, the most poignant loss of a man's life" (1900, p. xxvi). In this book he devoted a chapter to one kind of typical dreams: "Dreams of the Death of Persons of whom the Dreamer is Fond" (p. 248). The wishes that are represented in dreams do not always belong to the present. The wishes of the past have to be considered in the light of the child's beliefs. To children, death has little in common with the thoughts of adults on this subject: "a child's idea of being 'dead' has nothing much in common with ours apart from the word" (p. 254). He goes on to say that the dreams of the death of parents apply with preponderant frequency to the parent who is of the same sex as the dreamer. An investigation of Greek mythology recalls the examples of Kronos and Zeus. Finally, Freud gives his first formulation of the Oedipus complex, throwing light on the meaning of Sophocles' tragedy. He adds that as far as human beings are concerned, *wishful* dreams express wishes that are *unconscious*, "We live in ignorance of those wishes" (p. 263).

Freud realized that he had made a significant discovery, in fact the corner-stone of his theory, which he later called the "Vaterkomplex." He was so convinced of its importance – confirmed by clinical experience – that he wished to establish his theory beyond mere wishes. Just think of the Rat Man's father, already dead, whom the patient imagined standing behind the door while he was masturbating looking at himself in the mirror.

The 1910 publication of James Frazer's *Totemism and Exogamy* opened a wide debate in which Freud wanted to take part. After writing *Totem and Taboo* (1913), Freud oscillated between the conviction of having made a very important step forward, and disillusionment, as if what he had postulated was too good to be true.

Of his four essays, the last on the return of totemism in childhood, is the most important. I will not review in detail Freud's ideas that referred to Darwin on the primitive horde. Neither will I review the relationship between child and animal which Freud described in little Hans' phobia where the horse, as a phobic object, is taken as a symbol of the father who generates feelings of both fear and tenderness. And I won't give much credence to his belief in William Robertson Smith's ideas on the totem meal, following the murder of the tyrannical father, as the foundation for religion, morality and the laws of society.

Starting first by examining ideas, Freud proceeds to affirm them not just as hypotheses, but as facts. "One day the brothers who had been driven out came together, killed and devoured their father and so made an end to the patriarchal horde" (1913, p. 159). This was Freud's explanation of guilt and the consequences of it. And this is also where he asserts that "The dead father became stronger than the living one had been," adding "for events took the course we so often see them follow in human affairs to this day." From this moment, Freud will remain obsessed with the ideas of the origins of social institutions. In other terms, the past is still alive, is present in ourselves but unconscious; hence the "dead father." And the book ends with Freud quoting Goethe: "In the beginning was the Deed." Therefore in 1913 Freud moves from the indisputable presence of wishes in dreams to a postulate about the relationship of the wishes to a primal deed. He adds that "everyone possesses in his unconscious mental activity an apparatus which enables him to interpret other people's reactions, that is to undo the distortions which other people have imposed on the expression of their feelings" (p. 159). But there is still another problem that awaits an answer. If there is a primal deed, how has it been transmitted from one generation to the next until now? This is the last piece of Freud's construction, which he will deal with just before his death.

Moses and Monotheism (Freud, 1939) is a very rich and very disputable book. It can be read from many points of view. I think that Freud wanted indirectly to address psychoanalysts to express fears about the future of psychoanalytic theory, which he believed could be destroyed just as was Akhenaton's original idea of the first monotheistic religion. He admits that most of his ideas were already present in *Totem and Taboo*. Freud qualified his book as a "historical novel," a point that has been closely analyzed by Josef Yerushalmi (1989). In Freud's mind, the murder of the father was truly a historical concept, dealing with what he calls historical truth, trying to describe historical development. I shall limit myself to one point: the archaic heritage. After postulating an analogy between what is shown by human neuroses, related to individual psychology, and what is learned from the analysis of religious phenomena of mass psychology, Freud concludes that the traumas of the remote past of people's history are no different from the developmental traumas of the individual. So, he refers again to the murder of the father and says that it has also been repressed, forgotten or distorted.

What about the transmission of this important deed, in the form of an archaic heritage? Freud postulates this mechanism while being perfectly aware that it stood against science, which denies phylogenetic transmission as incompatible with Darwinian views. This answer was inevitable from Freud's point of view:

> Its evidential value seems to me strong enough for me to venture on a further step and to posit the assertion that the archaic heritage of human beings comprises not only dispositions but also subject matter – memory traces of the experience of earlier generations.
>
> (1939, p. 99)

Without a doubt, these views are unacceptable. Maybe Freud undervalued his own discoveries on the unconscious and underestimated the degree to which all the same questions about fundamental issues arise in each generation. Of course, times have changed and our answers are quite different from Freud's. In Western contemporary societies, we very often observe that the traditional family structures have disappeared. Families broken up by divorce are reconstituted with siblings coming from different fathers or mothers. Our methods of investigation have changed. We rely more on observation than on the symbolic significance of parental images which are affected by the changes. Freud was also aware of the impact of contemporary events on theory. In 1900 already he wrote: "In our society today [that is around 1900] fathers are apt to cling desperately to what is left of a now sadly antiquated *potestas patris familiae*" (1900, p. 257).[2] What about 2006, more than a century later?

The war interrupted the debate on Freud's view. After the war, psychoanalysis followed different paths. In the cultural world, "classical" psychoanalysis was criticized because of the failure of most historical systems of thought which led to such errors of interpretation and ignored the masked aspects of Marxism, just as those of National Socialism. These movements of ideas objected to psychoanalysis as being an enterprise of "normalizing" people (Whitebook, 2005). On the other hand, psychoanalysis was attacked by science. Structuralism was conquering the intellectual world. Lévi-Strauss's reading of *Totem and Taboo* led him to a radical rejection of Freud's ideas, though he accepted the existence of an unconscious, as in linguistics, as a system of unconscious links, but fiercely denied its relationship to any content. The idea of the predominance of the signifier paved the way for Lacan's ideas. Lacan shared many of the criticisms addressed to Freud and proposed alternate views. According to Lacan, we are wrong to assume that sexual wishes are symbolized. On the contrary, what comes first is the symbolic order and its signifiers. The symbolic order gets hold of the images and representations and gives them meaning. In other words, the processes of the dream work – condensation and displacement – compared to metaphor and metonymy, come into play, expressing the primacy of the symbolic over the imaginary. The symbolic order exists outside, independently and before the subject. In other words, the signifier necessarily precedes any symbolic act. No act can be given the role of a foundation. Moreover, to complete the assertion that the mother is the Other, Lacan adds: the father is not the Other of the Other. Only the "name of the father" can define its place, being at the root of the symbolic functions, which always identify the father's person with the figure of the Law.

Rosolato (1969) has described the Idealized Father as an entity of unlimited power, tyrannical, ignoring frustration, that protects and allows something else in the mother's desire: the phallus. This concept of the Idealized Father has to be distinguished from Lacan's concept of exchange, another example of the symbolic order, and according to Lacan, having to deal with a symbolic death. As Shakespeare wrote: "Thou owest Nature [sic] a death."[3] However, even if the symbolic order helps us to understand the symptoms of neurosis, it may prove very difficult to apply to non-neurotic structures, precisely because the role of the dead father is questionable in them.

The views held in France were long debated and long to be accepted in Anglo-Saxon countries. In Great Britain, Melanie Klein (1932) had revised Freud's views. For instance, re-examining the case of the Wolf Man in light of the Oedipus complex, Klein suggested that the fixations that were described in Freud's essay had to be understood in terms of the much earlier oral phase with its related anxieties and defenses. Ever since, psychoanalytic research has been oriented toward the study of pregenital stages. Experience demonstrated that the references to the castration complex and to the Oedipus complex failed all too often to cure the patients. For the most part, this period of analytic research was devoted nearly exclusively to earlier stages of psychic life, considered from the perspective of mother–child relationships. This original dyad was thought to exclude the father whose influence was thought to be felt only later.

This phase, still ongoing, led to interesting discoveries. It relied on a genetic point of view. The dyad of the mother–child couple was taken as the originary one. Few theorists were concerned with how the father figure could lead us to consider triangular relationships! In contrast, Lacan adopted an entirely different point of view, long limited to France and the French-speaking countries.

In the newer mother-centered perspective, the question of the dead father disappeared. The dead father was dead because, in order even to think of his murder, he must have some kind of existence that one would like to end. The patriarchal order, already weakening around 1900 as Freud observed, continued its decline, in tandem with other changes in the social condition of women. A working life was opening to them, contraceptive measures were developed in spite of the opposition of the Church. Children came to have another type of child rearing based on the joint participation of fathers and mothers, both having a role to play in parenting.

Compared with work on mother–child relationships, little has been written on the early aspects of paternity. The dead father in Freud is an outcome of the Oedipus phase. What we would like to know is what precedes it. In what way does the father figure in the picture and how can his role be intuitively grasped in such a context. Referring to Freud once again may help us find intuitions in his work that can serve as guidelines, guidelines we don't find elsewhere.

For instance, consider the following statement about the origins of the ego ideal: "for behind it lies an individual's first and most important identification, his identification with the father of his own personal prehistory" (Freud, 1922a, p. 31).[4] As far as I am aware, it is the first time that Freud mentions a personal prehistory and links it to an important identification with a father who is not yet involved in the complex web of intertwining ambivalent cathexes and relationships between mother and father. Freud explains, "it is a direct and immediate identification and takes place earlier than any object-cathexis" (p. 31). He had already considered this two years earlier, in 1921, when he distinguished taking the father as an ideal belonging to the "early history of the Oedipus complex" (1913, p. 104). We see Freud groping in the dark.

In Group Psychology, he shows how the child has two types of ties. He writes:

> At the same time as this identification with his father, or a little later, the boy has begun to develop a true object-cathexis towards his mother, according to the attachment [anaclitic] type. He then exhibits, therefore, two psychologically distinct ties: a straightforward sexual object-cathexis towards his mother and an identification with his father which takes him as his model. The two subsist side by side for a time.
>
> (Freud, 1922b, p. 105)

Here identification is related to a paternal model. Freud states that the boy deals with his father by identifying with him. In fact, Freud says that the boy appropriates, takes over, the father by identification, and suggests that the type of paternal identification implies a desexualization, a sort of sublimation. Even if Freud's statements are not always very clear, he seems to oppose two types of bonds from the very beginning: (1) those relating to the mother are directed, "straight forward" and (2) on the contrary, those related to the father, taken as his ideal, imply desexualization as some kind of relinquishment of the former tie. This, as I see it, is the consequence of the outcome of the Oedipal component of the murder of the father: the birth of the ego ideal and the superego, desexualization, sublimation, and, in culture, what is called civilization.

What is important in my view is Freud's persistent intention to build a picture of a three party relationship. I find this description more interesting than those of the supposedly exclusive mother–child dyad that makes no room for the father. Of course this dyad is related to what Freud qualifies as a "straightforward attachment," whatever its nature is. But I want to add another factor. The father, apparently absent from the scene, is far from being inexistent. In fact, he is an observer of the scene. And even if he joyfully participates as witness of his child's satisfaction, we also have to consider that given that he is not immediately included in and does not take part in this relationship, he stands in a sort of anti-sexual position. Even if he is not hostile, the simple fact of his exclusion from the direct exchange gives him a certain reserve about what is happening. Therefore the third party in the scene is the father's look, to which all the limitations of this supposedly entirely satisfactory situation can be attributed. This is more intuitively grasped by the child than stated openly. Moreover this situation may become connected with any other feelings having to do with unpleasure. If we add that it is inevitable that the father, witnessing the scene, experiences nostalgia for something forever lost to him that the child and the mother have the privilege of enjoying, we can imagine what takes place here. All the threats of separation and the effects of repression can be linked to this look. And if, from all the functions that Freud describes as constituents of the superego, self-observation is the most important one, we can guess that it might be the result of a turning-against-the-self mechanism. The baby is not looked at by the mother alone, but also by the father.

In the chapter called "An Advance on Intellectuality," in *Moses and Monotheism* (1939), Freud characterizes the patriarchal order as following the matriarchal:

> But this turning from the mother to father points in addition to a victory of intellectuality over sensuality – that is, an advance in civilization, since maternity is proved by the evidence of the senses while paternity is a hypothesis, based on an inference and a premiss. Taking sides in this way with a thought-process in preference to a sense perception has proved to be a momentous step.
>
> (p. 114)

Freud connects this with the "omnipotence of thoughts" linked with the development of speech. "The new realm of intellectuality was opened up, in which ideas, memories and inferences became decisive in contrast to the lower psychical activity which had direct perceptions by the sense-organs as its content" (p. 113).

This quotation can apply to our subject. Can we talk about the father in the same terms that we use to describe the relationship with the mother? This is something that the "new fathers" sometimes do not understand. These fathers have a closer relationship with the body of the child, giving attention and care in a proximity that he obviously enjoys. I will not go so far as to say that they are competing with the mother, but they sometimes seem to be doubles of the mother rather than finding what is expected of them as fathers.

The idea of the murder of the father is raised in the mind because the father is supposed to be the single possessor of something (the mother) that appears indispensable to the child. It is in this sense, standing for the indispensable, that it is called symbolic through the signs that are associated with it. We find so many varied circumstances concerning the father that we are not able to predict what emerges from them as an issue. The relationship with the father may have been marked in the past by sexual violence, transgression, rape, sodomy. These sometimes lead to an identification with the aggressor, not withstanding a strong fixation. At the other extreme, they can lead to masochistic fixations or feelings of emptiness as a reaction to an attitude of total neglect when the father desires to ignore the child's very existence. It is the relationship between the parents that determines whether the father's part will be one of total withdrawal or violence, as an ever-increasing tension paralyzes his thinking. It is essential to understand the relationship between both parents in order to understand the child's fantasies about his place.

I will consider these lost aspects through the clinical material present in most analyses of non-neurotic structures. I believe that all detailed treatments of patients showing psychotic structures, violent and delinquent behaviours or some psychosomatics, who have nonetheless sufficiently intelligible mental functioning, may open the way to clarification.

It is surprising that Freud, either in dealing with the murder of the father, or with other aspects of earlier phenomena, never considered the influence of the destructiveness, abundantly shown in all the cases I mentioned. Perhaps this is because he thought that the Oedipal murder of the father was an indispensable regulator in the prevention of extreme forms of destruction. Today we can no longer avoid the problem posed by the differential investment of mother and father. What I propose is less a description of the facts of what was supposed to have happened than a construction – in Freud's sense – of *this* lost father.

Today I believe Freud's words may be interpreted in the following way: that for the most part the father can only be reached through absence. Why is this? Why is it so hard to find room for him? Could it be because of the difficulty the child has in accepting that the mother might lack anything that the child itself could not provide? Indeed, to some extent, early on, the mother looking after the child tries to comfort it with the same thought. The concept of absence, though implicit since the beginning of psychoanalysis, was only later developed. Lacan put forward the idea that there was nothing concerning the mind that could be reached directly, especially when memories were not related to the senses. The subject therefore had no access to the most primitive events of psychic life. After Melanie Klein proposed her interpretation of what she believed to have occurred, Winnicott introduced the idea of "imaginative elaboration" of bodily functions. I consider that to be another way of expressing the idea of what comes to be called "representation." Perhaps the term "representation" sounded too sophisticated to Winnicott at the time. However, both of these terms relate to an activity supposed to happen after, rather than during, a given experience: in other words when "thinking" about it retrospectively. It is after the experience that one wishes to recall it, to relive the best aspects of it. It's as if one wanted to discover that they were still there and could be experienced once more, reassuring that they have not been lost forever in the flux of time. This internal reworking also gives a shape and a form to certain features of it. It adds some parts to the lasting memories that are, as it were, "corrected" in order to correspond with how the subject wishes them to appear. This process also reminds us of unpleasant aspects in order to avoid their return.

All these modifications are the familiar operations of fantasy. Taken together they refer to what Winnicott calls the "subjective object," which the child will not easily give up because of the omnipotent control that he exercises over it. When the child later "travels" from subjective objects to objects objectively perceived, absence will also be elaborated. What I mean is that some kind of splitting will occur between the capacity to represent and the strangeness of its outcome. Who represents and why? We must take possession of these things created by us. We must ask ourselves from whence they come.

We may feel that the presence of our selves is constant. We defend a homogeneous continuity of our beings. However, if we think about it, this is obviously false. For instance, we experience night dreams without requiring that either the dreamer or the world be present. Although we recognize some sort of presence of ourselves in the dream, it is of a different kind of presence than during the day. In dreams we discover someone else. Another self is unleashed that changes our experience of the world and how we belong in it. We discover that the transformation that the self undergoes is born of our wishes, new and old, even if not explicitly expressed. We wonder who we are while losing control of our thoughts.

Our attention fluctuates during the day. At times we let ourselves be absorbed by an activity similar to the dream thoughts. This inspired Bion to show that dream activity is not dependent on sleep. Barriers operate to prevent the thoughts of the day from invading dream thoughts; to keep them from being the thoughts of life while awake. The application of this notion was later extended to play. Freud had already observed this, and Klein utilized the idea when analyzing children. During a consultation with a depressed mother who had to bring her two-and-a-half-year-old son along, Winnicott discovered that the boy's play in the office was about what he overheard, even though the links were not direct. So play, like dreaming, is a repetition of subjective experience modified along lines that are meaningful to the player, even when no immediate connections are present.

Therefore, we are constantly shifting between different forms of presence. Some are linked to perception, and others to more evanescent modes of being attached to representation. An object that appears constant, its identity remaining essentially the same, is, at the same time, always undergoing per-mutation in our minds, changing shape and representation. Each of these ways of existing is distinct from and separated, absent, from the others. This is what I call the "third." As I have said elsewhere, the analytic object is composed of two parts, one belonging to the patient and the other to the analyst. The third here is not just another term to be added to the other two. Because of its alternative nature the third is mainly a question mark that stands for something for which no immediate answer is required. Yet it is the main promoter of psychic activity. Who, why, how? The gathering of these different psychic fields requires first and foremost a tolerance for contradiction.

A capacity for introjection is necessary in order to keep the different kinds of functioning together, not only to accept them, but also to imagine some sort of link among them. The subject is the attempt to make them coexist. The world is not reduced to what it simply is. Instead it opens itself to new possibilities, though not everything that is possible is realizable.

The connections made between ideas not based on real existence, but to aspects borrowed from existence, create another sort of reality. The oppor-tunity for alternative worlds in thought introduces us to the creative universe of cultural experience. The question "Have you created this or have you found it?" sometimes remains, though implicit and unformulated.

To summarize, the boundaries between the internal and the external worlds are flexible if, and only if, an activity of play is at work. Fundamentally, a search for the self can be seen as the motive for the therapeutic relationship. This must be experienced as a state of formlessness with no aim, a state of rest at the origin of which something creative might be elaborated. This is so only if that which is created is reflected and only if reflected. During a long session in which a patient had such an experience, Winnicott (1971, p. 61) said to the patient: "All sorts of things happen and they wither. This is the myriad deaths you have died. But if someone is there, someone who can give you back what happened, then the details dealt with in this way become part of you, and do not die." Winnicott profoundly understood the primacy of searching over finding or being found, which was the basis of what we seek. He came to this conclusion because of the patient's remark about a question she had been asking. Winnicott underscored it and the patient replied: "Yes I see one could postulate the existence of a ME from the question as from the searching" (1971, p. 64). Even in these extreme cases, the question is still there. Both patient and analyst share it, not awaiting an immediate response. The question is illuminated by the development of the analytic process, which throws light on it retrospectively.

We should by now have an idea of what absence is: it is the space between a listener and a reflector capable of resisting destruction. The subject is the latent organizer of the different types of representations (words, things, affects, drives, bodily states, acts), which become fused. They appear to the mind in the form of a questioning that first has to be translated into the common language of the partners. Unfortunately, we cannot take for granted that such a configuration is always available to the analyst. Working with violent and suicidal patients has taught us this. Lengthy treatments with psychotics show similarities with them (G. Kohon). Here, we have fewer questions than answers, but these answers are meant to conceal the questions that are behind them. They are meant to superimpose upon the analyst what the patient needs him to think, in order not to disclose the underlying ideas. So, all we can do is to try not to make assumptions about what we suppose to have happened. Instead we try to describe in a more or less coherent way what we hear, to try to imagine the world in which the patient evolves and to try to convey it to others. We have known for a long time that repetition can take the place of remembering. In these cases repeating is the way most often used actually to express mental contents that are disturbing, denied and given form only through action. It is as if the moment at which they come into existence coexists with their expulsion from the mind. One reason for this could be that action enables this kind of patient to put distance between himself and analyst (Rosine Perelberg). Regardless of its consequences, an act becomes an embodiment of something that might have started in the mind but becomes completely dissociated from it, as if the mere fact that it came into existence and became real disconnected it from any causal relationship. By interrupting the relationship to the mind, the act seems to have avoided an uncontrolled never-ending race to escape the fantasy that haunts the mind. At the same time, one can see the race is on for the realization of the same fantasy, one which will end in some sort of a collision between object and self in danger of disintegrating.

Experience with criminals shows that while they appear as to be mindful of their lives, their awareness of their action is actually variable. They can say, without a sense of contradiction, "Yes, I did it," adding, "it was not me who did it." When after years and years of a therapeutic relationship they are able to start feeling guilt, this change can be denied at a crucial moment: "Thus I was sure that I was right in doing it," even without rationalization.

No sense of self seems to be present. The self is confused with the body, and the body is treated as an entity to be hated and attacked. It is as if the patients stood outside of their skins, their bodies lost, while seeking an independence beyond their control. They fear close contact. Sometimes the patient cannot look at the analyst or talk to him for very long periods. Or he bursts into rages at any disappointment, expressing openly murderous feelings or a denial of the analyst's existence. He mixes hate, rage, and a desire to protect the analyst from his rage. The patient is restless, exhausting the analyst without letting on that he receives anything from him. This is in its own way a reflection of the patient's psychic life. The feeling that he receives nothing is the result of his destruction of anything he hears that may differ from what he immediately feels.

Understanding is associated with a danger of becoming mad. It is as if accepting a new light thrown on a situation would risk presenting himself to the mother as an independent mind. Any disagreement could lead her to accuse the patient of being crazy or, conversely, could imply that the mother is crazy. Needless to say, this is the patient's fantasy, but even delusions are based on a kernel of truth.

When the father begins to exist, not only in the mother's mind but also as a separate entity, a new space is created in which the child can imagine himself as separate. This situation is felt to be more frightening than hopeful. Absence and representation pose a threat rather than providing an opening up of the mind. Separation is experienced mainly as a loss. The child's fantasy is not only an expression of what he is supposed to think, but also a reflection of what the mother is expected to feel in retaliation for his acceptance of that unwished for third.

If the patient is to avoid being thrown into that deserted space of abandonment by the mother, he will have no other choice but to survive within one tolerable to her. When he feels confined, he opens the doors to devouring monsters meant to undo his budding unity by fragmenting his body. He is thus forced to admit that outside the mother no relationship can be helpful if openly manifested. But these monsters can be seen as a way of keeping the mother at a distance. It takes a long time for the patient to start to dream, beginning with nightmares that show some evidence of an independent mind. In the therapeutic relationship, he is not authorized to speak his thoughts. For instance, if a therapist – a third – attempts to relate to this kind of patient, the patient initially will respond with the voice of the internal mother rather than in his own name. He implicitly shows what she is supposed to think about this new presence introduced only to sever the ties between mother and child.

This hypothetical dialogue is in fact a denial of what the patient himself would like to have happen, but is not allowed to reveal in the slightest. Moreover, it is filled with such violence that it becomes unacceptable to him, as this liberation cannot be sought without taking revenge on the possessive mother. So in the end, he is bound to discourage anyone from joining the exchange with the mother.

One consequence of this is the lack of possession of one's own body. The body may suffer anxious transformations, such as changing its identity into that of someone else who might also have imposed his identity on the patient. Again, the self is submitted to a loss of boundaries, just as hallucinations invade the senses and perceptions. It is as if the inside, having invaded the outside through which the world was perceived, now turns against the inside to colonize it.

Gregorio Kohon, who has worked with psychotics, shows that behind the explicit descriptions of dual relationships one finds masked aspects that open ways of understanding which leave room for thirdness.

Lacan observed that even before a child came into existence, he was already there in the desire of his parents – not that he was always wanted or expected, but that he was in any case the object of desire before his own could be expressed in his individuality. Kohon reminds us that as soon as the baby is imagined in utero, the baby–mother dyad contains a third term as reference. Conversely, "the words of this pre-Oedipal mother constitute itself as a primitive third term in the baby's mind." To conclude, "Mother and baby can only exist in the context of a third person, which does not need to be physically present in order to be there" (Green and Kohon, 2005, p. 92). Further, Kohon says, "The mother's discourse did not include a father with a desire of his own, there was no father whose desire would take the mother away" (p. 71). Observe that Kohon did not write that this desire of the father was really non-existent, but rather that there was no place for it in the mother's discourse, as if there were nobody else but the child and she.

The influence of the father often seems negligible in clinical material. Yet when some fathers die prematurely, patients later confess, "When my father died, my life stopped." One image comes to my mind: Michelangelo's *Creation of Adam*. God and man are lying, facing each other, both pointing their index fingers at one another. A very small though visible space separates both fingers. This space is of extreme importance, forbidding any fusion between God and man, and compelling us to think about the discontinuity not only between deity and humanity but also between people. This leaves open the possibility of thinking about relationships without threat to the partners. As one of my patients once told me, "If it happened that they could touch each other, there would be a terrible explosion that could blow out everything." She was speaking of us, of course, but she was also communicating her fear to me that such communication would interrupt her feeling of being possessed by her mother, which she could not at any price give up. She was constantly complaining about her mother's tyrannical attitude, leaving her no independence. In fact, it was the patient who introduced her mother into almost all the acts of her life, directly or indirectly.

When a patient achieves a sense of reality, however uncertain, he comes to conclude that his belief, once held with absolute and indispensable conviction, was actually a reflection of what the mother was supposed to be through the child. It was an illusion directly communicated, one that suffered neither doubt nor delay. While this situation is evocative of a false self-creation, here the tragedy is greater. In these instances the mother's balance is preserved at the expense of sanity. Living in a mad world is chosen to protect the dyad. The individual not only feels compelled to adopt a false self, but he must also be part of a common madness or nothing.

Mirror relationships operate prior to and during the dyadic period. Even in a context of fusion, polarities that reflect one another come into play without a definite distinction that might contradict the dyad. It is essential that this situation be reflected yet again by someone outside the dyad. Peter Fonagy and Mary Target (1995) envisage the father's role as being the witness to the relationship between mother and child that fosters the capacity to present the child with a reflection of his position in the relationship.

As one of my patients said once: "When I look at myself in the mirror, I see nothing. Or I can see a very vague shape. But if this image in the mirror is reflected in another mirror, then I can see myself distinctly." The feeling of being looked at has itself to be looked at a second time as a reflection of the reflection. This may be one of the roles of the third. If the interposition of the father can be accepted, it is not only because of his role in the separation but because he gives himself as a compensation, as another being to love and be loved by. This leads to the question not only of the child's relationship to this third, but of the nature of the relationships between the two others, mother and father.

I wish to stress how this modification coincides with the arrival of a new partner. What happens in this case is the interposition of the father's body between mother and child at a point when the child to some extent is still involved in the previous fusional relationship. In most normal conditions this transition will occur gradually. The interposition mentioned here helps to establish the physical separation between mother and child.

What can help the child get through this passage? The father, by playing a separating role, by offering his own person in compensation for the loss of another, by tolerating the aggression that the child directs toward him, by standing firm and allowing himself to be hated because he has not permitted something to continue indefinitely, creates the necessary points of reference for the establishment of this conflictual situation. We can define this coming together with the father as an encounter with someone who introduces the idea of negation, of saying "No" in the same situation. Not that the mother didn't say "No" earlier, but it is quite different to hear this from someone outside the dyad who is not contradicted. Very ambivalent feelings sometimes accompany this passage. The giving up of the fusional relationship appears impossible to accept. What happens then is a violent rejection of this intervening third, with a fierce desire to maintain the earlier situation.

One can imagine the supposed reason for this rejection, the equivalent of an early murder of the father. It is not only to keep the fusional relationship going, it is also linked to the fear that accepting the father would be somehow robbing the mother, risking her retaliation. Or if the growing child tries to lessen his tension by clinging to the mother, he fears that he might create an opportunity for the other two to unite against him, perhaps coming to wish to destroy each other or him. What is unthinkable about the primal scene is thereby avoided: the child maintains the fantasy that he is still the focus of this situation.

The symptoms of which the patient complains – fears (phobias of all kinds, sometimes terrors), nightmares, threat of disintegration, murderous impulses following disappointment, hallucinations, oscillating identification between male and female, or projecting onto the other the same oscillations, search for closeness and dread of being rejected, fading into non-existence or being annihilated as a person and enslaved to some other – have the painful quality of alluding to events that occur in reality less often than in productions of the mind. It is as if there were a continuity between what belongs to the internal world, lacking containing limits, and the external. It is as if there were no boundaries that protect the self and no awareness that the symptoms are one's own productions. Therefore any other is dangerous, becoming inevitably an enemy rather than an ally. The only defense left is a kind of automatic mirror relationship. Others must reflect the dangerous internal world. They must be belittled, terrorized and paralyzed in order to neutralize the affects that they arouse.

Those working with these kinds of patients propose to understand their clinical picture as an expression of the persistence of an omnipotent internal mother who is still reigning in the child's mental universe. Several authors consider that one of the father's roles is to put to an end the fusional relationship that the dyad is willing to perpetuate. Winnicott thinks the father's role is to keep an eye on the mother's "voraciousness" for the baby. Is men's jealousy for not being able to bear children the cause of these remarks? Perhaps so; but one must note that the time of the intervention by the third coincides with early signs of a feeling of some unity and independent desire in the baby.

To understand what happens next, we must remember what Lacan described as "foreclosure": a radical rejection that does not allow early triangulation to be included in the process taking place among the chain of signifiers. Or we might recall what Bion tried to describe: the expulsion of mental contents in engulfing objects. This kind of murder leaves no trace, but can be identified in the return of the banished elements that come back to the mind that tried to expel them.

Sometimes the father is gone, having abandoned the child and the mother, refusing to be related to them anymore. In this case the father remains artificially present, but not internally included in any set of relationships. It is as if the mind of the child remains completely out of touch with him as an existing person. This is another figure of the lost father, one that escapes our understanding because its construction seems artificial, without internal resonance.

When independent psychic activity happens to appear, it links together imaginary contents ordinarily expelled. The unconscious becomes artificially conscious, simply for the sake of being evacuated. It is not that the patient is unaware of what he has grasped in the other's mind. He just must not, at any cost, reveal that it has become a matter of thought for him; nor can he draw conclusions about what he has thought. If someone were to discover what he was thinking, he would have to fiercely deny it. To do otherwise would lead him to accept that the thoughts were his.

The father has never been integrated into the internal world and seems to remain outside the self. The transference relationships show that he is potentially very important to the child. There are signs that show the child's need to protect him from others who deny his need for him, his wish to keep him alive even when dominated by the omnipotent mother. Fathers may remain external, but their existence must be secretly preserved.

So it actually is impossible to speak of an early father murder because, considering the situation from the inside, the father is not yet a father, but rather just a "would be" father. He may be prohibited from playing his role, but he will remain a secret companion of misfortune, even though he still appears as a threatening third. The silenced desires tell us that one can find him in the shade, offering progressively and slowly a space that resists the temptation to let hate invade the whole relationship. It is there that the therapist's persistence in the treatment is important. It's not that the patient can change the reality of his inner environment; but at least he can stop engaging in infinite quarrels with it, leaving him with a feeling of being lost in the wilderness. There is no murder of an early father here, but rather a deadening of his life to come. Ambivalence remains at work, not permitting reconciliation.

Attacks directed toward the father never cease, as if ceasing were an impossible task to achieve. If the father survives and seems to be reborn, perhaps it's because we think of him as somebody who is allowed to enjoy everything forbidden to us, those wishes that we know can't come true. We can't avoid idealizing him, and we continue to idealize him secretly in the unconscious. The mother is the only side of the triangle of relationships that has two carnal relationships. Even if those relationships are very different, they are still alive. Her carnal relationship with the father goes along with the carnal relationship with the child. For hidden behind all the things that the father has prohibited are also all the things that have not happened with him. We sometimes think that the fixations to the father are easier to overcome because the relationship is more distant. But this is not so. Think also about the things interrupted that remain, in longing, in nostalgia, forgotten but still very much present.

One of my patients said he had absolutely no memories of any rivalry with his father in childhood, though he had plenty during adolescence. He thought that the later rivalry was caused by his father's failure to recognize his right to be independent and to be rewarded for the quality of his work. One day he told me that as a child he had fits of somnambulism. During that period he regularly found himself waking, having slept on the carpet next to his parents' bed. When he was older, he had to tie himself to his bed in order to avoid some accident during such a fit. Still it was very difficult for him to recognize the meaning of this behavior. Ambivalent feelings towards the father remain lifelong, unrecognized. Displaced and disguised, their true meaning can be accepted only in the transference relationship.

Maybe this is the true function of transference: to concentrate onto one person all unsatisfied desire, thus providing an opportunity for some kind of acceptance. The analytic situation allows for the expression of those desires. Though the analyst interprets in the "here and now," he and the patient return to a remote and lost time where the analyst as father can both listen and be heard.

Giving up omnipotence is a heavy sacrifice. Even when apparently accomplished, a residual belief remains that *someone* has seen all of his wishes satisfied. The analytic father, the father in the transference, though able to speak to that which has never been addressed, is nonetheless unable to give answers. The form of the analytic exchange is meant to enable the formulation of new questions. Maybe one way of giving up omnipotence is to renounce the possibility that we can know all about the transformations that occur from our beginnings, namely those transformations that allow a shift from the dyad to the triad to an indefinite reproduction of thirdness. I shall take two examples of this change in our strategies. We give up the idea that we can witness our own past, becoming witnesses of ourselves. Perhaps accepting some basic constructs without exactly knowing how they originated actually tells us more.

Winnicott (1971, p. 152) concludes his work with a postscript. He proposes an unsolvable: "I postulate an essential paradox, one that we must accept and that is not for resolution. This paradox, which is central to the concept, needs to be allowed and allowed for over a period of time in the care of each baby." Winnicott also implies, in another part of his work, that it is a lifelong paradox between a subjective object and an objectively perceived object.

This gap between conception and perception involves something of the environment. But the important thing is to accept it without trying to overcome it. It is probably what helps the discovery of transitional objects and phenomena at the limit of the inside and the outside, both mother and not mother at the same time. These phenomena create the field of illusion and open the way to disillusionment. Disillusionment requires first having been illusioned.

Another example: Bion introduced along with Love and Hate (1962) a third category, Knowledge (1965), for something in the process of being known. He supposes that raw material derived from sense impressions cannot be used for psychic work. Needed first is the transformation through the alpha function, an unknown function in the system that must remain unknown. The mother's capacity for reverie gives an approximation of it. The result is the transformation of sense impressions into a material that brings this primitive activity close to the material of dreams, myths and passion. It is probable that linking is necessary to the development of these transformations. But Bion also matches the K function to – (minus) K, not knowing, as a form of omnipotence. –K seems preferable to K. K implies the conservation of what is taken in to be transformed, the fundamental dilemma being between the elaboration of frustration or the evacuation of it. This is not the simple outcome of one thing following another but of the acceptance of frustration and the relinquishing of the solution that prefers to remain ignored.

The analytic frame, i.e. the setting, can represent the father. Once Rosenfeld was asked by one of the people attending his lectures, "Where is the father in what you say?" He replied that verbalizing an interpretation could be seen as introducing the father into the material. In other words, literal references to the father are not required to introduce the father. The psychoanalytic setting itself, the analytic interpretive process itself, is experienced as a symbolic system that stands for the father.

Many authors emphasize the importance of making simple, descriptive interpretations which deliver as accurately as possible the patient's state of mind. The analyst must first send back to the patient what the analyst surmises that the patient is trying to express about his fears. The analyst should try to guess what the patient wouldn't dare say to himself. When the mediation of the third is missing, the distortion of the message keeps it undisclosed, lest it be deciphered by an enemy.

The patient may experience communication through language as fearful. Words seem to be used painfully, seemingly unable to contain the thoughts that want to escape their mental prison. But when words are returned, spoken, with the thinking that the patient unconsciously expects of the analyst, a reflection may occur. The discourse of the analyst reverberates with the patient's discourse. The analytic setting, with its fundamental solitude and tolerance for the unbearable, creates the conditions for the feelings, thoughts and impulses in want of mediation to be heard. Hence that setting has its own analytic third, making possible the operation of an internal mirror within the frame. This invites consideration of not only what the analyst understands from what the patient has communicated, but also what the analyst thinks of what he has understood and how he chose to formulate it. As Perelberg (1999) writes:

> I feel however that when the analyst formulates interpretations – of whatever kind – she is *inaugurating* something for the patient, independently of the content of the interpretation. The analyst introduces differentiations and separations into a territory previously more chaotic and undifferentiated. The theories present in the analyst's formulations are thus not there, present in the mind of the patient, available to be

uncovered, but become constructions made both by the analyst and the patients in the analytic process. In this process, the analyst is by definition creating the paternal function and breaking up the phantasy of a fusion with the mother.

(p. 105)

Here, thought processes also come to the fore, but they are not abstractions. They are about matters of life and death, survival, at any cost. The frame is not only a therapeutic tool but an analyzer too, "a procedure for the investigation of mental processes which are inaccessible in any other way" (Freud, 1913, p. 235).

Incidentally a strange remark comes to mind. In the beginning of *Moses and Monotheism*, Freud writes: "To deprive a people of the man whom they take pride in as the greatest of their sons" (1939, p. 7). In fact Moses is less the greatest of the sons of the Jews than their symbolic father. So, it seems that Freud wished to deprive the Jews of their father, just as he wished to contest Shakespeare's authorship, suggesting that Edward de Vere was the true author of Shakespeare's plays and poems.[5] Other examples can be found which relate to an essential theme in Shakespeare's work: *bastardy*. Bastardy, though very common at the time of the Renaissance, created in the bastard child feelings of resentment and a desire for revenge. Everybody remembers Edmund's cruelty towards his father Gloucester, leading to direct or disguised parricide. The hostility toward the father, ending in his assassination, is unconscious in *Oedipus Rex* in that Oedipus was unaware that the old man with whom he quarreled, and eventually slew, was his own father. Here the unconsciousness of the parricidal killings might explain such a dreadful deed.

Why must it to be unconscious? The obvious response is that parricide accomplished in full conscience is unthinkable. It was not even mentioned in Solon laws. Indeed, writing down its punishment would have been to admit its possibility. So, in conclusion, the murder of the father and the dead father are both unthinkable.

Final remarks

Why consider the dead father stronger than the living one had been? When alive, the actual father was more or less openly, if not a rival, at least an obstacle to any exclusive relationship between mother and child, for both sexes. He could not but inspire resentment or hostility whatever his loveable qualities, arousing the more or less open expression of negative feelings. The mother had her part to play on this score. She could either stand with the father, sharing the will to punish the guilty child, or she could defend him, not always on just grounds. In any case, we confuse the hostile feelings, or the feeling that the child has been unjustly treated, with their unconscious effects. It is impossible for the child to avoid guilt. But, and here is the point, unconscious guilt feelings are of another sort. Even the just feelings of revenge are seen from the unconscious as manifestations of prohibited emotions, just as the unconscious idealization of the father is an exaggeration of the conscious value and admiration (or envy) that he engenders.

In the idealization of mourning, the characteristic traits of the father are even more magnified and overpowered in order to deny any hostility that his memory raises. The longing for the father increases the loss. But why doesn't Freud ever argue this in the case of the dead mother? As I have already said, problems regarding the mourning of the mother and the father are very different. One would be tempted to understand this in terms of the different statuses of mothers and fathers in Freud's day. The patriarchal order was the explanation. However, the predominance of the father figure is insufficient to account for the ambivalence. Behind the father stood a god, just as the god evoked the image of the father. The project of reaching God was only possible through the lens of fatherhood. The father, like God, was the creator. To lose a father was like the punishment of being abandoned by God and expelled from the garden of Eden (the mother). Freud added that the loss of a father was the realization of a repressed wish, i.e. eliminating his presence as an obstacle to the enjoyment of the mother's body.

All the reasons for the hatred of the father – authoritarianism, rigidity, harshness – hide the main motive. The father stands between the bodies of the mother and the child and has a limiting influence on the pleasure born from bodily contact, skin to skin, smile with smile, laughter, joy and bliss shared, created together. From this the father should be absent, not only because the child would like to be the only one, but also because an absent father does not limit the joy in the fantasy that the father could actually disappear, perhaps due to an unpredictable accident. But the real loss of the father would also mean the loss of his protection.

So, in all circumstances, the relationship with the father is more distant and more intermittent than the one with the mother. His "presence" is felt more as a return of the repressed, a reaction carrying the forbidden wish to get rid of him as an obstacle. All the symbolism linked with his power, the fear he inspires and the love, respect, and awe due him are linked to his distance. Distance is necessary to worship him, the keeper of the sacred order. Though modern fathers play more joyfully with their children, I doubt that this can modify fundamentally the nature of the core conflict. In the end, the parents share the same bed.

The father's distance from the child is not just something external. More important is the distance in psychic space between the unconscious repressed desires (and their punishment) and the conscious manifestations dictated by education, civilized behavior, the dictates of conscience, etc. Remember that all of this is linked to an absence of awareness, except in some circumstances. Unconscious guilt, obsessive manifestations, tormenting feelings, uneasiness with the authority figures are experienced consciously as implausible because they have been cut off from their roots. This mystery is tormenting. The consequences of the death wish precede any allusion to death aimed at the father (not to say anything about their connection to a limitless pleasure).

It is difficult to conceive of mourning for the dead father, because it does not resemble mourning for an object in the present. The presence of the dead father is of a very special kind of presence. Not linked to memories, it is not a representation, nor linked to any perception. It is as if one were haunted, inhabited by a ghost, whose reality is both a doubtful and overpowering kind of unthinkable presence seen with the eye's mind (Hamlet). The ghost is hardly about a real father, who is rather like a ghost himself. So we have the ghost of a ghost, of an incomprehensible psychic reality, the result of unconscious guilt and longing for a father figure, who may never have existed. The death of an already dead figure is very different from the death of someone who once was a living person. Freud was very good at suggesting this type of psychic reality. After him, I see no one who has succeeded in continuing this train of thought.

Things have changed. No more are today's fathers kept from physical contact with their children. On the contrary, they have very close relationships with them. But the father as an entity is still an object with whom an indirect relationship is still more important than an immediate close relationship like that with the mother. Intense pleasurable physical contact with the father is in fact another source of guilt and fear. It can stimulate defensive reactions against feelings created by sensuous contact.

Moreover, when negative relationships predominate, aggressive fantasies directed toward the mother are more accessible than fantasies addressed to the father. In other words, the father figure is more subject to unconscious fantasy than the mother is. It is as if fear of retaliation (castration) obliged the child to hide his hostile fantasies. Perhaps the circumstances of contact with the mother are more difficult to refrain from, disguise or repress. They are more natural. Why forbid playing with the mother's breast if the child is breastfed? Fathers have no breasts, but their body structure is more suited to a kind of play that is closer to a fight. There is a point at which the child wants to measure the father's power and strength against his own. Even when the father pretends to fight, the child seems to realize that no real fight is possible under these conditions. So, play-fighting is a way of maintaining knowledge of what would happen in the case of a real fight.

The unconscious conflicts between the repressed negative feelings of childhood and the conscious feelings of tenderness, admiration and recognition of the father's superiority in the rivalry for possession of the mother, result in two issues. The death wish toward the father and the desire to replace the father are overcome by the solution of identification. Freud qualifies it as a momentous step when the child borrows from the father the force necessary to relinquish forbidden wishes in favor of becoming like the father. The conflict cannot be totally resolved because the child must admit a contradiction: "Be like father but stop wanting to be totally like him in your most cherished desires." So, a certain amount of hostility remains, detectable in an ever-lasting ambivalence. Another problematic issue is the negative Oedipus complex. The negative Oedipus complex does not just represent the opposite constellation, but pregenital fixations as well. Strongly anchored in the unconscious, these stand in the way of the classical Oedipal outcome. Not only does pregenital aggression dominate the picture; those early fixations take the form of what I have called "primary anality" (Green, 1993, pp. 284–291), in which the trends belonging to the anal phase bear the impact of narcissism. Aggression is often directed toward women and latent homosexual fixations, mixed with aggressive fantasies, are more widespread. These fantasies often spare the father and are focused on the mother.

Repression is more necessary with the father because he is seen as the purveyor of security, and he permits access to the mother. Of course, some fathers are not protective. They can become threatening in fits of anger or under the influence of alcohol, unpredictable and even sexually dangerous. Furthermore, the old family picture is no longer universal. Now mothers usually work. They are as absent as fathers used to be. They contribute their share to the frustration imposed on the infant. So, what does remain of the old picture?

As important as these modifications in the family structure are, they don't account for the consequences to the structure of the mind of the child. It is not relevant to underline behavioral or psychological effects, or to describe observed changes. That is not what psychoanalysis is about. It is not so important to describe those changes through observations. All of this must be interpreted by the mind of the psychoanalyst, still shaped on the axiomatic lines of modes of desire and unconscious identification.

One consequence is that unconscious parental images are more difficult to decipher. They are more ambiguous and their characteristics become more difficult to interpret. If we argue that things are not so clear as in the past, those differences must be clarified and their importance recognized. In other words, fathers are not pals. Playing games with children emphasizes that someone has to make the rules and ensure that those rules are respected. Unfortunately, in real life, we often find a mimicry of these supposedly respected rules of sacred value.

Though I grant that relationships have changed, I still insist that the father cannot be apprehended without mediation. The question is whether these changes affect the basic features defining the relationship between the child and the father. The specific nature of this relationship is such that it is contingent upon the primitive relationship between the child and the mother. Furthermore, even this relationship must be considered in relation to the father. Yet there are differences. In the mother–child relationship, the mediation that must be evaluated is the place of the father for the mother, her desire for him, the way she leans on him in his complementary role. All these parameters organize and structure the direct, immediate relationship between mother and infant. In non-neurotic structures, the father is unable to play his role as mediator, as separator of mother and child. What is striking in these structures is that the father as separator seems to be absent. He cannot even be thought of in the light of the concept of mediation, i.e. as a model for the constitution of relationships. Without some idea of mediation, the very notion of relationship is mutilated.

The love of the mother or for the mother has an unmistakable, evident quality, while in the case of the father, he always stands as an enigmatic third whose function is not evident. So, even in an apparently direct relationship, the question "What is he doing right there?" is still raised. Despite all the love he displays, the father cannot avoid playing the role of the embarrassing additional third. His love can always be questioned, answered only by still another question, unarticulated, about the relationship between the parents: "What is it that is going on between *them*?" The mystery of the hidden aspects of love remains a secret one quite inevitably unbearable for the child. So there is the real unquestioned question: "Love for the mother, love for the father, love for the child but how about the love *between* mother and father?" Infantile sexuality cannot fathom what adult sexuality is. Therefore the father is not seen simply through *his* absence; rather he is seen mainly through his absence *with* the mother, in a relationship from which the child is excluded. This situation knows no healing, only painful elaboration. No trust can be placed in "nice" or "adorable" answers that only testify to the strength of defenses, of lies and of rationalizations as transference shows.

Here, no hostility can be avoided, because the child has some obscure intuition that the excessive closeness to the mother without any prohibition is a threat to his independence. And the hostile wishes frequently take the form of a retrospective reproach of the father for not having done anything to limit the situation. Given that the dual relationship is never totally given up, it remains cause for ambivalence. The father can be too fragile to bear the child's reproaches. Moreover, these reproaches can be dangerous, damaging the weak thread of the positive relationship between child and father that has to remain outside the domain of the powerful mother, for whom being the sole available partner is a necessity. In this instance, the father is only an appendix required for procreation who must remain backstage. Hopefully the child and the father know what is happening and are united by a secret bond. This is not enough, however, to promote identification with him. The only genuine hope is in the transference, in meeting an analyst who can face the ambivalence. Though there is a difference between mother and father from this point of view, mothers are normally inclined to what I have described as "maternal madness" (Green, 1975) from which they also must recover as the child grows up.

In the very regressive states that we have tried to describe, in which violent psychotic fixations are refracted through the omnipotent mother figure, we can observe all the transitions from the negative Oedipus complex to earlier fixations, where the voice of the self seems to be covered by the mother's discourse, who uses the child as a channel through which she can express all her regressed hatred without taking responsibility for that hatred. She puts aside the father whom she finds incompetent. In these situations, it is as if the child was deprived of the possibility of fighting the father figure, because it looks as if the mother already swallowed him usurping his paternal functions. Borderline cases particularly demonstrate the distorted distribution of parental functions. Imagine also, how in these mother–infant relationships, the child can become the stake of a pervert game. The omnipotent mother cathexes invest the child with many of the cathexes that are ordinarily devoted to the father, love and hate. So high is her frustration at not being able to be the self of the infant or its father, that her feelings become very destructive. Here the father cannot be put to death, in that he is already half dead. What remains of him will be worshipped in silence, unconsciously, and hidden from the "voracious" (Winnicott) mother when she dangerously denies her narcissistic hunger. The father cannot be put to death, only embalmed. The lost father has to be constructed from the remaining destroyed fragments. So the father is neither absent, nor hated. Rather he is lost.

I close with the idea that the lost father may be someday found in the transference. It has to be kept in the analysis as a kind of weary psychic object, neither past nor present, neither existent nor dead. The thread-like fragile tie to him must be maintained as his ghostly existence is pursued like a relic. He is not a fantasized object but a dead object kept artificially alive during the child's life.

I am not accusing the mother of making the father responsible for the child's pathology though it may seem to the reader that I have. What I have described is the construction that occurs in the mind of the analyst. In order to understand the patient and to identify with him, the analyst must have a sort of script, a scenario, which he believes has been built by the patient he sees in treatment. It is probably because things are too complicated to understand "from above" that the identification with the patient helps the analyst to organize the plot of an unwritten tragedy that he is too weak to imagine. Psychoanalysts such as Bion have gone ahead of us into remote sectors of the psyche of the patient. But here the attempt to put oneself into the patient's mind builds up a bizarre and unthinkable story, because in the wish to go to the deeper layers, we have had to enter a place where there are no limits: a confused body of threads all jumbled together. We try to follow them to find a way out to a world with thinkable relationships at hand. We need a father to show us the way. With the help of repression, this has always been so in our Western civilizations. We did not yet know Samuel Beckett and Sarah Kane. Was the world the same?

Notes

1 Presented at the New York Symposium on "The Dead Father", organized by the Association for Psychoanalytic Medicine, April 29, 2006.
2 The paternal power as head of the family.
3 What Shakespeare wrote is (1H4: v.i.127): "Thou owest God a death." It is Freud who misquoted Shakespeare.
4 Freud adds in a footnote: "Perhaps it would be safer to say 'with the parents' for before a child has arrived at definite knowledge of the difference between the sexes, the lack of a penis, it does not distinguish in value between its father and its mother."
5 Richard Kuhns (an Emeritus Professor of Philosophy at Columbia University) has brought this parallel to my attention (in the course of a personal communication).

References

Bion, W. R. (1962) *Learning from Experience*, London: Karnac.
—— (1965) *Transformations*, London: Maresfield.
Fonagy, P. and Target, M. (1995) "Understanding the Violent Patient: The use of the body and the role of the father", *International Journal of Psychoanalysis* 76: 487–501.
Frazer, J.G. (1910) "Totemism and Exogamy", reprinted (2000) in *Totemism and Exogamy: The Collected Works of James G. Frazer*, London: Routledge Curzon.
Freud, S. (1900) "The Interpretation of Dreams", trans. James Strachey (1953), *Standard Edition*, Volumes 4–5, London: Hogarth Press.
—— (1913) "Totem and Taboo", trans. James Strachey (1955), *Standard Edition*, Volume 13, London: Hogarth Press.
—— (1922a) "Beyond the Pleasure Principle", trans. James Strachey (1962), *Standard Edition*, Volume 18, London: Hogarth Press.
—— (1922b) "Group Psychology and the Analysis of the Ego", *Standard Edition*, Volume 18, London: Hogarth Press.
—— (1939) "Moses and Monotheism", trans. James Strachey (1964), *Standard Edition*, Volume 23, London: Hogarth Press.
Green, A. (1975) "La sexualisation et son économie", *Revue Française de Psychanalyse*, 39, 5–6, La Bisexualité Psychique [translated into English 1980].
—— (1993) "Primary Anality", in *The Work of the Negative*, trans. Andrew Weller (1999), London: Free Association Books.
Green, A. and Kohon, G. (2005) *Love and Its Vicissitudes*, London: Routledge.
Klein, M. (1932) "Obsessional Neurosis and the Superego", in *The Psychoanalysis of Children*, revised as H. A. Thorner (revised in collaboration with Alix Strachevby, trans.) (1975) *The Psychoanalysis of Children*, Volume II of the Writings of Melanie Klein, New York: Free Press, pp. 158–161.
Perelberg, R. J. (ed.) (1999) "A Core Phantasy in Violence", in R. J. Perelberg (ed.) *Psychoanalytic Understanding of Violence and Suicide*, London: Routledge, p. 105.
Rosolato, G. (1969) "Du père", in *Essais sur le Symbolique*, Paris: Gallimard.
Whitebook, J. (2005) "Against Interiority: Foucault's Struggle with Psychoanalysis", in G. Gutting (ed.) *The Cambridge Companion to Foucault*, Cambridge: Cambridge University Press.
Winnicott, D. W. (1971) *Playing and Reality*, New York, London: Tavistock/Routledge.
Yerushalmi, Y. H. (1989) "Freud on the 'historical novel' from the draft (1934) of Moses and Monotheism", *International Journal of Psychoanalysis* 70: 375–394.

Chapter 2

Fatherhood revisited

The dead father, fraternal pact and analytic filiation in the work of André Green

Fernando Urribarri

The prolific work of André Green can be defined as a search for a new contemporary psychoanalytic thinking capable of overcoming the impasses and fragmentation of post-Freudian models. From "The Freudian Unconscious and Contemporary French Psychoanalysis" (1960)[1] to *Key Ideas for a Contemporary Psychoanalysis* (2002), his writings can be seen to be directed, even propelled, by the issue of the contemporary. This investigation results in the construction of a personal theoretical and clinical model that articulates a reconceptualization and renovation of both the metapsychological foundations and the method of psychoanalysis.

Psychoanalyst and historian Martin Bergman was right when he said that Freud, for better and for worse, left behind a psychoanalysis that is much less definitive and complete, and more open to new problems and developments than his early disciples believed. After Freud's death, his depth psychology was fortunate enough to see the rise of some original post-Freudian authors who made very valuable contributions. But it also encountered the misfortune in that each of these authors created a militant "school" proclaiming itself Freud's legitimate heir. The "three great post-Freudian dogmatisms: Ego Psychology, Kleinism and Lacanism" (Laplanche, 1987) repeated the process of setting up their own reductionistic model, converting it into a dogma, adopting a particular technique and presenting an idealized leader as the head of the School.[2]

André Green wrote that the crisis of post-Freudian psychoanalysis is a melancholic one, marked by the interminable mourning of Freud's death. Symptomatically, each post-Freudian author wanted to replace him as the great figure, and each militant movement believed that it re-experienced the original situation of the pioneers and the (re)founding Father. As in a reaction formation, a paternalistic mythology (or ideology) replaced the historical sentiment of orphanhood.

Three pioneering anti-dogmatic movements struggling with post-Freudian sectarianism and reductionism arose, one in England, one in France and one in Argentina.[3] In France, in the 1960s, when Jacques Lacan went from renewing thinker to Head of School, many of his major followers, according to Roudinesco, some of the outstanding members of the third generation of French psychoanalysis, broke away from him. Some of these were J. Laplanche, J.-B. Pontalis, D. Anzieu, D. Widlocher, P. Aulagnier, F. Perrier, J. McDougall, G. Rosolato, C. Stein and A. Green. This Freudian movement, intellectually pluralistic and institutionally diverse, inaugurated an "after Lacan." Based on a kind of "fraternal pact," it established a generation that developed a new theoretical and clinical synthesis out of a critique of post-Freudian reductionism.

This contemporary movement constructs a novel historic (and historicizing) filial position in relation to Freud. It postulates an unavoidable and potentially fruitful distance from the founding father. (As Goethe and Freud said: what you have inherited you must make your own.) This means that every relationship with Freud's work is necessarily and irremediably mediated by the selection and preferences of each theoretical model. Consequently, the contemporary model transforms the issue of the father doubly. On the one hand, at the imaginary institutional level, the relationship with the "founding father" and the filial regime insists that the fraternal pact is the condition for filial work and that the labor of continuity and rupture is the only road to autonomous thought. On the other hand, at the theoretical level, the metapsychological conception of the father and the "father complex" (*Vaterkomplex*) itself varies.

To review these developments, I will examine them in three successive stages: "with Lacan," "after Lacan" and "beyond Lacan." The question of the father in the works of André Green will provide the guiding thread.

With Lacan

The stage "with Lacan" covers the 1950s and 1960s, characterized by the "return to Freud." At this time, adherence to Lacan is, or seems to be, compatible with filiation with Freud. Lacan's deep and innovative reading of Freud, especially his theorization of the Oedipus as a structure, marks and inspires his eminent disciples. We see this effect, for example, in *Hölderling and the Question of the Father* (Laplanche, 1961), *Desire and Perversion* (Aulagnier, 1966) and *The Tragic Effect* (Green, 1969).

At this stage, two significant group traits become clear. The first is that Lacan's leading disciples reading him with a critical heterodox attitude, express criticism. In reference to the theme of the father, we find that in *Hölderling and the Question of the Father* Jean Laplanche critiques the disavowal of the signifier of the name of the father. In 1960, at the Bonneval Colloquium on "The Unconscious," André Green debates the paper by J. Laplanche and S. Leclaire (designated to represent Lacan for the colloquium): he objects to the reduction of the unconscious to language and to the assimilation of primary repression into the paternal metaphor. He also takes up positions that form the basis of his future work. He states:

We may observe that, whereas for Freud unpleasure intervenes as the dynamic motor of repression, in Laplanche and Leclaire this role is assigned to the *paternal metaphor, the Name of the Father* or its symbolic signifying attribute, the phallus. This interpretation of the text does not absolutely contradict Freud; what is experienced as unpleasure is signified as an expression of the prohibited, imposed by the father as the embodiment of the Law, to which the mother submits. But this neglects the importance, in the intervention of repression, of the effects of impotence that the obstruction of the child's desire generates in the child. If the unconscious and repression can be affirmed, with Freud, to be contemporaries, then it is necessary to establish the same correlatively for the symbolic and drive activity, discernible when the primary defenses (reversal into the opposite and turning round upon the subject's own self, inherent to primary narcissism) are set in motion.

In contrast to Lacan's position, ours tends to place more value on the role of the drives: their economic aspects, basic organization and aims, while also considering the structuring role of repression, to grasp the subject's manifestations in the conflict between positivity (drives) and negativity (defenses). (. . .) Actually, Lacan's reconstruction of Freud is built upon grounds that differ radically from those of the founder of psychoanalysis. Lacan seems to follow a particular desire: to find an ontological status for psychoanalysis based on philosophical consistency, which requires the reinterpretation of a whole aspect of Freudism: everything that is usually labeled as biologistic. In spite of the impasses to which it apparently leads, it seems to me to be indispensable to preserve it, since this perspective is practically the only attempt to give psychic reality *body* without reifying it.

(Green, 1960, p. 374)

The undeniable importance of the drives, of the dynamic and economic dimension, is also highlighted in "Primary Narcissism: State or Structure?" (Green, 1967). Lacan attacks its irreverent autonomy, thereby provoking the break in his relationship with its author. The central line of this text is an articulation of the theory of narcissism with Freud's second drive dualism (synthesized by the opposition between "life narcissism" and "death narcissism"). But it also involves the question of the father on several levels. One of the most important is the role of the father in the constitution of primary narcissism: it is seen as the combined result of the "mother's negative hallucination" (which constitutes the ego's framing structure) and primary identification with the father (as an ideal). The other level is the relation between the death drive (seen as a non-sexual force and a process of normal decathexis and unbinding, not reduced to destructivity) and the dead father (the symbolic basis of separation, renunciation, desexualization and ideals). Green postulates this articulation in "the work of the death drive," an antecedent of his future concept of "the work of the negative," as the "structural basis of the un-mixture of the drives – which permits renunciation and aim-inhibition of the drive – for the creation of lasting, permanent cathexes" (Green, 1967, p. 100).

The 1960 Bonneval Colloquium (which brings Green, Laplanche, Leclaire and C. Stein together) also illustrates the second important group trait, namely the relationship and exchange among peers, dialogue and intergenerational debate, cooperation and fertile rivalry; ultimately, the development of a horizontal, fraternal and institutionally intersecting weave of relationships.

After Lacan

This second stage is characterized by Green's break with Lacan, by a search for intellectual independence that leads him to a confrontation with the "Maître" and the critique of what he considers a reductionistic theoretical system and an unacceptable clinical practice (short sessions). Actually, the essential meaning of this stage is defined, on the one hand, by the dialectic, critical and creative use of the contributions of Lacan and other post-Freudian authors for an autonomous personal syntheses. On the other hand, supported by a fraternal pact, this stage institutes a new psychoanalytic current, Freudian, anti-dogmatic, plural, cosmopolitan and institutionally transversal. Green comes to define, après-coup, the richly productive period between the late 1960s and the end of the 1980s, as "post-Lacanian" (Green, 1986).

The innovativeness of these two decades is represented by such noteworthy books as the *Language of Psychoanalysis* (1964) by Laplanche and Pontalis, and Green's *The Fabric of Affect in the Psychoanalytic Discourse* (1973). But it is particularly typified by the journals like *Topique* (edited by Piera Aulagnier, with collaborators F. Perrier and J. P. Valabrega), *Psychanalyse à l'Université* (edited by Laplanche with G. Rosolato and P. Fedida), *Études Freudiennes* (Conrad Stein), *Confrontation* (René Major) and quite especially, the *Nouvelle Revue de Psychanalyse* (the "flagship" piloted by Pontalis with Anzieu, Green and invited English editor, Masud Kahn). These post-Lacanian journals (with the participation of some of the major French intellectuals of this generation, such as J. Derrida, J. F. Lyotard, C. Castoriadis and G. Deleuze) were the vanguard and motor of psychoanalytic thinking at that time, when their contributors published the central texts of what were later their major books.

When we examine the post-Lacanian production, its first outstanding feature is the critical current that proposes to re-establish the difference between Freud's and Lacan's thought. The rejection of the formula "the unconscious is structured like a language" is one of its starting points. The Freudian thesis that the psychic apparatus cannot be reduced to language is recovered in favor of a conception of "the heterogeneity of the psychoanalytic signifier" (Green, 1973, p. 253). The different post-Lacanian authors enrich the Freudian theory of representation by elucidating and multiplying its components e.g. Aulagnier's pictograms, Rosolato's signifiers of demarcation, etc. They propose new processes or modes of functioning such as the originary, the semiotic, and tertiary processes. In this context, in contrast to Lacan, Green defines affect as a mode of primary symbolization a "signifier of the flesh, and flesh of the signifier" (Green, 1973, p. 239).

In regard to the subject of the father, these authors try to deconstruct what they take to be Lacan's formalistic idealism. They dismantle what they see as the reduction of the process of symbolization to the Symbolic order, of the latter to the Oedipus complex, of the Oedipus complex to the paternal metaphor, of the paternal function to the signifier of the name-of-the-father, and of Freudian castration (anxiety and fantasy) to symbolic castration, whose ontological status devolves into a kind of Heideggerian metaphysics of "lack" (*manque*). Green quotes Laplanche who states – not without irony – that Lacanian theorization itself slides into a phallic, binary logic. Green also critiques Lacanian practice, in which he sees an exploitation of the idealized paternal transference, taking sadomasochistic deviations of "symbolic castration" to be the goal of psychoanalysis (Green, 1991). At the same time, the post-Lacanians are interested in the work of D. W. Winnicott and W. Bion. Furthermore, they are especially sensitive to the concept of the psychoanalytic frame (or setting) as understood by J. Bleger (1967), developing both its both technical and epistemological vertices.

Post-Lacanian Greenings

The works of André Green richly illustrate this stage of creative counterpoint. At this juncture, he publishes a series of foundational works whose center is frequently the Oedipal structure. His work on borderline structures leads to the study of the particular kind of triangularity found in these pathologies. In one of his first books, he formulates the idea that in non-neurotic structures, the structure of the Oedipus complex takes the form of "tri-bi-angularity" (Green and Donnet, 1971): the subject relates to two idealized objects, one absolutely good (and impotent) and the other absolutely bad (omnipotent). In contrast to the Kleinian line, Green rejects the idea of a dual or dyadic (mother–baby) relationship as a theoretical and clinical model:

> Every subject, whatever their psychopathological structure, reaches the Oedipus. The centrality of the Oedipus comes first, before children have their own experience, when they occupy a place in their parents' Oedipus. Also, every subject, as Freud says, was germinally, in childhood, an Oedipus.
>
> (Green, 1986, p. 286)

This line of thought is one that Green continues to elaborate in his chapter of this book.

Referring to clinical work with non-neurotic structures, Green maintains that it is not a question of the passage from two to three, from dyad to triad, but of transition from the state of potential thirdness (as long as the father is present only in the mother's mind) to effective or real thirdness. To this point, he writes:

> The future of psychoanalytic theory, clinical work and technique does not consist in replacing the Freudian problem centered on castration with a modern problem in which other referents intervene (dismemberment, disintegration, annihilation, etc.), but in the articulation of these two problems.
>
> (Green, 1986, p. 191)

Open triangularity and the object's other

In 1981, the year that Lacan died, Green wrote "Freud, Oedipus and Us" (Green, 1992), a foundational article in which he distinguishes the Oedipus as a complex, a structure and a model. As a model, he proposes the idea that the Oedipus is an *open triangle with a substitutable third*, and introduces the notion of the "object's other" (the first "third" object, which may or may not be the father), aiming to define more precisely an originary triadic scheme.

Although it may be obvious that the baby's major relationship is initially with the mother, the situation is triangular: the father is inscribed as a figure of absence. "His essential role in the structuring of the mother–child relationship stems from the place the father occupies in the mother's mind. More precisely, it depends on how she situates him with respect to the Oedipal fantasms of her own childhood" (Green, 1992, p. 134).

The primal scene is theorized as the psyche's triangular matrix, before the Oedipal phase in which it must be articulated with the castration complex. The primal scene and the castration complex are therefore postulated as two nuclei of the Oedipus complex, two poles whose relationship determines the subject's position. This is a way to construct a non-"phallocentric" theory of symbolization that differentiates and articulates the notions of absence, lack, loss and castration. It also elucidates the structural and historical dimension of the Oedipus, thus avoiding both the potential negative theology of a transcendent symbolic structure as well as the genetic trap of the dual relationship.

This conception of the Oedipus as an open triangle with a substitutable third underlies and is developed in Green's most famous article: "The Dead Mother" (1982). It is important to remember that this paper not only introduces the idea of a "maternal function" (related to the constitution of the

Ego's "framing structure"), but it also aims to establish a structural theory of anxiety, and therefore implies a theory of symbolization. This theory of anxiety defines "red anxiety" corresponding to the castration series and "*blanc* anxiety" inherent in object loss and primary narcissism. Further, the paper illuminates the triangularity of non-neurotic functioning, establishing the relation between the narcissistic trauma and the fantasy of the primal scene. Insofar as it is impossible to mourn the dead mother, it is also impossible to renounce the incestuous object, preserved by a "frozen love." The two impossibilities are inseparable.

The fabric of discourse

In *Language in Psychoanalysis* (1983), Green introduces an original theoretical model of the functioning of analytic practice. Although it is not yet a general theoretical model, one can find most of the general perspectives (the articulation between the intra-psychic and the inter-subjective), theoretical options (representation as the psyche's basic function) and original concepts or notions (tertiary processes, the objectalizing function, etc.) that he later develops. It is a true milestone in the intellectual career of this author, who "aspires to the inscription of this paper as a cenotaph for Jacques Lacan." As a filial work, it is an inflection point, one of both continuity and rupture with the author of the Rome Speech, paving the way to works with a personal signature.

This "Report" analyzes the Lacanian system and goes on to construct an original model of the psychoanalytic process based on a metapsychology of the analytic frame and symbolization. Green accomplishes this by discussing both the question and the answer that is found in Lacan's model. "Why does the talking cure work? Because the unconscious is structured like a language" (Miller, 1990, p. 148). This Lacanian thesis, based on a general conception of language (grounded in the structural linguistics of Saussure and Jakobson) is countered by Green's specific theory of discourse and language in psychoanalysis, determined by the particulars of the frame and the transference: "the analytic word," he writes, "un-mourns language . . . by effect of the setting" (Green, 1983, p. 132).

The frame is called the "language apparatus," since its aim is the most extreme transformation of psychic production into language through free association. Because it is hyper-cathected by the transference, language functions as a mediator in the direction of what is not language and not the unconscious. The word changes status and itself becomes a singular "third" object, born of the communication between analyst and analysand: it is the analytic object (a discourse object, composed of the representations and affects that knit together the transference and the countertransference). As a third element (between analyst and analysand), it is defined as a matrix of transitional and tertiary symbolization:

The setting brings together the three polarities: the dream (narcissism), maternal caregiving (the mother in Winnicott) and the prohibition of incest (the father in Freud). The word is therefore the symbolization of the unconscious structure of the Oedipus complex, and is made to speak by the psychoanalytic apparatus (the setting).

(Green, 1983, p. 147)

The section on "The Symbolic Order: The Tertiary Processes" discusses the key question of symbolization:

Lacan was wrong when he linked the symbolic to language – since it is actually to the psyche that the symbolic is consubstantially joined . . . What Lacan tried to do was to surpass Freud in the conceptualization that the latter essayed when he opposed the primary to the secondary processes. However, this kind of "improvement" through the Symbolic excluded not only the signified but also the affect. We propose a different solution. We postulate the existence of relationship mechanisms between the primary and secondary processes, which circulate in both directions: we call them tertiary processes and attribute them to the preconscious of the first "topographical scheme" and to the unconscious ego of the second. Therefore, the symbolic order is based not on language but on all the bindings–unbindings–rebindings that operate in the three agencies of the psychic apparatus. The tertiary processes form the bridge between the language apparatus and the psychic apparatus.

(Green, 1983, p. 153)

Before leaving the "Report," we return to its opening, which nicely demonstrates the conjunction of theoretical and filial work. In both, we also find explicit recognition of the support of the fraternal pact:

Rome 1953 – Aix-en-Provence 1983 . . . Thirty years have gone by . . . We are no longer living in those agitated times, and Lacan's voice is silent. It is taken over with great difficulty by his disciples, who dispute his remains, and many of his traveling companions – myself included – have gone their own way . . . Lacan's filiation? Or is it the diaspora of his people? The following text does not do justice to all those who helped me to think about this subject, which I have chosen deliberately, my first reflections on it going back to 1960, to the Bonneval Colloquium: J. Laplanche, S. Leclaire, G. Rosolato, J.-B. Pontalis, O. Mannoni, P. Aulagnier and S. Viderman, among the psychoanalysts. To this list I must add the names of M. Merleau-Ponty, P. Ricoeur, J. Derrida and G. Deleuze. . . . This mention is less of authors than of interlocutors. Our lively exchanges have undoubtedly enriched this text, and nourished it throughout its long gestation.

(Green, 1983, pp. 176–7)

The authors Green cites are more than simply sources he has read. They are living interlocutors in a new generational space, co-protagonists of the construction and development of a new disciplinary matrix.

Beyond Lacan: contemporary psychoanalysis

This stage of Green's intellectual trajectory is labeled "Beyond Lacan" because Lacan is no longer *the* central reference, either positive or negative. It also describes getting beyond the crisis of post-Freudian models. At this stage, filial work moves forward too, from an orientation to the past and into its definition by projection by a projected future. Post-Lacanism becomes contemporary psychoanalysis, the project of a new Freudian paradigm, pluralistic and complex.

The new contemporary disciplinary matrix has the following four bases: (1) a renewed reading of Freud (defined by Jean Laplanche as "critical, historical and problematic") that revalues Freudian metapsychology and method as the foundation of psychoanalysis; (2) a critical and creative appropriation of the major post-Freudian contributions (and dialogue with contemporary authors of diverse currents); (3) an extension of clinical work to meet the challenges of practice with predominantly non-neurotic patients; and finally (4) a tertiary clinical model, which is a new synthesis of the Freudian model (centered on transference) and the post-Freudian model (centered on countertransference), grounded on the concept of the analytic frame.[4] It also establishes a Freudian vocabulary as its lingua franca and common ground. As Green observed recently:

> In France, the thinking of post-Lacanians is now dominant. What they have in common is having been and no longer being Lacanians, radiating a fertile diversity that allows them to refer to each other without dogmatism, to the great benefit of all.
>
> (Green, 2006, p. 247)

Since the 1990s, when they were reaping acclaim both nationally and internationally, these contemporary authors have been producing major mature works, in which they propose a personal version of the contemporary model, for example, *New Foundations for Psychoanalysis* (1989) by J. Laplanche or *Psychic Causality* (1996) by A. Green. In them, they demonstrate the value of this new disciplinary matrix as a potential space and a platform for the theoretical and clinical imagination of today's psychoanalysts.

Key ideas for a contemporary psychoanalysis

Green's work achieves new milestones in his more recent efforts to construct a general theoretical model (which takes up and extends the "basic model" of 1983). In a first phase in the early 1990s, Green introduces two new lines of thought, accompanied by a general review of metapsychology and a broad reorganization of his own thinking. They are first "On Thirdness" (1990) and *The Work of the Negative* (1993). In yet a second phase of theorizing, Green writes *Propaedeutics: Metapsychology Revisited* (1995) and *Psychic Causality* (1996). As their titles suggest, they present a general formulation of the Greenian theoretical model.

Green continues to deepen and develop the conceptualization of the father and the Oedipus along two central lines of investigation, perhaps the most original and distinctive being that on thirdness and the work of the negative. In relation to the work of the negative, he discusses the question of what says "No" to drive discharge and what opposes destructivity and sexuality, leading to transformational psychic work. Not considered only in relation to prohibition and the law, the paternal figure emerges as one of the primary sources of the work of the negative, since the primary relation with the father's image (in contrast to the primary relation with the mother's body) is an indirect relation that takes him as an ideal (an object of primary identification, in contrast with the object of desire). Thus, a paternal lineage in the work of the negative runs from identification to sublimation, by way of the function of the ideal: processes and functions that permit renunciation of the object, change or inhibition of the drive aim and the creation of substitute satisfactions and objects; in sum, they allow the subject's liberty to expand in relation to the drives and the object.

Going deeper into his "theory of generalized triangularity with a substitutable third," Green adopts (from Charles Peirce) and elaborates the notion of thirdness as a triadic matrix of meaning and symbolization. More than a notion, thirdness is a conceptual line or a meta-concept. It aims to integrate convergent but heterogeneous ideas, as proposed by the contemporary epistemological current of "complex thought" (Morin, 1996). The author of *Key Ideas for a Contemporary Psychoanalysis* describes it:

> When examining Lacan's reflections more deeply, I realized that triangular relations had been left arbitrarily and negligently restricted to the Oedipus complex. At that point, the work of C. S. Peirce contributed decisive light, through his notion of triadic relations that lead into the more general concept of thirdness. *Thus, I attempted to apply them to ideas I had expressed without referring to any theory in particular, and to cases I had not analyzed from that angle.*
>
> (Green, 2002, p. 231)

Considering it a conceptual line, Green (Green, 2002, p. 232) speaks in terms of "configurations of thirdness" in which "the triadic nature of relations can be observed." Into this frame, we can place the Oedipal triangle (Freud), the Imaginary–Symbolic–Real triad (Lacan) and transitional phenomena (Winnicott).

In Green's theoretical model, we find that thirdness is part of a new "general theory of representation." In it, mental functioning is viewed as a heterogeneous process of representation that binds and symbolizes relations within and between the intra-psychic (centered on the drive) and the inter-subjective (centered on the object). Thus, he presents a tertiary matrix of the psyche, composed of the triad: drive–object–representation (the intra-psychic vertex) and the triangular scheme: subject–object–object's other (the inter-subjective vertex). In the dynamic nucleus of this matrix we find the work of the negative and the tertiary processes, sources of the creative, poetic dimension of the psyche.

Green's itinerary culminates here, having journeyed from his critique of the reductionism of the Oedipus complex to his development of a more complex Oedipus theory that offers a tertiary model of the structural and historical relations involved in the constitution and functioning of the subject.

Acknowledgement

This chapter was translated from Spanish by Susan Rogers.

Notes

1 Bibliography dates correspond to the first (usually French) edition.
2 Many authors have pointed out that Heinz Kohut took a similar historical turn: from heterodox innovator to leader of a new dogma. More recently, the new version of the post-Freudian militant tendency seems to be the North American intersubjective movement.
3 In the UK, Winnicott's middle group; in Argentina's early 1970s, the pluralistic Freudian movement that renewed the Argentine Psychoanalytic Association, led by J. Mom, W. Baranger and M. Baranger.
4 See F. Urribarri (2007) "The Psychic Work of the Analyst and the Three Countertransference Conceptions", in A. Green (ed.), *Resonance on Suffering*, London: Routledge.

References

Aulagnier, P. (1966) *Desire and Perversion*, Paris: du Seuil.

Bleger, J. (1967) "Psicoanálisis del Encuadre Psicoanalítico", in *Simbiosis y Ambiguedad*, Buenos Aires: Paidos.

Green, A. (1960) "L'Inconscient Freudienne et la Psychanalyse Française Contemporaine" [The Freudian unconscious and contemporary French psychoanalysis], *Les Temps Modernes*, 195.

—— (1967) Le narcissisme primaire: structure ou etat? [Primary narcissism: state or structure], *L'inconscient* 1. Also in *Narcissisme de Vie, Narcissisme de Morte* [Life Narcissism, Death Narcissism] (1982) Paris: du Minuit.

—— (1969) *Une Oeil en Trop* [The Tragic Effect: The Oedipus Complex in Tragedy], Paris: du Minuit.

—— (1973) *The Fabric of Affect in the Psychoanalytic Discourse*, London: Routledge.

—— (1982) *Narcissisme de Vie, Narcissisme de Morte* [Life Narcissism, Death Narcissism], Paris: du Minuit.

—— (1983) *Language in Psychoanalysis*, Paris: Belles Lettres.

—— (1986) *On Private Madness*, London: Karnac.

—— (1990) "Sur la tercieité" [On thirdness], in A. Green *La Pensée Clinique* [Clinical Thinking], Paris: Odile Jacob.

—— (1991) *Le Complexe de Castration*, Paris: PUF.

—— (1992) *La Déliaison*, Paris: Belles Lettres.

—— (1993) *Le Travail du Négatif* [The Work of the Negative], Paris: du Minuit.

—— (1995) *Propédentique: La métapsychologie révisitée* [Propaedeutics, Metapsychology Revisited], Seyssel: Champ Vallon.

—— (1996) *La Causalité Psychique* [Psychic Causality], Paris: Odile Jacob.

—— (2002) *Idées Directrices Pour une Psychanalyse Contemporaine* [Key Ideas for a Contemporary Analysis], Paris: PUF.

—— (2006) *Unité et Diversité de la Pratique des Psychanalystes*, Paris: PUF.

Green. A. and Donnet, J.-L. (1971) *L'Enfant de Ça. La Psychose Blanche*, Paris: Editions du Minuit.

Laplanche, J. (1961) *Hölderling and the Question of the Father*, Paris: PUF.

—— (1987) Prologue, in S. Bleichmar *Aux Origines du Sujet Psychique*, Paris: PUF.

—— (1989) *New Foundations for Psychoanalysis*, trans. David Macey, Oxford: Blackwell.

Laplanche, J. and Pontalis, J. B. (1967) *Vocabulaire de Psychoanalyse* [Language of Psychoanalysis], Paris: PUF.

Miller, J. A. (1990) *Matemas II*, Buenos Aires: Manantial.

Morin, E. (1996) *Introduction a la Pensée Complexe*, Paris: du Seuil.

Urribarri, F. (2007) "The Psychic Work of the Analyst and the Three Counter-Transference Conceptions", in A. Green (ed.) *Resonance on Suffering*, London: Routledge.

Part II

The father embodied

INTRODUCTION
Maria Cristina Aguirre

The theme of Part II is the "body" set in the larger context of this volume's exploration of Freud's notion of the symbolic or Dead Father. The concept of the imaginary body is a difficult one to grasp. However, this part of the book, "The Father Embodied," brings that idea to life. Most people relate to the body as though it were brute fact, something that hurts, hungers, or requires medical attention. This is particularly true these days given that neurochemistry increasingly dominates the field of psychiatry. Patients often enough report that they are suffering from a "chemical imbalance" or that they need more serotonin rather than describing themselves as suffering from a conflict over one matter or another. Nonetheless certain psychiatric disorders actually make the case for a body that exists outside of the laboratory and in the imagination, in the self-image, of the individual. Take, for example, "body dysmorphic disorder," anorexia nervosa, and conversion hysterias where psychogenic symptoms can impair physical functions such as sight, hearing, and ambulation. Of course, having an image of "an imbalanced brain" is in and of itself imaginary, regardless of what the biochemistry might be.

Bear in mind that even the "self," the "me," is a rather recent concept in mankind's history (Taylor, 1989). Fourth-century Bishop Augustine of Hippo is generally given credit as the earliest philosopher to have embraced the standpoint of the first person, the "I," in his turn from the outer world to the inner one in his quest for truth. Going beyond the perspective of consciousness embedded in that standpoint to thinking of mind in the complex terms of the unconscious and psychic structure was, for the most part, left to the last century or so. And although "imagining" things about the body was certainly a rather common idea, the notion of the body as constituted by an imaginary axis was not.

Psychoanalyst Jacques Lacan put flesh to the bones of the idea of the imaginary body with his landmark (1938) paper "The Mirror Stage," in which he describes the moment of jubilation when the infant recognizes his own image in the mirror. Through an external reflection, through what Lacan called the signifier of the Other, the baby has the illusion of completeness. No longer a jumble of unintegrated physical sensations and faceless body parts over which he has little motor control, he sees a unified entity. This, says Lacan, is the basis for narcissism. That entity is "me," the *"moi,"* that is to be my "ego." For Lacan the ego has an imaginary status (which hardly means unimportant!). It is the view of one's self in one's own eyes, reinforced by or undermined by the gaze of the Other – the mirror, the mother, the father, and society. This also establishes the basis for the relationship to our siblings, peers, our counterparts, relationships often dominated by aggression and rivalry; it is either you or me.

According to the prominent Lacanian Jacques-Alain Miller, Lacan attributes the pre-eminence of the image of the "own-body" for the human being to the subject's intuition that he lacks something, has a hole, of something missing in Being, that the image of the body covers up or fills. Received wisdom tells us something analogous in the rather ordinary understanding that arrogance or extreme physical narcissism is usually a defense against "in-security." In other words, they cover a lack, a *manque* as the French would put it. Chatter among teenagers, so involved in the construction of the imaginary body, certainly affirms that!

This imaginary axis is traversed by the symbolic composed by signifiers – phonemes, words, the spoken language of the (m)Other. Those signifiers create an effect in the bodies of speaking-beings, naming it, sculpting it, cutting it up, forming and transforming it according to the demand of the Other. The "Other" is understood in both the restricted and extended sense of the term. The Other, Lacan's term for the Unconscious, includes the voices of the early objects as well as the whole of current culture and civilization. Thinking about the ideal body promoted by culture today makes this idea rather obvious. The exigencies of the perfect body are the bases of multiple contemporary symptoms, such as those listed above. Bear in mind, however, that the traversing of the imaginary by the symbolic organizes the body image. The functions of the symbolic create psychic structure. The paternal function, the function of the Dead Father, is central to the normative structuring and functioning of the mind.

Freud's drive theory, postulating both Eros (libido, life instinct) and Thanatos (death instinct), has created generations of disagreement among psychoanalysts worldwide. Mainstream American psychoanalysts by and large reject the death instinct while accepting most other aspects of Freudian theory. The Europeans, particularly the French, take the concept very seriously. Lacan found a way to unify libido and the death instinct through his understanding of *jouissance* (Miller, 2006), which knots together pleasurable satisfaction as well as pain, suffering and discontent in multiple forms. Lacan's formulation of *jouissance* distributes the experience over two forms:

(1) the *jouissance* obtained through the body of the other, the other's parts, for satisfaction; and (2) the *jouissance* of the organ of the "own-body." The latter is called "phallic *jouissance*." In contrast to *jouissance*, which can be of the body, desire requires an encounter with another, an Other, through the path of love. For Freud, the object is lost; for Lacan it is total satisfaction by the object that is lost. This "castration" keeps desire alive (Miller, 2006).

The chapters that follow in Part II examine the effect of the representation of the Father on the body from several perspectives. Marilia Aisenstein, coming out of the psychosomatic school of thought in Paris, looks at how the absence of the father and his symbolization affects the real body, the actual soma. Eric Laurent, Parisian Lacanian psychoanalyst, looks at how recent changes in cultural norms and advances in contemporary knowledge have impacted the representation of the father and his symbolization. And noted historian Thomas Laqueur writes a personal memoir that painfully demonstrates the impact of culture, the Dead Father writ large, on his own father's experience of his life and his body as he confronted his rejection by his beloved Germany during the time of the Third Reich.

Aisenstein finds that the failure of the paternal function creates devastating clinical manifestations in both the lives and the bodies of the patients that she describes. Both have serious physical illnesses that bring them for psychoanalytic treatment. Starting with a review of the Oedipus myth and focusing on the father–son relationship, she goes on to pose an interesting question about the connections among the search for identity, for fantasmatic filiations and popular voluntary body alterations such as tattoos. She demonstrates the interface between the imaginary body and the real one, separable only conceptually.

In the case of Xavier, who presented with severe idiopathic hypertension, the failure of the paternal function leaves him unprotected and at the mercy of a terrifying mother, whom he described through memories of his distressed childhood replete with humiliating punishment. Because of his arrest record, he would under ordinary circumstances be considered a "sociopath." Apparently paradoxically, in his quest for the father, he represents the policeman who arrests him for a minor crime as a "good man." In Aisenstein's chapter the reader will see her working to give Xavier's actions the status of psychic events through the shared narrative of their work together. Her goal is to make it possible for Xavier to inscribe himself "at least into a fantasy of a filiation bearing mourning."

Aisenstein's second case is clearly one of a more neurotic structure. Monsieur Z, suffering from a rivalry with his rejecting father, came to treatment because of kidney disease so serious that it required dialysis. Her third is that of a young man who tattoos almost all of his body. He attempts to re-create himself "by means of corporeal transformation" in an effort to spare himself the need to seek psychological treatment. Laurent picks up this point later in his chapter when he demonstrates how the modern subject, confronted with the collapse of cultural ideals and the decline of the paternal function must find unique ways, personal solutions by which to reinvent the self. Aisenstein's tattoo artist finds his solution through finding a way to write what would otherwise be impossible to say or to inscribe.

Laqueur has written extensively on the body and the history of sexuality and masturbation. He is currently working on the culture of death and its history, how society deals with the dead, the changing rituals and customs surrounding death and burial. He is therefore no stranger to the concept of the body as imagined. Taking as his starting point a photograph of his father found after his father's death amid boxes of memorabilia in the garage, what he wryly calls an "auto haunting," he traces the trajectory of the imaginary through several preceding generations, searching for and finding the ultimate symbolic inscriptions on ancestral tombstones. His narrative follows changing paternal images over his family's remarkable history, documenting changes in the family name, the Name of the Father (le Nom du Père) as well.

Laqueur compares the "physically successful," proud young German student in his father's dueling club photo to the frail and dying abject body of the father that the son remembers. These memories evoke those of Freud of his own humiliated and ill father. He contrasts this father to the father of psychoanalytic theory – the Oedipal father, the father of the primal horde in Totem and Taboo, to the father of fatherhood, Vaterschaft, in Moses and Monotheism. Laqueur's moving account illuminates just how flesh of the living, unlike the remains of the dead, is a creation of Geist, of Spirit, of culture.

Laurent's chapter complements both Aisenstein's and Laqueur's as he articulates how Lacan's distinction among the three registers of the Father – the symbolic, the imaginary and the real – contribute to sorting out the contemporary cultural situation with its lifestyle choices and new reproductive technologies. He examines the place of psychoanalysis in the post-paternal era in this time of the global market, where the father of authority of tradition and patriarchy, the Father of the Law is finished. Using the Lacanian deconstruction as described above, Laurent says that the primal totemic father, the real father of the Freudian myth who becomes the agent of castration, disappears behind the imaginary father, the father who has created "this particular inadequate child who I am." Lacan states in the Seminar The Ethics of Psychoanalysis that it is this imaginary father who becomes the foundation for the providential image of God (1960).

Using the story of the sacrifice of Isaac, Laurent discusses the Akedah, illustrating that this is precisely where Lacan situates a fundamental change in humanity. The totemic father becomes the Father of the Word. Through the effectiveness of his speech, this father becomes the father that names, is transformed into the symbolic function of the Name-of-the-Father. As the Oedipal conflict diminishes, the real, "totemic" father hides behind the imaginary one, the particular father who made me so inadequately so. From then on the loved Father who names coexists with the hated Father.

Laurent explores the opposition between the universal of the dead father and the peculiarity of the real living father, reminding the reader of that distinction as drawn by Laqueur. He reviews the function of the father and his role in the distribution of *jouissance* and then looks at everyone's need to invent a father and his function. It was this that Aisenstein attempted to do for her patients through a shared psychoanalytic construction.

From the analytic perspective both Marilia Aisenstein and Eric Laurent agree that the paternal function is in decline in the Western world. All three chapters that follow are persuasive to that point. Furthermore, Aisenstein argues that the body has become the site of a "ferocious care" because of the disintegration of filial and community ties in the death of the communal body. Thomas Laqueur's remembrance of his family's history reveals the immense transformation in the role of cultural norms in the construction of the self. His sweet memories, including listening to Beethoven in his father's arms, poignantly show that the son cannot heal the wounds of the real father, especially when that father has been betrayed by his culture, the symbolic father.

Eric Laurent develops what Lacan calls the *père-version*, a version of the father, who makes the objects of a woman's desire his own, providing them with paternal care. He concludes that "to be father is not a social norm but an act which has consequences, sumptuous or severe."

This era therefore demands deciphering the new forms of loves for the father now found in new families, fathers themselves born of the new procreative possibilities.

References

Lacan, J. (1938) "The Mirror Stage", trans. Bruce Fink (2007), in J. Lacan *Ecrits: The First Complete Edition in English*, New York: W.W. Norton and Company.

—— (1960) *Le Seminaire, Livre VII L'Ethique de la Psychanalse, 1959–1960*, Paris: Les Editions du Seuil. Republished as J.-A. Miller (ed.) (1992) *The Seminar, Book VII The Ethics of Psychoanalysis, 1959–1960, English Edition*, trans. Dennis Porter, New York: W.W. Norton and Company.

Miller, J.-A. (2006) *Introduccion a la Clinica Lacaniana*, Barcelona: RBA.

Taylor, C. (1989) *Sources of the Self: The Making of the Modern Identity*, Cambridge MA: Harvard University Press.

Chapter 3

The death of the dead father?

Marilia Aisenstein

The question asked here implies a reflection on the undeniable waning of the patriarchal nucleus in our Western societies. Does this waning and change inevitably lead to a collapse of the paternal function as that which inscribes the subject into a symbolic line of descent, the succession of generations, and culture? Put differently, do the changes in social and imaginary representations of fathers irremediably affect the symbolic function of the father as Freud described it? Should we not stop confusing the transmission of a "paternal cultural" with a contested and contestable predominance of the masculine in our time?

In *Moses and Monotheism*, Freud (1939, p. 114) describes how "this turning from the mother to the father points in addition to a victory of intellectuality over sensuality – that is, an advance in civilization, since maternity is proved by the evidence of the senses while paternity is a hypothesis, based on an inference and a premiss." In a book that appeared recently in French, *La Fonction Paternelle* [The paternal function], Jean-Claude Stoloff (2007, p. 89) condemns with great precision the invariable amalgam between a theory of cultural and symbolic parenthood and the primacy accorded to patriarchy throughout history. In modeling again today the "paternal function" on current representations of a real father, we risk reproducing this very telescoping. On the contrary, it is a question of identifying the distinctiveness of a function that concerns mothers as well as fathers, men as well as women: "the interposition between the human subject and his two biological progenitors, the real mother and father, of a symbolic and social progenitor responsible for introducing him into the human community."

One may speak of a "social and cultural third party" of the concept of the father which concerns both parents. How might a failure of this "paternal function," tied to social, historical, and psychic conditions, affect the subject's body? I will try to illustrate this question by drawing on Greek mythology, some fragments of Freudian theory, and two short clinical examples from my practice as a psychoanalyst working with patients suffering from somatic illnesses. I will then ask a few other questions concerning voluntary infringements on the body as we find them in tattooing, body piercing, scarification, and, lastly, body art.

Two fathers, two sons

In Greek mythology the Sphinx is above all associated with the Oedipus legend and the Theban cycle. The Sphinx is a feminine monster depicted as having a woman's face and chest, but its body, paws, and tail are those of a lion. Moreover, it has wings like a bird of prey. It was sent close to Thebes by Hera in order to punish Laius, Oedipus's father. Fatherless and chased from his kingdom, young Laius sought refuge from Pelops, but he seduced his young son, Chrysippos. Pelops then damned Laius. This is the origin of the curse of the Labdacides, and Oedipus was its victim even before he was born. Pelops complained to Hera, who sent the Sphinx to the Thebans. The Sphinx devastated the country, asked enigmatic questions, and then devoured the passers-by. Oedipus was the first and only person to give the correct answer to the riddle: "What is the animal that walks on all fours, then two, and then three?" Man, obviously. Defeated, the monster then fled.

Another riddle no one could find the answer to went: "Two fathers and two sons walk together, how many are there?" The answer would obviously be: "There are three." One can imagine that Oedipus, parricide, son of a fatherless father and pedophile seducer of the son of the one who was a substitute father to him, could have eluded this riddle's trap as well.

The *Urvater* in Freud's oeuvre

The father question – the question of the originary father (*Urvater*), of the murder of the father – fills Freud's entire oeuvre. In 1896, in a letter to Wilhelm Fliess, Freud (1896, pp. 238–39) writes, "It seems to me more and more that the essential point of hysteria is that it results from *perversion* on the part of the seducer, and *more and more* that heredity is seduction by the father." In 1908, in the second preface to *The Interpretation of Dreams*, we read that the death of one's father is "the most important event, the most poignant loss, of a man's life" (p. xxvi). In his letter of May 1912 to Karl Abraham, Freud (1912, p. 116) writes, "You are right to identify the father with death, for the father is dead, and death itself [. . .] is only a dead man."

However, it is above all in *Totem and Taboo* (1913) that Freud works out the concept of the originary father tied to that of parricide. The latter concept takes on a particular amplitude in his theoretical reflections in *Moses and Monotheism*. As Guy Rosolato (1969) has emphasized, the question of the order of inheritance, of three generations, is then immediately raised. In the myth the zero point is the death of the father, but heredity and transmission must be questioned in this order. In the paradigm of Abraham, what is handed down is life, but also phallic power, going from God to Abraham to his son. The transmission is made by surmounting differences, differences of sex and generations. The three terms are important, as the riddle attributed to the Sphinx indicates.

The conjunction between the Freudian notion of the murder of the father and the idealized father, death then, already noted by Freud, was developed by Lacan (1955, p. 556) who wrote that "the necessity of his [i.e. Freud's] reflections led him to relate the appearance of the signifier of the Father, as author of the Law, to death, indeed, to the murder of the Father – showing thus that if this murder is the fecund moment of the debt through which the subject ties himself to the Law for life, the symbolic Father, insofar as he signifies this Law, is in fact the dead Father" (free translation).

In other words, after Oedipus and the castration complex, the dead father, according to the law, succeeds the idealized father of primary identification like a universal *ananke*. When this does not occur, the lack may give rise to certain classic configurations, such as paranoia, as Freud shows in the Schreber case, in which the subject, so as to nullify his filiation, creates a megalomaniac genealogy which places him in a direct line to God; or certain sexual perversions of which the aim is the disavowal of sexual difference and castration.

I will not dwell at any more length on Freud, but will turn instead to the focus of this section. "The dead father and the body" impels me to proceed with two complex psychical histories in which one may perceive the failure of the constitution of the father – dead according to the law – in the impact that it has on the body through illnesses or even sometimes voluntary affections.

Clinical material

Xavier

I would like to describe a few moments in the cure of a patient whom I treated for five years in the setting of the Paris psychosomatic institute (IPSO) day hospital.[1] The patient was about 30 when I first saw him. He was a tanned, handsome young man of Italian parentage. He was dressed like a young executive, in a dark suit and tie, and he always carried an attaché case in which he packed what he needed for the night, but his sneakers and anorak added a rather unusual aspect to his appearance. He had worked in various offices "but they didn't keep me on anywhere." When he came to see me he was an unsuccessful martial arts teacher and on his way to becoming a bum because he could no longer earn his living. He had severe idiopathic high blood pressure which was not controlled, and diffuse anxiety described as a permanent state of alert. The cardiologist who was treating him at the hospital referred him to the IPSO and made it clear that he did not know if this young man took his medication as he had a hard time imagining what kind of life he led. (Note: the doctor thought he was "crazy.")

Xavier, as we shall call him, appeared to fit with the descriptions of the Paris psychosomatic school: a crushing of the preconscious, an invading of the real, i.e. that which could be perceived. There was not, it appeared, a protective shield against excitation; the preconscious was no substitute for a filter. Thus there was no identifiable trace of the regular topography. What we call the superego did not seem to exist. In classical psychiatric nosography, he would in all probability be described as a psychopathic personality.

He did not have a police record, but he had committed certain criminal acts: at night he had set fire to the warehouse of a business from which he had been fired. Xavier had violently beaten a prostitute: he became deeply afraid when she lost consciousness because he thought she was dead, "which could have caused me some trouble." When he told me this, I asked him if it had been pleasurable for him or if, on the contrary, he had to make something unbearable stop: "Nothing like that at all, I just didn't want to pay."

Notwithstanding the high blood pressure and the diffuse anxiety, he was obviously the kind of patient that a psychoanalyst has little occasion to meet. The work I carried out with him consisted in listening to the flood of information he poured forth, trying at least to put some spatial-temporal order to it, and to give it some meaning, to make connections or, rather, to suggest to him that such connections could be made. The quasi-permanent state of alert he lived in effectively yielded, we saw together, when he felt himself to be in a "benevolent" setting. As he was incapable of wondering, even for a second, what was happening in another person's head, he made people uncomfortable. He vaguely perceived this. Hence he had a sensation, not quite with the status of an affect, of moving in an often hostile world that made him violent.

My patient manifested great difficulty in restraining, holding back, and waiting. He recounted how much a perceived object which he desired became overwhelming. One morning, when he saw a beautiful pair of fur-lined leather gloves in a car, he broke the window in order to take them. He was then stopped by a plain-clothes policeman who took him to the police station, where he was beaten up and held for 24 hours, and allowed to go, once they'd taught him a lesson. Xavier seemed very happy about this experience: "A good man," he said, to which I suggested, "The father you would have wanted to have." In fact, he had never known his father. His mother, a drug addict, was described as incoherent, unemotional, and frequently sadistic. A terrible, humiliating memory then came back to him. When he was learning toilet training and soiled his underwear, he was sent into the courtyard with his bottom naked and his dirty underwear on his head like a hat. Xavier cried when he recalled this.

Based on these two elements, which I had connected by showing him that to be corrected by a benevolent man had led him to recall the story of a cold, humiliating punishment that had failed to make him understand that he had to wait and to restrain, we were able to construct a history of the distress of the child he had been. The work of reconstructing a past which was meaningful to what he had become seemed to interest and even fascinate him. Some time after, he would tell me violent and crude dreams, that he recounted in urgency at the beginning of the sessions, as if he wanted to get rid of them. Here is an example: "He walks in the street and a tall and heavy man overcomes him from behind; he feels that he is being raped and penetrated. He is furious but it is not disagreeable."

The next night he dreamed that he was "in the street, he was walking and looking for his keys in his pocket. He finds something flabby and sticky which he looks at and identifies as a cut and bloody penis. He throws it into the gutter."

I never intervened directly concerning the content, but rather I asked him about the affects accompanying the dreams, or I emphasized their lack. I thus suggested to him the connections between the two dreams, the scene at the police station, the father's absence, and his desire for a male's grasping hold of him. I also showed him that his very great need to recount his dreams, as if he had to rid himself of them, was perhaps tied to a worry about what was happening inside himself. What was strange was the treatment he made of his dream material, which did not appear to me to assume a much different status from his narratives of factual events. Thus he once dreamed that he "was breaking my little black car," which he had spotted in the hospital's parking lot, "with a big hammer." He was so afraid to recount this dream that he had first spoken to the secretary about it and asked her if I was going to get angry. I then said to him, "Get angry to the point that I would send you without your pants into the courtyard where you spied my car?"

The other side of this unusual face-to-face psychoanalytic treatment consisted in interventions that I would qualify as "psychodramatic," namely those aimed at forcing work in the arena of identification, apparently non-existent; for example, "You've asked yourself what this person could feel when you told her what you did?" or "What effect do you think your narrative has on me?"

In thinking about this case, I see three essential dimensions to our work: one consists in the work of mentalization, that is, seeking to give, by means of a shared narrative, the status of psychic events to his acts or behavior, thus, initiating a drive temporality so that the perceptual mosaic could become a weaving of related representations; two, the work of historicizing, showing that there is a past which affects the present. And three, objectalization or re-objectalization in order to make the other exist, thus initiating a drive circuit such that it might generate a subject.

At the beginning of the cure, Xavier had no past, no history, no object. How, in this condition, could he feel himself to be a subject? To become one, he had to inscribe himself, at least in fantasy, into a filiation bearing mourning.

A dream about Heidegger

"Heidegger invites me to Tübingen, I meet him in the university library. He is sitting in a black armchair, like yours. He is wearing a beautiful, very light beige gabardine. He tells me he likes my articles and asks me to do a thesis with him. I feel deeply happy." This dream was told to me during the penultimate session of a long analysis whose end had been anticipated months earlier. While very cultivated, the patient was, however, neither a philosopher nor a writer. He was a very successful businessman whose entire analysis turned on the "murder of the father."

His parents divorced when Monsieur Z was two years old, and then his father disappeared and started another family. He only saw his son again when Monsieur Z finished first in his class from a prestigious school. The father then hired him in his business. Ten years later, his father thanked him for his work but fired him, giving him a significant severance package, for he wanted to make room for his second son, who was born out of his second marriage. The furor and hatred of Monsieur Z drove him to start his own company in the same domain that, seven years later, bought out the father's, which was then in difficulty. A few months after, Monsieur Z fell ill with a serious kidney disease. He underwent dialysis and then a transplant. Such is the context for the beginning of the analysis.

I will only speak about the dream. The patient told me, "I am substituting you with a more prestigious father, but this great thinker was also a Nazi shit, which reminds me of my father." There was a short silence and then he said, "What is important is the light beige gabardine. It's the same one I bought last week. I think that in the dream, Heidegger is my idealized father but is also me. I too was a bastard with my father, even if I didn't feel guilty . . . But I fell ill. In the dream I give myself a son, myself, whom I recognize. Such is the feeling of happiness. I owe all that to my body, otherwise I would have never gone into analysis."

Discussion

In this short chapter, I cannot go into the complexities of these clinical treatments, nor into psychosomatic theory. I will say, however, that both these patients, while they had completely different psychic structures, had an "absent father." This "absence" is obviously experienced more by the capacities for psychic working-through of the mother than by the reality of the absence. For example, one can very well imagine that Xavier's mother had no access to a third party. Both patients were obliged to confront themselves with the question of the symbolic father by means of a somatic disorder. My hypothesis is that somatic disorders are correlative to the temporary, or long term, overflowing of the subject's capacity to engage himself in psychic working-through.

Inspired by Thomas Laqueur's impressive book *Making Sex: Body and Gender from the Greeks to Freud* (1992), I will now explore the question of "the dead father and the body" with more general and anthropological thoughts, and questions on the possible connections between identity, the search for identity, and ultimately for a fantasmatic filiation, and the present vogue – one might even say, industry – of "body transformation."

My reflections on the subject, rarely treated by psychoanalysts, began during a very "unusual" congress. As I had long been interested in masochism and pain, and had also written on these themes, I was invited in the year 2000 as a "psychoanalyst specialist" to an enormous international congress of practitioners of sado-masochism. It took place in a provincial city in France. The other invited speaker from outside the milieu was a very well-known sociologist, David Le Breton, the author of *Anthropologie du Corps et Modernité* [Anthropology of the Body and Modernity] (2005) and *Signes d'Identité* [Identity Signs] (2002). Le Breton has for years investigated tattooing and body piercing.

Those attending the congress came from across the world, and many from the United States. I can tell you that I learned a great deal and was even led to rethink certain preconceived ideas, even dogmas, about masochism. But what I would like to describe here is a long conversation with a man, Amaury, who said he was 32 years old. He was impressive because, given that he was wearing only shorts, it was possible to see that not a single inch of his skin was free of piercing or tattoos, or both. He came to see me after my round table in order to tell me that since his "re-creation" by means of "corporal transformations," he felt better and did not need a "shrink." Nevertheless, he was quite ready to answer my questions. Amaury did not want to speak about his childhood; he had succeeded in effacing it. He said that what he had created was "a work of personal art that had no past." He had neither history nor mother nor father. He considered himself "self-engendered."

I then asked him about the process of transformation and the physical pain which accompanied it. It had been very great. He had invested it like an initiation. The physical pain effaced the past, but through the traces, the scars left behind, it opened up "a new memory" for him. He spoke about the pain like an obligatory but saving rite of passage.

What Amaury told me that afternoon ties into the analyses of David Le Breton (2001) who, relying on a great deal of interview material, speaks of the "Self's identity DIY (or do-it-yourself)" and sees in such practices twin attempts at abolishing filiation, all the while seeking to rediscover connections.

Le Breton's works, well documented and highly interesting, show how, after the waning of tribal bodily marking in traditional societies, there now follows a vogue for marking. While its practitioners think of themselves as dissident, the fashion is nothing other than a search for identity by means of individual and anarchic rites of passage. Le Breton is also interested in the question of pain related to the acts of tattooing and, especially, body piercing. He is astonished that in the hedonistic Western world, inclined toward the suppression of suffering and pain, the craze for body marking is accompanied by a search for, and indeed, a sublimation of, physical pain. He acknowledges the connection between pain and sexuality, but denies however any relation to masochism. I believe that this is due to his use of a socio-logical definition of masochism. I think, moreover, that though he has read Freud, his knowledge of masochism stops in 1915, before, that is, what is called Freud's "turning-point of 1920."

In my view, in contrast to Freud's, originary masochism has an import-ant role in binding the drives together in the pain that accompanies bodily modifications. Originary (or "primary" in Strachey's translation) masoc-hism, which, personally, I relate to the Lacanian concept of *jouissance*, was described by Freud (1924, pp. 159–70) in a fascinating article of just over ten pages. Failures in clinical treatment, the compulsion to repeat, the negative therapeutic reaction, masochism, and psychosis, all led Freud to revise his theory of the drives and then to replace the first topography with the second. In 1924 he grappled with what he called the "enigma of masochism." He asked himself, if pain and displeasure could become a goal of mental life, what then becomes of the pleasure principle? As a result he had to revise not only his theory of masochism, previously understood as a secondary reversal of sadism on to the individual proper, but also the pleasure principle as well. The pleasure principle, which was economic, related pleasure to discharge and unpleasure to the (painful) tension and build-up of excitation.

In 1924, Freud recognized that pleasure and excitation could actually blend; painful excitation could be enjoyable. This seemed to puzzle him and led him to imagine what he had until then refused, namely the existence of an originary masochism beginning at the dawn of life. Originary masochism would thus be, to quote Freud (1924, p. 164), "evidence of, and a remainder from the phase of development in which the coalescence, which is so import-ant for life, between the death instinct and Eros took place."

Put more simply, and in my own words, from the founding of mental life, the painful expectation of the hungry baby who hallucinates the pleasure of the breast must be, so as to make it tolerable, *masochistically invested*. There must exist an originary masochism in order to invest oneself in expect-ation, in thought, in desire, in the path of mental life. This idea seems to me to be fundamental in that it enables us to understand some secondarily masochistic behaviors as attempts to catch up on the construction of origi-nary masochism in instances where the mother was incapable of helping or allowing her child to invest in expectation, delay, or the modality of representation.

The works of Stoller (1991, pp. 239–40) and Benno Rosenberg (1991) are not far from the hypothesis I suggest: *bodily modifications, dearly and deliberately acquired through pain, should also be considered as a secondary recapturing or recovering of a failed originary masochism, which is equivalent to*

personal and unconscious attempts at experiencing what was missing, specific-
ally, the masochistic investment of a painful expectation. Painful and dangerous behavior manifestly aimed at the abolition of history, filiation, and
castration, can from then on be understood as an effort to re-create and to
rediscover a "symbolic order," which in turn opens up the imaginary.

In the Western world, in which a crisis of meaning and values has carried the
day, we are witnessing the waning of the paternal function (see Michel Tort,
2005, *La Fin Du Dogme Paternal* [The End of Paternal Dogma]) and the
"death of the dead father." The body seems to have become the site of frenzied and ferocious care, as if investing in it was correlative of the disintegration of filial and community ties.

Would marking, which can be destructive, "the exposed flesh," thus, be the
mark of a lack, a call to an inconceivable, missing "dead father"? To that
question I would personally answer "yes." Freud put the father's function at
the core of the "culture process" as well as at the center of the construction of
the individual subject. In addition, anthropologists generally agree that a
"transcultural paternal function" exists. In every culture the relationship with
the father is fundamental. It marks the evolution of a direct cathexis of the
object to a more complex relationship based on identification. The child takes
possession of his father through identification, resulting in the most ambivalent relationship, characterized by love and hate. But above all, the process of
identification opens the way to otherness (Stoloff, 2007, Chapter 4).

In his essay "Ethique et Infini," the philosopher Emmanuel Lévinas (1988,
pp. 63–4) writes about fatherhood: "it is a relationship with a stranger who
while being someone else is also a part of me."

Acknowledgement

This chapter was translated from French by Steven Jaron.

Note

1 During the 1950s a team of medical doctors and psychoanalysts joined Pierre
Marty to found the Paris psychosomatic school. Their point of departure was the
principle that patients stricken with physical illnesses should also be apprehended
psychoanalytically. Pierre Marty was struck by the absence of mental symptoms
during intercurrent illnesses.
  In the theoretical model of the Paris school, instinctual drives have their source in
bodily excitation. Their role is to deal with the tensions thus created. If the sum of
excitations continues to be excessive, the functional drive system becomes disorganized and the mental apparatus overloaded, thus leaving the way open to somatization. The notions of disorganization, fixation, and regression are therefore central
to this tightly woven and complex conceptualization (see Aisenstein, 2006).

References

Aisenstein, M. (2006) "The Indissociable Unity of Psyche and Soma: A View from the Paris Psychosomatic School", trans. Steven Jaron, *International Journal of Psychoanalysis* 87: 667–680.

Aisenstein, M. and Smadja, C. (2001) "Psychosomatics as an Essential Current of Contemporary Psychoanalysis", *Revue Française Psychanalyse*, supplement.

Freud, S. (1896) "Letter of 6 December 1896 to W. Fliess", trans. James Strachey (1966) *Standard Edition*, Volume 1, London: Hogarth Press.

—— (1908) Second preface to "The Interpretation of Dreams", trans. James Strachey (1953) *Standard Edition*, Volume 4, London: Hogarth Press.

—— (1912) "Letter of May 1912 to K. Abraham", *A Psychoanalytic Dialogue: The Letters of Sigmund Freud and Karl Abraham, 1907–1926*, trans. James Strachey (1965), London: Hogarth Press.

—— (1913) "Totem and Taboo", trans. James Strachey (1955), *Standard Edition*, Volume 13, London: Hogarth Press.

—— (1924) "The Economic Problem of Masochism", trans. James Strachey (1961), *Standard Edition*, Volume 19, London: Hogarth Press.

—— (1939) "Moses and Monotheism", trans. James Strachey (1964), *Standard Edition*, Volume 23, London: Hogarth Press.

Lacan, J. (1955) "D'une question préliminaire à tout traitement possible de la psychose" [On a preliminary question for any possible treatment of psychosis], *Ecrits*, Paris: Le Seuil.

Laqueur, T. (1992) *Making Sex: Body and Gender from the Greeks to Freud*, Cambridge, MA: Harvard University Press.

Le Breton, D. (2001) "Self's Identity DIY (or do-it-yourself)", *Cultures en mouvement* 38.

—— (2002) *Signes D'identité: Tatouages, Piercing et Autres Marques Corporelles* [Identity Signs: Tattoos, Body Piercing, and other Body Marks], Paris: Métallie.

—— (2005) *Anthropologie du Corps et Modernité* [Anthropology of the Body and Modernity], Paris: Presses Universitaires de France.

Lévinas, E. (1988) "Ethique et Infini" [Ethics and Infinity], in E. Lévinas, *Biblio-essais*, Paris: editions Fayard.

Marty, P. (1976) *Individual Movements of Life and Death*, Paris: editions Payot.

—— (1980) *L'ordre Psychosomatique* [The Psychosomatic Order], Paris: editions Payot.

Rosenberg, B. (1991) *Masochisme Mortifière et Masochisme Gardien de la Vie* [Mortifying Masochism and Life-Preserving Masochism], Paris: Presses Universitaires de France.

Rosolato, G. (1969) *Essais sur le Symbolique* [Essays on the Symbolic], Paris: Gallimard.

Stoller, R. (1991) "XSM", *Nouvelle Revue de Psychanalyse* 43.

Stoloff, J.C. (2007) *La Fonction Paternelle* [The Paternal Function], Paris: Editions in Press.

Tort, M. (2005) *La Fin du Dogme Paternal* [The End of Paternal Dogma], Paris: Aubier.

Chapter 4

A new love for the father

Eric Laurent

In the post-paternal era proclaimed by those who say that the old fathers have disappeared, psychoanalysis strives to maintain the gap between the socio-logical narrative and the lived experience of subjects. Gone is the father of authority, of tradition, of patriarchy – gone is the father of the Law. In his place has emerged a new paternity, one that is contractual, negotiated and responsible. This paternity would be nothing more than an equilibrium between rights and duties, negotiated by contracts. In the near future we might thus imagine a pacified paternity, devoid of the excesses of passion aroused by the old system. Paternity diffracted, defined by eminently variable norms, would especially suit the new arrangements of reconstituted families. This is a reformist version of the father who is finally led back to a function as instrument of social utility, divorced from his drama. The reverse side of this pluralization, of his reduction to an instrument, is a new version of the humiliation of the father, the father who is evaluated, for example, with regard to his authority. Traditionally tied to the paternal function, the ques-tion of authority returns through external demands for the old social order: "Control your children!"

The father in the era of the global market

Sociology pursues the deconstruction of fatherhood through the description of customs, while suspending all axiological[1] positions on what the father is or should be. This descriptive enterprise was more or less supplanted in the twentieth century by projects attempting to do without fathers. At the threshold of the twentieth century, André Gide cried out: "Families, I hate you!" (Gide, 1897, p. 67).[2] And again: "Nothing is more dangerous for you than *your* family, *your* room, *your* past." (p. 44).[3] He exclaimed this to break from the "natural" conception of the family that Bernardin de Saint-Pierre perfectly expressed in the eighteenth century: "Melons . . . are divided into [ribs] . . . and seem destined to be eaten in families: There are even those [like] the pumpkin . . . which one could share with one's neigh-bors" (Bernardin de Saint-Pierre, 1836, p. 594). Do not think, however, that de Saint-Pierre, one of the inventors of the travel book, was not a subtle mind. He also wrote: "Women are false in the countries where the men are tyrants. Everywhere violence produces deceit" (Bernardin de Saint-Pierre, 1984, p. 232). Moreover, while now the family is less in harmony with nature, Pope Benedict XVI has just consecrated it as "the patrimony of humanity," "the irreplaceable institution according to the project of God, of which the Church cannot stop announcing and promoting the fundamental value."[4]

Throughout the twentieth century, there were attempts to eliminate the family father, first in the communal experiences starting in the 1920s, then in the Russian experiments of the 1930s, for example, those of Anton Makarenko (from *Le Petit Robert des Noms Propres*, Paris, 1994, p. 1289).[5] Next came the kibbutz, then the communal utopias of the 1960s, both American and European. These experiments failed in that they remained only experiments. But as Jacques-Alain Miller noted *à propos* of marriage, there remained something that was not entirely discouraged. Thanks to reinforcement by the gay and lesbian communities, the demand for marriage is increasing. A call for a father accompanies the demand for marriage in these communities, even though they have not particularly wanted to be included in this category. We now must deal with new configurations, new models, of the desire to be father. Renewing the legal fiction of paternity, it creates work for lawmakers and dislocates the old ideals.

Like the law, science also pluralizes the Name of the Father. The real father ironically can be reduced to sperm, as Lacan emphasized. Precisely this, father as sperm, has enabled an alliance between the global market and science, thereby producing distinct phenomena in ways that differ from those created legally. The global market now makes sperm an object of exchange like any other commodity. Sperm now replaces the father in multiple ways. To take a novel recent example, a laboratory at the University of Newcastle has produced mice starting only from undifferentiated cells removed from the seminal vesicles. "Born without a father!" proclaims the Italian journal, *La Repubblica* (July 12, 2006). In France, we are sticking with the anonymous donor, and thus equality in the face of the unknown. In contrast, in the United States sperm is stocked and sold. Sperm banks are ranked according to various criteria. Willingness to pay more will acquire the sperm of a Nobel Prize winner or a handsome young man, depending upon the buyer's taste.[6]

Women's clubs meet to exchange their experiences with sperm banks. They evaluate the quality of the service, the substantiation of claims and the freshness of the product. This suits those busy young women who want children, but no longer have time to deal with the complications of a shared life with men and their imperfections.

The Lacanian father transmits the effectiveness of the spoken word

The Lacanian deconstruction of the Freudian father is achieved quite differently. It proceeds first by dividing up the Freudian father into the three dimensions: the real, the symbolic and the imaginary. In his seminar "Introduction to the Names-of-the-Father" (Lacan, 1990), Lacan commented on what is called "The Sacrifice of Abraham" in the Catholic tradition and the *Akedah* ("The Bondage of Isaac") in the Jewish. The story captures the moment that defines the alliance between the father and the son. Lacan locates a first Name-of-the-Father, the totem father. Rachi[7] writes, and Lacan underscores, that the ram must be present, ready for sacrifice, from the beginning of time (Lacan, 1990; Gallia and Yerid ha Sefarim, 2000).[8] The sperm from the lineage of Abraham, it is he who at first is the divine name. The *Akedah* brings about the passage from the register of the totemic name to a Name-of-the-Father, which will function in a way opposed to the totem. The totem designates a lineage through identification with a name, an unending animal lineage, while the *Akedah* implicates a name that only sustains itself through the effectiveness of its statement. It sustains itself in the particularity of a relationship.

Beginning with this second moment, the *Akedah* incarnates the effectiveness of a spoken statement of God through the intervention of the angel. The angel is the power of speech itself, which says "No" to the ideal totemic line. In this sense, says Lacan, it is the father totem which is sacrificed. The operation produced a remnant, the horn, a piece of the ram that endures and which will be transformed into a ritual instrument; the *shofar* is a remnant of the operation of substitution. Nothing animal remains in Abraham's lineage. Now it is a lineage tied to an act of speech, the transmission of the benediction, of the *berakhah*, such that the father transmits to the son the effectiveness of the spoken word in its particularity.

Let us reconcile this first division by means of Lacan's explanation of the Freudian myth of *Totem and Taboo*, which he elaborates in his Seminar, *L'Ethique de la psychanalyse* (1986). The Freudian myth of *Totem and Taboo* posits a primal totemic father who becomes the agent of castration. According to Lacan, when the threat of castration occurs, a subject appears who is captured in a new relationship with the father who then becomes imaginary. Imaginary in this context means that the father no longer appears in the universal. He becomes the father who has created *this* child, *this* inadequate child who *I* am. Lacan writes:

> [This] real and mythical father, does he not disappear, at the decline of the Oedipus complex, behind . . . the imaginary father, the father who has so badly formed this kid? Is it not around the experience of deprivation that the child undergoes – not so much because he is small but because he

is human – is it not around that which for him is deprivation, that mourning for the imaginary father is fomented and forged? That is to say, of a father who would be really someone. The perpetual reproach that is thus born, in a manner more or less definitive and well formed according to the case, remains fundamental in the structure of the subject. This imaginary father, it is he, and not the real father, who is the foundation of the providential image of God.

(Lacan, 1986, p. 355)[9]

From this point on, there will coexist the symbolic father, the father of love or the Name-of-the-Father, and the imaginary father or the father of hatred and reproach. This hatred is simultaneously the hatred of oneself and the hatred of him, for having made me in my miserable particularity. I will spend my life trying to separate myself from all that is failed in me, all that I hate about myself and about this God who has made me. I will pass my life in aspiring for a separation from the *kakon*[10] that is in me and which I hate. This separation, this expulsion of the object from the body, can extend to mutilation. Similarly, the *Akedah* permits the passage from totem to the castrating father. As Rachi said, restated by Lacan, in this alliance it is necessary to cut off a piece of the body, to tear out something from the body, to mutilate it. This ritual piece will serve to cover the object of self-hatred, which simultaneously incarnates all I am deprived of as well as excess *jouissance*. The religious operation of the alliance itself will consist of veiling this object by disguising castration as castration rite.

The father captured by the function

This double commentary valorizes the isomorphism of the Freudian myth of *Totem and Taboo* and Judeo-Christian tradition. It introduces us to the opposition between the universal, which Lacan will call "the eternal," and the particular. Hence it is necessary to consider the myth beginning with the logic of quantification. In totemism, the name totem defines a god. Every father is a ram, according to his totem. Before the *Akedah*, Abraham was part of the lineage of the ram. Every father is God in this sense, if he connects with his totemic identification. The paradox presented can be articulated as "Every father is God," on the condition not *one* existing father be God. The non-existence of such a father verifies that "Every father is God." As soon as the existence of the father is not in quotation marks, the objection raised by the castration complex appears along with the imaginary father, in no way a god, since he is the limited being who badly created me. Lacan thus stages the opposition between the essence of the function – the function as it defines a totality, a "for-all" (*pour-tout*) – and existence. Introducing tension between the two levels is part of the Lacan's radical anti-Hegelian project, which refuses to reduce particular existences to parts of the whole. Lacan boldly articulates this at the time of the Seminar, "Introduction to the Names-of-the-Father": "The entire Hegelian dialectic is fabricated to fill in this fault and to demonstrate, in a grand transmutation, how the universal can particularize itself through the path of the scansion of the *Aufhebung*" (p. 74).[11]

This unfastening of the Hegelian totality aims at enabling us to consider the particularity of our existence. Lacan pursues this approach when he defines the Name-of-the-Father by starting with a function. The great advantage of a function is that it avoids defining a totality or whole. A function only defines its domain of application. It is useless to define the nature of a logical function by beginning with an essence. Furthermore, modern logic considers the question of infinite sets. One only has to take into account the infinite to appreciate that one can never completely define the totality of all cases of a function; one will never arrive at the end of its domain of application. Contemporary logic explores an entire series of paradoxes on this subject. The function then is definable only through manifestations of the variables that constitute its development. Lacan uses the term "model" in this context. We understand the paternal function only via the models that it realizes. If to be is to be the value of a variable, to be a father is to be one of the models realized, one of the values (a, b, c, etc.) of the function $P(x)$. To say, "The father as the agent of castration can only be a model of the function," means the access Lacan chooses to the question of fatherhood is thinking about actual fathers on a case-by-case basis. Therefore, to define a father Lacan speaks of *père-version*,[12] versions of a father, taken one by one.

From the name to object "*a*"

Consequently, it is no longer a matter of beginning with the name, but rather with the object "*a*". In modern physics, an elementary particle can always be grasped according to its double nature, either as a wave or as a particle. For us, a psychoanalytic notion can be approached either through the signifier or through the object. The definition of a father starting with the object *a* can be achieved through different means, including the following:

> A father has the right to respect, if not love, only if the aforesaid love, the aforesaid respect is ... *perversely* oriented, that is to say, makes of a woman the object *a* who causes his desire. But that which a woman thus *a*-ccomodates has nothing to do with the question. That which occupies her is other objects *a*, which are children.
>
> (Lacan, 1975, p. 107)[13]

So to be a father is to have the particular perversion of attaching himself to the objects *a* of a woman. The formulation leaves open whether or not this woman is the one with whom the father had the children. It is a formulation that especially suits reconstituted families. Note the chiasmus, the structural criss-crossing. Normally, according to the structure of masculine desire, the man attaches himself to the objects *a* that induce his *own* desire. For example, the fetishist attaches himself to the phallus that the mother lacks, actualizing it in a particular fetish, such as the shoe, the "shine on the nose", etc. Lacan defines the father according to a particular fetish. It is not a matter of an object out of place, that *ex-ists*,[14] but of an object that a woman has produced. But the child is an object *a* of the *mother*. One can now speak of the intertwining of the *père-version* – a version of the father and the perversion of the father – and the mother's perversion. The father must take special care, called "paternal" and understood in the largest sense, of this object *a*. It is a kind of care that can be defined as beneficially separating the child from the mother. He who makes this choice is a father. Lacan adds, "whether he wishes it or not," underlining that this has to do with a decision on an order other than volition. To occupy this position, the father is a model of the function. What is really at stake is the way in which the woman is the cause of his desire – or the cause of his hatred.

In the Seminar, *D'un Autre à l'Autre*, Lacan proposes another definition of a father beginning with the object *a*. He distances himself from the father defined by the family in leading him back to a myth relating to the neurotic:

> If for the pervert there has to be an uncastrated woman, or more exactly, if he makes her such, is not the *famil*[15] figured at the horizon of the field of neurosis, this something which is a *He* somewhere, but of which the *I* is actually the issue that is being dealt with in the family drama?
>
> (2006, p. 293)[16]

An approach through femininity

In "Preface to *Spring Awakening*," a commentary on the play of Frank Wedekind, Lacan approaches the reversal of perspectives between the universal, or eternal, and the particular, but starting with the feminine: "How can one know if, as Robert Graves formulates it, the Father himself, our eternal father for everyone, is only a Name, among others, of the White Goddess,[17] she who by her word loses herself in the night of the times, so as to be the Different one, the Other forever in her *jouissance*?" (Lacan, 2001, p. 563).[18] The White Goddess marks the place of *jouissance* as "losing oneself in the night of times," having its own kind of eternity. It is the inverse of the Name-of-the-Father as totem, the father as animal or as eternal. Here it is a matter of naming two modes of the eternal. Jacques-Alain Miller situates their equivalence in the following way:

> Freud, establishing the genealogy of God, stopped at the Name-of-the-Father. Lacan, in contrast, bores into the metaphor all the way up to the desire of the mother and all the way up to the surplus *jouissance of*

the woman. From there comes the notion ... that it would be possible that the father be only one of the names of the maternal goddess, the White Goddess, who remains Other in her *jouissance*.

(Miller, 2003, pp. 26–27)[19]

The feminine religions especially fascinated Graves, who believed in them more willingly than in the masculine religions centered on the father and the law. Graves, first militant pacifist then worthy soldier, described in his war memoirs, *Goodbye To All That!*, the reasons that compelled him to reject the lies of civilization. He thought of himself as an outcast among men. Nevertheless, he redeemed himself by creating a god in the form of this belief in *jouissance* before the Law. Next, he tried to identify it in the development of his work.

If this equivalence is posited, how then can the difference be maintained between the place of the Other of *jouissance*, which pertains to all religions, and the adventure of the patriarchy which began with the *Akedah*? It begins at the moment where *jouissance* – of which the totem qua animal is one of the names – is replaced by a particular alliance. Lacan articulates the passage from the universal to the particular in another way during his speech at Yale: "Atheism is a malady of the belief in God, the belief that God does not intervene in the world. God intervenes all the time, for example under the form of a woman" (1976, p. 32).[20] It is not a matter of *The* Woman, The White Goddess, who will grant access to supreme *jouissance*. It is a matter of *a* woman with whom a particular alliance is knotted such that the man believes in it. Of this woman, Lacan creates a god who acts in the world, an incarnation of the desire of the Other under the form of faith in a woman. One must compare this declaration of Lacan with that which he advances on faith in a woman as symptom, during his Seminar "RSI":

> You will see that a woman in the life of a man is something to which he attaches faith. He believes that there is only one, or sometimes two or three, and it's exactly there the interesting part – he cannot believe only in one, he believes in a kind ... One believes in her because one never had proof that she was not absolutely authentic. But there one blinds oneself. This *to believe in her* serves as an obstructing cork for *to believe in it* – something which can be very seriously called into question. To believe that there is a *One*, God knows where that leads you – that leads you to the point of believing there is a *The*, a belief that is fallacious.
>
> (1975, pp. 109–110)[21]

It is not a question here of a guarantee, but of faith. That faith consists of leaving to chance what took place in the encounter. In this sense, modern kinship cannot be atheistic, in the meaning given to the term atheist by the Enlightenment. Within democratic kinship, in order to put oneself at a distance from the "for all" that the universal God or the father of eternity introduces, the tendency is to say that paternity supposes no belief. As a pure legal device, kinship would only be the norm. In fact, kinship cannot be atheistic, because it assumes an act of faith which bases itself on a belief in a particular *jouissance*. The *jouissance* of a woman, *just as she is*, as proposed by Lacan in 1975 reformulates his earlier thesis on perverse *jouissance* which he articulated in 1964 in the Seminar on the Names-of-the-Father:

> It is here that the accent I placed on the function of perversion in relation to the desire for the Other takes its importance. That is to say, perversion takes at face value the function of the Father, the Supreme Being. Eternal God is thus taken literally, not by his jouissance, always veiled and unfathomable, but by his desire as interested in the order of the world.
>
> (p. 89)[22]

What better description is there of a woman's intervention in the order of the world than the figure of Anna Karenina? For her desire achieves the destruction of an order that passed itself off as natural. She is as destructive for traditional Russian society as the Napoleon of *War and Peace*. But she proceeds through particularity. The first sentence of the novel expresses this well: "Happy families all resemble each other; unhappy families are unhappy each in their own way" (Tolstoï, 1951, p. 61). From this perspective, we are far from the world of the gods and the exceptional fathers. We are in a democratic world in which each one can become father, be a value of this exceptional function: "Whoever achieves the function of exception that the father has, we know what the result will be, that of his *Verwerfung*[23] in the majority of cases by the descendants that he engenders, with the psychotic result that I have denounced" (p. 107).[24]

Lacan therefore makes use of the three clinical categories – neurosis, perversion, psychosis – in order to explore the subjective consequences of the irreconcilability of the two levels of quantification. The principal virtue of a father is not to identify himself with the function. He must protect himself from that, confining himself to the contingency of his encounter with the woman who became mother due to the intertwining of each other's causal objects. If the father identifies himself with the function, he can imagine he is God, indulging in domestic tyranny like President Schreber. Or, like the paranoid genius Jean-Jacques Rosseau, he might devise an ideal system of education. It is also possible, from the standpoint of perversion, to object to the universality of the function, to the "magnificent" republican order founded on the grandeur of reason, and to its distributive justice guaranteeing equality of *jouissance* for everyone.

What must be maintained is the distance between actual existence and the "for all." Then one can deduce a notion of paternal virtue, which Lacan amusingly situates as "épater (sa) famille" ("to astonish his family"). The

French verb *épater* means simultaneously "to produce a sort of admiration," "to create an effect," but above all, in playing with the Latin *pater*, "to step aside" in relation to the ideal of the pater familias – to "ex-father" or "de-father" the family. It causes its effect through staying at a distance from the belief that the father can be "for all." Remember that *épater* does not mean "to play the hero." Generally a father is not the hero of his family, precisely because he meets the operation of castration. Nonetheless exceptional fathers might exist; a place for them should be reserved.

The father facing the communities of *jouissance*

Approaching the father through his existence demands that his incarnations be considered case by case. But how can *this* father guarantee access to *jouissance* as the father-God of the Freudian model did for *all* women? Now it's a matter of making *one* woman the cause of the father's perversion. Through the particular alliance, the subject can have access to the real *jouissance* at play.

In thinking about this only from the standpoint of particularity, are we so easily liberated from the deceptive semblance that the Name-of-the-Father comes to represent. The function at the level of the "for all" will not cease to exist under the form of this *semblant*. We are led to ask: How are we sure that a model, an example in the flesh, really results from the general function?

Contemporary hedonism in its multiple variations proves that it is impossible to define correctly sexual relations between the sexes, or between members of the same sex. The *jouissance* here is never what should be the ultimate *jouissance*. There is no norm that can stabilize the drive toward *jouissance*.[25] Distributive justice can support the dream of the guarantee of an equal distribution of *jouissance*. The welfare state was in fact a religious hope, the foundation of a secular religion that could show us how to build on the ideals of a republic. The ideal of universal distributive justice is now confronted by communities of *jouissance* that do not want to become assimilated in the common good. They simply hope for a society with laws that affirm the right to difference. Each community wants to define itself starting with its own *jouissance*.

In a patriarchal utopia, it is possible to dream that such *jouissance* would be equally distributed among all. Each could claim his share, based on his love for the father and the parity of the father's love for his children. This utopia having met its limit, contemporary hedonism, in its polymorphism, is confronted with the absence of guarantee. Modernity does not make happiness the goal, contrary to what the Enlightenment thinkers believed. Instead, the quest is for the ultimate *jouissance*. This is why we are now dealing with what Judith Butler calls the "gender trouble" (Butler, 1990) of our civilization. The heterosexual utopia was defined by a belief in a father who distributes the sexes and guarantees that *she* is made for *him*, in a bijection[26] of the principle of the natural or just order.

Unbelievers of the religion of distributive reason are rising up. They don't want to define themselves by a distinguishing trait, by a sexual identity. They want instead self-definition based on a sexual practice. This new Adamic nomenclature would come from the subject himself, acting as such, and no longer from the Other. "Gender trouble" translates a large spectrum of sexualities: gays, lesbians, transvestites, transsexuals, sadomasochists, all part of the grand parade where the known sexual practices can inscribe themselves. The Pride Parade provides a place of communal association for the demand for equal rights to the child, no matter the sexual identity of the partner or the sexual identity chosen. This could be a version of the end of the history of sexuality, a Hegelian whole panoramically filmed under the camera of the modern democratic master. Of course, one ought always to be able to add one more position, that of she or he who does not want to be identified, a sort of pure Deleuzian identity according to Butler. Contrary to other militants who demand communities of *jouissance*, this Butler favors psychoanalysis. But she resolutely calls for a psychoanalysis that would aim at, in the language of Freud, a polymorphous perverse pre-Oedipal ideal. We will not follow her to this other utopia. Some dream of a pre-Oedipal world, but we in fact live in a post-Oedipal world in which the neurotic love for the father, the paternal perversion and the more or less generalized rejection of fathers coexist. If this world can be defined by its disbelief in the father, it is above all defined by its connection to the paternal guarantee, but retroactively, *après coup*. Though without guarantee, it does contain the impossibles.

There is no ultimate *jouissance* that could definitively relieve us of our anxiety; such is the impossibility that confronts the discourse on *jouissance*. The community that pursues the quest for *jouissance* can function as an imaginary basis for a symbolic neo-guarantee. Nevertheless, point of the real remains intact. The subject must submit to this hole in the universe in the sexual sense in which he wishes to live. We could say that he submits to the paradox of *Kripgenstein*, as Hilary Putnam called it.

For each to invent the father who recognizes him

Under the most celebrated form, which Kripke gave to it, the argument consists of interpreting the philosophy of the rules of Wittgenstein as the "skeptical solution of a skeptical argument". Wittgenstein would have brought to light an unseen and powerful skeptical argument by virtue of which it is impossible to determine the rule followed by an agent in the course of an action. According to Kripke, Wittgenstein "has shown that *all* language, *all* concept formation is impossible and in reality unintelligible". An agent performing an addition could as well be in the middle of doing something completely different, and neither we *nor he* have any means to know it. There is not a single given, neither observational nor introspective, which would permit saying that it is a matter of an addition or even of some completely different operation which in this precise case gives the same result as the addition, but which follows completely different rules and of which the results differ from those of the addition in a great number of cases. There are no "facts in the world" . . . which would permit one to say what rule has been followed. The skeptical solution of this skeptical paradox is therefore the community view: To follow a rule can be nothing other than to conform to the established usage in a community. It is the community which determines or which *constitutes* what is a false calculation.

(Laugier, 2002, pp. 557–558)

Jacques-Alain Miller, in his Course entitled "Donc" ("Therefore"), developed the consequences of this paradox, and the matter of overcoming it, for psychoanalytic practice.

For Lacan, every human community comprises a limit to *jouissance*. This limit can take the form of a demand for recognition of the sexual rules that each one follows. The most radical inventions, those breaking most sharply with tradition, wish to be recognized in their particularity. A transsexual will detest being put in the same category as a transvestite. This recognition can be obtained with or without the aid of tradition, religion, or the usual standards that ordinarily define the function of recognition. Both an authorization and a barrier, it is the function of the father. We all have to invent for ourselves the father who recognizes us or rejects us, even if we want to be self-engendered because of the uniqueness of our sin. The creation of this paternal perversion in each case should be the subject of our clinical inquiry.

Each one surrenders to the contingency of the encounter with the partner, hetero or homo. He never succeeds in reducing her to the terms of a norm, or knowing exactly which rule she obeys. It is impossible to reduce the encounter to a description. It is also impossible to reduce the question of the real father to the place of the object *a*. The lure of Lacan is instead to reduce this place to a logical characteristic:

That the dead father be the *jouissance* presents itself to us as the sign of the impossible itself. And it is indeed in this that we rediscover here the terms which are those I define as affixing the category of the real . . . the logic of that which, in the symbolic, articulates itself as impossible . . . Indeed, we recognize well there, beyond the myth of Oedipus, an operator, a structural operator, the one of the real father . . . advancement then to the heart of the Freudian system, of that which is the father of the real, which places a term of the impossible in the center of the Freudian articulation.

(1991, p. 143)[27]

A remnant incommensurable with the norms

The "real father" thus becomes the presence of the real in the symbolic, "a sign of the impossible." He operates so as to create a radical separation between the discourse of science, which offers its services as knowing absolutely who the biological father is, and the discourse of psychoanalysis, which makes of it an impossible point in knowledge and in social norms. The Name-of-the-Father is that which covers over this impossible, this veritable hole in the symbolic: "*I am what I am*, this is a hole, isn't it? A hole ... it swallows up and then sometimes spits out again. What does it spit out? The name, the Father as name" (1976, p. 54).[28] Lacan also says it in this way:

> Papa, this is not at all necessarily he who is – it is the case of saying it – the father in the real sense, in the sense of animal nature. The father, it is a function which refers to the real, and it is not necessarily the truth of the real. This does not impede that the real of the father is in fact absolutely fundamental in psychoanalysis. The mode of existence of the father partakes of the real. It is the only case where the real is stronger than the truth.
>
> (1976, p. 45)[29]

The Name-of-the-Father is a *semblant* in the sense that we "call '*semblant*' that which functions to veil nothingness" (Miller, 1997, p. 7). This nothingness or this hole can also articulate itself as something that is insoluble in knowledge, something that is impossible to know.

Perhaps Donald Rumsfeld, whipping father if there ever was one, wanted to identify with this point when he performed his exercise of dazzling logic in masking the lack of reference to weapons of mass destruction: "There are things we know that we know. There are known unknowns; that is to say there are things that we now know we don't know. But there are also unknown unknowns. There are things we do not know we don't know" (quoted by Cohen, R. in *International Herald Tribune*, July 7, 2006, p. 2).[30]

To be a father is not a social norm but an act that has consequences, sumptuous or severe. Contemporary filiation refers beyond the norms to the particularized desire of which the child is the product, whatever be the complexity, and to the impossibility of describing it. The contemporary father is a residue, a name, but he remains incommensurable with norms. Therefore, he remains passionately at stake, and the pacification of paternity will remain as utopian as the end of history. Our era requires deciphering these new loves for the father, whether they are unveiled by political or sociological approaches, or whether we bring them to light through our clinical inquiry.

To make use of the Name-of-the-Father in order to transcend it still harbors many surprises. We can reclaim as epigraph for our inquiry the word of love devised by Martial, strange Roman poet of the first century, "unexpected classic" as his biographer calls him. It figures in his epigrams and proclaims, "Neither with you, nor without you" (Hennig, 2003).

Acknowledgements

This chapter was translated from French by Edward Kenny. The translator wishes to thank Maria Cristina Aguirre, Lila Kalinich, and Catherine Maheux for their valuable contributions.

Notes

1 Axiology – The study of the nature of values and value judgments. From *The American Heritage College Dictionary*, 4th edn, New York: Houghton Mifflin, 2004.
2 The French reads: "Familles, je vous hais! Foyers clos: portes renfermées; possessions jalouses du bonheur."
3 The French reads: "Rien n'est plus dangereux pour toi que ta famille, que ta chambre, que ton passé."
4 Audience with the participants of the General Assembly of the Pontifical Counsel for the Family, Rome, May 13, 2006, and Speech proclaimed at the 5th World Family Meeting, July 8, 2006, Valencia, Spain.
5 The works of Makarenko created a particular echo in France. Louis Aragon described his *Poème pédagogique*, the story of a colony of criminal and vagabond children, as "one of the most poignant documents that humanity has produced." From *Le Petit Robert des noms propres*, Paris, 1994, p. 1289.
6 On this subject, consider the article "Cercasi 401 disperatamente", in the July 13, 2006 issue of *La Stampa*, in which Marina Verna, the Berlin correspondent, recounts the fate of "donor 401," of German origin, from the Fairfax Cryobank in the United States. A myth is in the midst of being born: He is not only tall with blue eyes, but he also loves his mother.
7 AKA Solomon Ben Isaac (circa 1040–1105), a commentator on the sacred Jewish written texts and oral tradition (from Wikipedia, online).
8 Lacan, 1990, p. 100, and also *Houmach, Tora Temima, avec Rachi – Berechit*, Jerusalem, eds Gallia and Yerid ha Sefarim, 1998–2000.
9 The French reads:

> [Ce] père réel et mythique ne s'efface-t-il pas au déclin de l'Œdipe derrière [. . .] le père imaginaire, le père qui l'a, lui le gosse, si mal foutu [?] N'est-ce pas autour de l'expérience de la privation que fait le petit enfant – non pas tant parce qu'il est petit que parce qu'il est homme – n'est-ce pas autour de ce qui est pour lui privation, que se fomente et se forge le deuil du père imaginaire? – c'est-à-dire d'un père qui serait vraiment quelqu'un. Le reproche perpétuel qui naît alors, d'une façon plus ou moins définitive et bien formée selon les cas, reste fondamental dans la structure du sujet. Ce père imaginaire, c'est lui, et non pas le père réel, qui est le fondement de l'image providentielle de Dieu.

10 From the Greek, *kakos*, "bad."
11 From Wikipedia online: "In Hegel, the term *Aufhebung* (translated as 'sublation') has the apparently contradictory implications of both preserving and changing. The tension between these senses suits what Hegel is trying to talk about. In sublation, a term or concept is both preserved and changed through its

dialectical interplay with another term or concept. Sublation is the motor by which the dialectic functions."

12 Note the pun in French on "perversion."

13 The French reads "Un père n'a droit au respect, sinon à l'amour, que si le dit amour, le dit respect, est [. . .] père-versement orienté, c'est-à-dire fait d'une femme objet a qui cause son désir. Mais ce qu'une femme en a-cueille ainsi n'a rien à voir dans la question. Ce dont elle s'occupe, c'est d'autres objets a, qui sont les enfants."

14 Note the etymology of "exist": Latin *ex-*, outside, out of, away from + *sistere*, to stand. From *The American Heritage College Dictionary*, 4th edn, New York: Houghton Mifflin, 2004.

15 *famil*: Lacan's word play here is between *famille* (family) and the homophonous *femme-il* ("woman-he", or he-woman). The pun aims to deconstruct the evidence for the existence of a family which consists of a father and a mother, and to replace it by the relationship of a man and a woman. In the quote that follows, Lacan contrasts the uncastrated woman as the pervert's ideal and the ideal of the "mother of the family" that tries to explain away the feminine enigma, reducing it to an ideal function. In that sense the neurotic's family ideal produces a unisex version of womanhood, the "femme-il" or "famil." This avoids the subjective division of the ego.

16 The French reads: "Si, pour le pervers, il faut qu'il y ait une femme non châtrée, ou, plus exactement, s'il la fait telle[,] le famil n'est-il pas notable à l'horizon du champ de la névrose, – ce quelque chose qui est un Il quelque part, mais dont le Je est véritablement l'enjeu de ce dont il s'agit dans le drame familial?"

17 Robert Graves' book *The White Goddess* describes the matriarchal religions of the Mediterranean which existed before the patriarchal ones. Graves proposes the existence of a European deity, the "White Goddess of Birth, Love and Death," who, he argues, lies behind the faces of the diverse goddesses of various European mythologies. J.-A. Miller offered Lacan the revised edition of the book and Lacan used it in his commentary on Wedekind's play, *Spring Awakening*. The feminine goddess seemed an adequate incarnation of the mystery of the *jouissance* which is not "eternal" but which "loses itself in the night of times." (Portions of this footnote text were adapted from Wikipedia, online.)

18 The French reads: "Comment savoir si, comme le formule Robert Graves, le Père lui-même, notre père éternel à tous, n'est que Nom entre autres de la Déesse blanche, celle à son dire qui se perd dans la nuit des temps, à en être la Différente, l'Autre à jamais dans sa jouissance?"

19 The French reads: "Freud, établissant la généalogie de Dieu, s'arrêtait au Nom-du-Père. Lacan, lui, fore la métaphore jusqu'au désir de la mère et jusqu'à la jouissance supplémentaire de la femme. D'où la notion [. . .] qu'il se pourrait que le père ne soit qu'un des noms de la déesse maternelle, la Déesse blanche, qui reste Autre dans sa jouissance."

20 The French reads: "L'athéisme, c'est la maladie de la croyance en Dieu, croyance que Dieu n'intervient pas dans le monde. Dieu intervient tout le temps, par exemple sous la forme d'une femme."

21 The French reads: "Vous y verrez qu'une femme dans la vie de l'homme, c'est quelque chose à quoi il croit. Il croit qu'il y en a une, quelquefois deux ou trois, et c'est bien là l'intéressant – il ne peut pas ne croire qu'à une, il croit à une espèce. [. . .] On la croit parce qu'on n'a jamais eu de preuves qu'elle ne soit pas absolument authentique. Mais on s'y aveugle. Ce la croire sert de bouchon à y croire – chose qui peut être très sérieusement mise en question. Croire qu'il y en a Une, Dieu sait où ça vous entraîne – ça vous entraîne jusqu'à croire qu'il y a La, croyance qui est fallacieuse."

22 The French reads: "C'est ici que prend sa valeur l'accent que j'ai permis de mettre sur la fonction de la perversion quant à sa relation au désir de l'Autre comme tel. C'est à savoir qu'elle représente la mise au pied du mur, la prise au pied de la lettre de la fonction du Père, de l'Être suprême. Le Dieu éternel pris au pied de la lettre, non pas de sa jouissance, toujours voilée et insondable, mais de son désir comme intéressé dans l'ordre du monde."

23 *Verwefung* (German): buckling, dislocation, dismissal, rejection.

24 The French reads: "N'importe qui atteint la fonction d'exception qu'a le père, on sait avec quel résultat, celui de sa *Verwerfung* dans la plupart des cas par la filiation qu'il engendre, avec le résultat psychotique que j'ai dénoncé."

25 Le "pousse-à-jouir."

26 In mathematics, a bijection, or a bijective function, is function f from the set of X to the set Y with the property that, for every y in Y, there is exactly one x in X such that $f(x) = y$. (Adapted from Wikipedia, online.)

27 The French reads: "Que le père mort soit la jouissance se présente à nous comme le signe de l'impossible même. Et c'est bien en cela que nous retrouvons ici les termes qui sont ceux que je définis comme fixant la catégorie du réel, [. . .] logique de ce qui, du symbolique, s'énonce comme impossible. [. . .] Nous reconnaissons bien là en effet, au-delà du mythe d'Œdipe, un opérateur, un opérateur structurel, celui dit du père réel, [. . .] promotion au cœur du système freudien, de ce qui est le père du réel, qui met au centre de l'énonciation de Freud un terme de l'impossible."

28 The French reads: "*Je suis ce que je suis*, ça c'est un trou, non? Un trou [. . .], ça engloutit et puis il y a des moments où ça recrache. Ça recrache quoi? Le nom, le Père comme nom."

29 The French reads: "Papa, ce n'est pas du tout, forcément, celui qui est – c'est le cas de le dire – le père au sens réel, au sens de l'animalité. Le père, c'est une fonction qui se réfère au réel, et ce n'est pas forcément le vrai du réel. Ça n'empêche pas que le réel du père, c'est absolument fondamental dans l'analyse. Le mode d'existence du père tient au réel. C'est le seul cas où le réel est plus fort que le vrai."

30 Rumsfeld, D., quoted by Cohen, R. in "Rumsfeld is correct: The truth will get out", *International Herald Tribune*, July 7, 2006, p. 2.

References

American Heritage College Dictionary, 4th edn (2004), New York: Houghton Mifflin Company.

Butler, J. (1990) *Gender Trouble: Feminism and the Subversion of Identity*, New York: Routledge.

Franceschini, E. (2006) "Nati Senza Padre, Rivoluzione in Laboratorio", *La Repubblica*, July 12, 2006.

Gide, A. (1897) "Les Nourritures Terrestres", in *coll. Folio, 1917–1936*, Paris: Gallimard. 44, 67.

Lacan, J. (1975) "Le Séminaire, Livre XXII, "RSI", Leçon du 21 Janvier 1975", in *Ornicar?, n° 3*, Mai 1975: 107, 109–110, Paris: Lyse.

—— (1976) "Le Séminaire, Livre xxii, "RSI", Leçon du 15 Avril 1975", in *Ornicar?, n° 5*, Hiver 1976: 54, Paris: Lyse.

—— (1976a) "Conférences et Entretiens dans des Universités Nord-Américaines, Yale University, 24 Novembre 1975", in *Scilicet, n° 6/7*: 32, Paris: Le Seuil.

—— (1976b) "Conférences et Entretiens Dans des Universités Nord-Américaines. Columbia University, 1er Décembre 1975", in *Scilicet, n° 6/7*: 45, Paris: Le Seuil.

—— (1986) "Le Séminaire, Livre VII", in *L'Éthique de la Psychanalyse*: 355, Paris: Le Seuil.

—— (1990) "Introduction aux Noms-du-Père [Introduction to the Names-of-the-Father] Seminar", in D. Hollier, R. Krauss and A. Michelson (eds) *Television: A Challenge to the Psychoanalytic Establishment*, New York: W. W. Norton, pp. 74, 89, 100.

—— (1991) "Le Séminaire, Livre xvii", in *L'Envers de la Psychanalyse*: 143, Paris: Le Seuil.

—— (2001) "Préface à *L'Éveil du Printemps*" [Preface to *Spring Awakening*], *Autres Écrits*: 563, Paris: Le Seuil.

—— (2006) "Le Séminaire, Livre XVI", *D'un Autre à l'Autre*: 293, Paris: Le Seuil.

Laugier, S. (2002) "Wittgenstein et la Science: Au-Delà des Mythologies", in P. Wagner (ed.) *Les Philosophes et la Science*, Paris, pp. 557–558, Paris: Gallimard.

Le Petit Robert des Noms Propres (1994) Paris. 1289.

"Martial, Épigrammes, xii, 46", in J.-L. Hennig, (2003) *Martial*, Paris: Fayard.

Miller, J.-A. (1997) "Des Semblants dans la Relation Entre les Sexes", in *La Cause Freudienne, n° 36*, Mai 1997: 7, Paris: Navarin/Le Seuil.

—— (2003) "Religion, Psychanalyse", in *La Cause Freudienne, n° 55*, Octobre 2003: 26–27, Paris: Navarin/Le Seuil.

Saint-Pierre de, J.-B. (1836) "Etude Onzième", in *Etudes de la Nature, Tome 1*: 594, Paris: Lefèvre.

—— (1984) "Paul et Virginie", in *Imprimerie Nationale, coll. Lettres Françaises*, Paris, p. 232.

Tolstoï, L. (1951) "Anna Karénine", *coll. Bibl. de la Pléiade*, Paris: Gallimard, p. 61.

Chapter 5

Unmastered remains

Fathers in Freud and me

Thomas W. Laqueur

"He wasn't clever at all," says W. H. Auden of Sigmund Freud on the occasion of his death in 1939,

> he merely told
> the unhappy Present to recite the Past
>   like a poetry lesson till sooner
> or later it faltered at the line where
>
> long ago the accusations had begun,
> and suddenly knew by whom it had been judged,
>   how rich life had been and how silly,
> and was life-forgiven and more humble,
>
> able to approach the Future as a friend
> without a wardrobe of excuses, without
>   a set mask of rectitude or an
> embarrassing over-familiar gesture.
>   (W. H. Auden, *In Memory of Sigmund Freud*,
>   1995, pp. 100–101)

What follows is a "recit[ation] of the Past" and more specifically a case study of me and of an archive about two centuries of dead fathers that has sat in boxes in my garage until the occasion of this literary talking cure. It is an exercise in what we might think of as "auto-haunting" – calling up ghosts rather than waiting for them to appear – and at the same time in putting the dead to rest so as to be able to "approach the Future as a friend."

I begin with a picture of three young men dressed in high riding boots and what seem to be Prussian military uniforms – white jodhpurs, dark, possibly blue, gold braided tunics, a white sash. They look no older than their 20 years. They stand with an easy weightiness on a low flight of stairs bounded by an iron railing. One of them, thin with perhaps a certain aristocratic insouciance, is on the upper step; his head is cropped by the picture frame. The other two are one step down, both their hands firmly around the hilts of unsheathed sabers.

Two things tell us that these boys – just shy of 20 – are not Prussian cadets but students in a dueling fraternity: they are wearing at the appropriate angle so as not to look like party hats the small caps that German university students adopted in the nineteenth century; and, their hands are shielded by white gloves with long sleeves, rather like those worn by laborers who shovel dirt or cement. The boy on the top step, the one without a saber, is identified on the back as "Coco." In another picture he is coming in second near the finish line of a 100-meter dash at the 1931 *Burschentag* – student day – in Berlin. The boy on the left is identified as "Ego": my father.

It is 1929 and these three are making a statement that they would have expected their parents as well as strangers to understand. Max Weber's mother slapped his face when he came home from university with a dueling scar, taking her son's interest in such matters as a sign that he was gravitating away from the sensibilities of her pietism and toward the physicality and boorishness of his father (Meyer, 1979, p. 23; Diggins, 1996, p. 48). I do not think my father thought that the choice was so stark. He thought, a letter I will talk about in a moment suggests, that he had no such choice to make.

But for now I want to say only that in almost all the pictures that I have of him before he came to the United Sates he seems physically comfortable in his world: he is with a group of his school fellows age 14 or 15 on rocks in the harbor of Hamburg; he is in an open car with a girlfriend; he stands in his *Abitur* picture with a small group of classmates and the headmaster grouped around the bas relief of an eighteenth-century bewigged worthy. The three buttons of his fashionable jacket are closed; he knows he looks good in these clothes. It is a sweet happy picture of young men born too late to have suffered in the Great War. My father was always extremely proud of having graduated during the four-hundredth anniversary year from a school that one of Luther's followers wrested from the monastery of St. John in 1529 and renamed the Johanneum. Great figures of the German Enlightenment had taught or studied there; C. E. P. Bach and Georg Philipp Telemann had been music masters. Maybe I am projecting this pride into his face at age 18 or 19.

I say all this to make clear that my image of my father in the world before I knew him was of a rather beautiful and physically successful young man. My brother has the silver cup he won in a Hamburg citywide tennis tournament. And indeed both from pictures of me with my father and of almost every memory I have of him, he is in my psyche as someone at peace with his body. It is a tender body in relationship to me. It is a body that is already embraced by culture, by something elevating, by something more than matter.

Freud's dreams, interpretations and memories of his dead father's body have an entirely different valence. Of course, when he wrote about his dream of being offered a drink by his wife from an Etruscan urn and the water tasting salty – "obviously from the ashes," he says – he had not yet written about the band of brothers devouring the primal father. That would be more than a decade later. But he does write already in 1900 about the death wish of the son for his father, about the "dark tidings that reach us in myth and legend from primeval days," and about the necessity of Zeus castrating his father as Cronus had eaten his children (Freud, 1900, 4, p. 256). (An odd version of the story: in Hesiod's *Theogony* it is Kronos who castrates his father Uranus and then swallows all his own children to prevent the same thing happening to him; only Zeus escaped this fate and when he grew up gave his father an emetic which caused him to vomit up the others. The nastiness of the rival stories is the same; Hine, 2005, pp. 59, 69–70.)

But even if Sigmund in *The Interpretation of Dreams* did not yet think of ingesting dead fathers, the Jakob Freud who his famous son imagines in his first, epochal book is unrelievedly abject. The most famous instance, of course, is the resonant story of humiliation that the son recalls being told by the father: Jakob as a young man is walking in the Moravian town where Sigmund would be born. "He was," the son reports, "wearing [his] best clothes and a new fur cap on [his] head. Then, a Christian comes along, knocks [the] cap in the mud with a single blow, and shouts 'Jew, get off the pavement!' " "And what did you do?" Sigmund remembers asking: "I stepped into the road and picked up my cap," came the impassive reply. From this much follows in the psychic life and self-understanding of the son.

But that is not my interest here. It is rather how relentless Jakob Freud's abjection needs to be for Sigmund to take his own place in the world. Killing the father was a nasty business. The aged man, half blind, "plainly my father, now urinating in front of me as I once did in front of him" in the revolutionary Dream. "I am making fun of him: because he is blind, I have to hold the bottle for him." A patient's dream of his father in a railroad accident, his head jammed crosswise between collapsed seats, prompts Sigmund to remember a dream about his dead father as a Magyar leader looking like Garibaldi on his deathbed. But, as he says, exalted thoughts are a warning that "the thing we shall encounter is vulgarity." Then comes a memory of his dying father's bowel obstruction and the recollection of a friend's telling him about a relative whose father died in the street and whose bowels were discovered when the body was brought home to have emptied post mortem. There is the dream of his father drunk, jailed, and subject to ridicule (Freud, 1900, 4, pp. 209–11, 216–17; 5, pp. 426–29).

There is a great gap between this father – pitiful, abject, and dead – and the great immaterial *Vatershaft* – fatherhood – that will in later works reappear as the superego or as god – small "g" or large. In *Totem and Taboo* he makes the case that psychoanalysis teaches that god is "in every case modeled after the father and that our personal relation to god is dependent upon our relation to our physical father." In short: "God is at bottom nothing but an exalted father." The longing for the murdered primitive father grows in the band of brothers as bitterness toward him subsides; the sons come to long for him and an ideal arises "having as a content the fullness of power and the freedom of restriction of the conquered primal father, as well as the willingness to subject themselves to him." Ontogeny recapitulates a mythic phylogeny; the father of every son – in the living flesh or dead – will come in the imagination to be transcendant and again all-powerful, a being to be struggled with but never put to rest (Freud, 1913, 13, pp. 147–48).

In *Moses and Monotheism* (Freud, 1939), published 25 years later in the year of his death, Freud would shift to an analysis of *Vaterschaft* – fatherhood – at its most abstract and the apotheosis would be complete. Here Freud takes Orestes' defense against the charge of murdering Clytemnestra, his mother in Aeschylus' *Eumenides*, to be the founding myth of patriarchy and a critical moment in human evolution and in the evolution of culture. Mothers constitute but the earth-like seedbed for a son, and all that really matters is the incorporeal seed. *Vaterschaft*, Freud claims, like belief in the Jewish God, is based on inference and supposition while *Mutterschaft*, like the old gods, is based on evidence of the senses alone. The invention of paternity, like that of a transcendent God, was thus, *"einen Sieg der Geistigkeit über die Sinnlichkeit": "einen Kulturfortschritt"* – "a triumph of the spirit – of the unseen – over materiality – over the stuff of the senses." It is "a great step forward for Culture" (Bonaparte, 1950, 14, pp. 220–21).[1]

The father in me feels never to have not been inflected by *"Geistigkeit,"* by standing for a culture in which I am embedded, however much I might want to escape. I do not mean by this that I, like Freud – or any son – do not have to kill the father or did not fear castration in some symbolic sense but rather that, unlike Freud, I can conjure no corporeal correlative of these desires in my imagination. The abject, murdered body of the – my – father is little in evidence for me. Whatever abject images I have of my father are in the realm of the emotions, failures of the heart. My father in the flesh, now long dead, remains for me – as I think it stood for him until death conquered *Geist* – an abstraction – even as I, and I suspect he, knew and felt that this was an impossibility.

The frightening thing about the picture with which I began is precisely how far from abjection and from social historical reality it is. It is the expression of a wish on his part for the transcendence of ideals over facts. My father does not stand here as proto-Nazi; he was too conservative for this and the class with which his dueling uniform allowed him to identify was generally speaking not keen on Hitler. Anyway, very very few – although there were some – Jews thought they could become Nazis. But my father could, and, I suspect did, imagine himself as deeply and thoroughly and passionately German as anyone because it had nothing to do with the body. Being German was about something higher and more abstract. Of course, the uniform and the saber dressed the flesh, but it was *Geist* that mattered.

On this matter he was more or less explicit. His twentieth birthday was November 4, 1930; five days later, November 9, he wrote to his uncle Ernst Laqueur, a distinguished endocrinologist, the discoverer of estrogen, the future rector of the University of Amsterdam, to thank him for a wallet and card.[2] My father confessed that it was very difficult for him and for his fellow students to remain optimistic for themselves or for Germany: "One's will and hope are hard to focus on anything in the current situation . . . But if we young students can't, despite everything, be at least optimistic for ourselves then we may as well pack it up." Their fate and that of their country are linked: "On the contrary, my university comrades and I are wracking our brains as to what kind of interventions in the life of civil society that we might make. We are completely at loose ends, where we, especially as Jews, can somehow make our convictions felt." On this point the only way out, he seems to suggest, is "*Geistigkeit*," that which fatherhood represents. "We feel ourselves to be German," my father writes, although "people are taking German to mean a German race or breed [*Stamm*] and indeed to be claiming that the two are somehow identical."

He then makes a remarkable *reductio ad absurdum* argument. "It is a huge mistake that people should make the distinction between Jews and Germans rather than between Jews and Christians," because "if one takes Jews to be a race then it is out of the question to even consider Jews in relation to Germans because a German as race does not exist. The concept of being German is of an essentially higher order [*das Deutsche sein ist ein durchaus übergeordneter Begriff*]." To speak in this way, he tells this uncle, is to make a category mistake. (One hears in this passage echoes of Lessing's famous Enlightenment play about toleration – *Nathan the Wise* – with its famous claim that to be human is the general and relevant category while to be Christian, Muslim or Jew is of a different and wholly less important order.) My father laments that "people don't understand this" and that "many of the Jews in Germany are angry with us because we are not sufficiently conscious of our Jewishness. But now on to other things."

The entire second page of this densely written letter is optimistic about his personal future in the life of the mind: he is tutoring some boys in Latin, French and English for their *Abitur* examinations and earning ten DM a week; he is enjoying his rotation in a neurology clinic where he has seen interesting syphilitic paralysis and in a regular ward where he has been allowed to perform various lab tests and take part in primary care.

In retrospect this reversion to everyday life might seem ridiculous. Gershom Scholem seems to have been clear already before the Great War that those who chose assimilation "chose self deceit," but this was clearly neither my father's nor his father's view (Scholem, 1976, pp. 3, 61–70). My father does not say so, but it was not delusional for him and for many others, still in 1935, to hope that the ridiculous new Nazi regime would surely be over soon. The average length of a Weimar regime in the late 1920s and early 1930s, after all, had been only nine months. There is, however, also more personal and direct evidence that his optimism was not entirely phantasmic; the Jewishness of his body might still be transcended. I have a form – *Aktenzeichen* (Documentary certification) U 146 – dated September 19, 1935, that admits my father, upon payment of 250 DM and other fees, to stand before the examining body for medicine in the University of Hamburg and present his credentials. He must for this occasion have gathered all his certificates of clinic attendance – little chits stating that Werner Laqueur had from this to that date attended the gynecology or the surgery or the pathology clinic. Or perhaps he had collected them for an earlier hearing: he had stood for his examination already in Basel in 1934 because, I assume, he was initially barred from doing so in Germany. In any case the evidence of his medical studies is neatly assembled in an envelope.

The second paragraph of form U 146 sets out one more condition: "Your ultimate [*endgultige*] admission depends upon presenting proof, complete and without any gaps [*lückenloss*] of being of Arian descent. Any missing evidence must be provided by the end of the examination." This – and the following paragraph that offers the consolation of being allowed to take a year of further practical training and qualifying as a dentist should the candidate fail the medical exam – are crossed out by a neat, ruler-guided, dark line drawn from the left corner of the first one to the bottom right of the second. Someone in the office of the registrar in the university of this traditionally liberal city still thought that *Geist* and hard work were what mattered. This gesture, this tidy negation of the new barbarity – was a last stand. When my father was on a train to Amsterdam to seek the advice of his uncle – he could not enter upon the academic career he dreamed of in his homeland – he was harassed by an SS officer and never returned alive to Germany. (I will speak in a moment about what became of a few molecules of his ashes.)

My father, I suspect, absorbed the idea that "*das Deutsche sein ist ein durchaus übergeordneter Begriff*" very early in his life. I have a reading diary that must date from when he was still very young because its earliest entries were written by his father; later additions are in his hand. The first entry was in 1915 when my father was five and records that epitome of dark mystic German-ness produced in the burst of nationalistic fervor that followed the Napoleonic Wars: the "*Märchen der Brüder Grimm*" read with his sister – my Tante Eli – in Schierke, a town in Anhalt-Saxony near where my grandfather was a medical officer at one of the typhus hospitals serving the eastern front of the Great War. The classics of German literature follow upon the fairy tales, read with "*Vater.*"

Until recently I knew relatively little about that father. Because he did not live "long before the days of photographs," I was not quite as dependent on the imagination as was Pip at the beginning of Dickens' *Great Expectations* when he tried to picture his father dead in the ground from the shape of the letters on his grave marker. In fact, I grew up with a picture of his tombstone in the great Ohlsdorf cemetery in Hamburg, an Elysium of the burgherly dead; black granite: "Walter A. Laqueur, MD" inscribed in Jugendstil lettering, the same as on the "Dr. Laqueur" plaque that was once on his radiology office and is now on my gate in Berkeley. Just from the lettering he must have been a very solid central European character. My grandmother sent money regularly from West Virginia to keep up the grave.

But there were also two pictures of him on my grandmother's desk: one, fairly anodyne, of a balding man with a goatee in his forties. The other is more like my father's dueling fraternity picture. It shows my grandfather dressed in a fashionable winter coat and hat; he is descending the front stairs of a large house; in one hand is a walking stick, in the other there is a handsome Doberman who nudges a little at the leash, the universal canine reminder that enough of whatever is occupying the human mind; time for a walk. Like my father in the picture with which I began, this is the image of a man deeply rooted and comfortable in his world; he is not quite the Freiherr that Freud remembers seeing in the train station when he is interpreting his revolutionary dream, but he is a commanding figure.

I now have another photograph of this same man, my father's father. In this one he is lying on his funeral bier; I know it is he because his head is clearly visible in profile peering out from white drapery; a filigree of fern next to a small bundle of three flowers that lie on the hidden corpse. And I have a copy of the speech given at the funeral on December 16, 1927, by my father's Uncle Ernst, the famous younger brother of the dead man. I know that my father, then a 17-year-old gymnasium student, heard it. The first part speaks of Walter's great love – my grandmother – his professional success, his kindness. Except for the relative lack of sentimentality in the account of his marriage – he met Olga when they were both still in their teens and fell madly in love – much of the speech is unremarkable. (This love, represented by the Bechstein grand piano that my grandparents were given on their silver anniversary nearly cost her her life. Unwilling to leave it, she stayed in Hamburg another 12 years after her husband's death and left under duress only in December 1939; the Bechstein stayed. She did take some of their music scores – the famous, pocket book sized, yellow covered Eulenberg editions – with her to Istanbul and on to the United States where they now sit on my shelves in Berkeley. A few weeks ago, in an act of self-conscious ancestor worship, I took the appropriate one to a performance of the St. Matthew Passion knowing that even if I had the skill to follow along I would not be able to see the notes in the dark.)

Ernst's funeral oration soon takes a strange turn away from the more or less conventional matters he had been rehearsing. I will quote him in full. He speaks about how his brother, my grandfather, had found only a certain measure of comfort in his work and his family. His soul had not been at rest:

> On one point he could not master himself so as to find inner peace; there was something that stirred in him the deepest sentiments, raised in him bitterness, even hatred: it was the so-called peace conditions under which we live [i.e. the Versailles Treaty and particularly the war guilt clause

no 231]. He suffered under the resolution of the world war more than many others. He was a German to his marrow. He loved Germany and therefore hated its enemies. Although a Jew – something he never denied, indeed something that he was even proud of – he never allowed the fact that some – even a goodly number – of so-called Germans believed it to be their duty to take a stand against, yes to revile and distain (*bekämpfen, ja beschimpfen und verachten*) those of Jewish belief, to make him love Germany any the less. [Notice the piling up of invective against which his love stands.] He loved Germany and therefore every form of internationalism was to him repugnant. To be sure Nationalism was for him not an end in itself because he believed fundamentally in the unity of all mankind; it was a necessity of the moment. In this sense he was a Humanist, someone who was grateful for the noble pleasures that were offered humanity.

"*Unsere grossen Meister, Bach and Beethoven*" (our great masters Bach and Beethoven) Ernst continued a little later, "were from youth his constant companions . . . he could hear Beethoven's 'Appassionate' already as he climbed the stairs when he visited his ageing grandmother." (I cannot help hear this line resonating with one of the repeated lines of Paul Celan's "*Todesfuge*": "*Der todt ist ein meister in Deutschland.*")

The father before this one – my great grandfather – now makes an appearance. Ernst in the funeral address remembers that his brother and their father had tears in their eyes as my grandfather on his wedding day in 1895 left his parental house to music from Beethoven's "Ninth." (Mothers are largely absent from the oration although I know this was not the case in real life. My grandfather's last words were "I want to go now and write my mother." He died at his desk.)

With this great grandfather I recently had a Pip-like encounter. I came upon my father's father's father's grave by accident when my wife and I toured the German Jewish cemetery in Wrocław, formerly Breslau. There is an irony in the fact that a Jewish burial place is one of the very, very few public signs that there had ever been Germans in what is now a thoroughly Polish city.[3] (The many so-called German ones were unceremoniously bull-dozed under at the first opportunity.) My great grandparents – Siegfried and Anna – are in good company: a Greek helmet adorns the gravestone of a fallen Jewish officer of the Great War; there are monuments to soldiers who died at Sedan in the war that founded the empire and to one who died in the Napoleonic *Freiheitskriege*. The parents of the Carmelite saint Edith Stein are here, as are those of Fritz Haber, the Jewish Nobel prize winning chemist who invented poison gas; Ferdinand Lasalle, founder of what became the German Socialist Party, is 20 meters away and Abraham Geiger, founder of reform Judaism, is not far distant. I imagine this Siegfried to be not unlike my grandfather.

We are almost to the last dead father, the one about whom my father would have heard the following at the funeral of his father, the one who spoke again through him in his letter to Ernst. This would be Moritz Laqueur, who was invoked by Ernst who was determined to prove that the dead man, his brother, was the scion of *Geistigkeit* all the way down. He tells his listeners:

> It must be just 80 years ago [that is 1847] that our [his and his dead brother's] grandparents moved away from the Hamburg in whose earth he now rests: the grandfather a superb philologist (*Sprachförscher*), the grandmother a charming, artistically cultivated and refined woman. They brought the culture of the spirit [*geistige Kultur*] to their circles in the east of Germany where it was still foreign and passed it on more or less intact to their eight children who in turn were able to create families themselves [this referred directly to his parents' home] in which cultural riches [*geistige Güter*] were esteemed more highly than material ones.

It seems almost pre-ordained that the child of such a tradition, Sigmund Freud, would have equated *Vaterschaft* with *Geistigkeit*.

And now the final father, one that we – my wife and I on our academic visit to Wrocław – have only recently discovered and who was not known to my father or, I think, to his. This final father is David ben Elizer, who sometime in the late eighteenth or early nineteenth century took the name Laquer, which soon acquired a "u" and became my name. His grave is known through the studies of German researchers on the Jews of lower Silesia and Polish scholars of Jewish history and culture who are transcribing names from Jewish gravestones. This rabbi, my father's great, great grandfather, seems to have been a man of considerable learning – secular as well as religious – who spent his whole life in a tiny village now called Miejsce, then Stadel, set among potato fields 70 km south east of Wrocław. It still has both a Protestant and a Catholic Church between which sat the manor house of the local lord who, perhaps because his people already had pluralistic allegiances, would tolerate a third religion. This rabbi's tombstone has a few pockmark-like bullet holes from the Second World War but is otherwise remarkable only in that a fairly long epitaph in the third person turns to a familiar second person "you" and addresses the rabbi as "You who managed in wisdom for thirty six years . . . you will harvest with joy." He is almost conjured back to his body; it is almost as if he were there to listen. (This gravesite also stands as evidence for why dead mothers are harder to think with. David's wife, like Pip's mother, gets little more than "and also" with a few words about her virtues. Abraham's first real estate purchase in Canaan may have been a cave for Sarah's burial, but from then it is the tombs of the patriarchs that draw notice.)

Let me end with my case. In fact, the actual death of my father left me numb, as did his final illness. I remember distinctly feeling very little when I got the news of his death. During the months that he was dying of cancer I remembered every clinical detail but forgot much else about daily life: where I had parked a car, what I was doing somewhere on an errand. My father, the German trained anatomical pathologist, so effectively translated his own dying into the life of the mind that it took me years to understand that he was not a case out of Robbin's *Principles*. Huge amounts of our relationship, at least on the surface, were then and always had been mediated by learning. We talked about his symptoms – difficulty in swallowing, shortness of breath, fainting, as a problem in differential diagnosis. I think that he was irritated that he missed the final call but then, to give him the benefit of the doubt, hypernephroma is notoriously difficult.

What I do remember from his dying is less his physical weakness, although I did find it distressing, but the fact that even at the end he was unable to live in some sort of harmony with his emotions or his body. Of the body I would need to say more. Of course as the cancer progressed he became weaker, but in fact I never knew the young man who was Hamburg tennis champion and a fraternity dueler. My father never exercised; did no sport; seldom walked more than he had to. I never knew the emotionally focused, passionate young man who had written to his uncle and who still seemed alive in some early tender pictures taken in Istanbul with my mother. By the time I knew him he was, I came to feel consciously by the time I graduated college and my first love left me, emotionally abject. And I was furious at him for it. The one time I wished him dead was when, within a couple of years of his death, I heard him furtively or not so furtively whining to a woman – not someone with whom he was having an affair; he was past that – who I knew was manifestly inappropriate. It is, on reflection, almost as if my father – having been so brutally rejected by his great, ultimately unrequited love for Germany could never really allow himself to love again. Except me. I have both the sweetest of memories of lying in his arms listening to "*the* ninth" [*die* – the only possible – *neunte*] on my birthdays. But they are mixed with the feeling that I could never really heal the wounds in his soul. I could not requite his love. What was he saying to or through me?

I end with a "recitation of the past" that calls forth the ghost of a me beyond my memory, words that are fictively mine. On November 8, 1945, my father wrote a birthday letter to my mother in my name: "An Meine Mamma von Thomas Laqueur." [I am named Thomas after my father's best friend and fellow pathologist who died of hepatitis after cutting himself at an autopsy.] Two bars of music, for coloratura or baby cries, opus I, no. 1 moderato, begin my missive. I thank her for her tender care of my skin and my bottom; I tell her how much I appreciate always having as much milk as I would like; I promise to make every effort to be a joy to her; I tell her I love her. By November 8, 1946, I have adopted a different voice, still loving but the voice of *Vaterschaft*.

"My dear, good mama," I begin. "I have watched you several times now eat many large pieces of chocolate one after the other from which I can see that you really like it." I explain my reasoning: she knows that when I eat a lot of something I like it. I also explain my dilemma: that I would probably want to eat some of the chocolate that I am giving her. "I have," I say through my father's text, "come up with something to deal with these issues. With three of the bars of chocolate you can do what you want; the others you will give to Oma, because you know that she is very orderly. She will give you every week one bar from me. Think about it. You will thus have a bar of chocolate every week until the New Year. Isn't that fine."

I assume, although my letter does not say so, that the infant me will somehow get his share of sweets as well.

As for the physical father, there was one final encounter. When he died in 1984 we mixed his ashes into a flowerbed by the cottage in Virginia where his life ended. More than a decade later I was invited to lecture in Germany. Encouraged by my wife, I decided to take a small bag of dirt in which there might have been a homeopathically small number of inorganic molecules that had once been in my father and to mix these with the soil of his father's grave in the Jewish section of Hamburg's great Friedhof Ohlsdorf. I knew well my grandfather's black tombstone with "Walter A. Laqueur, MD" Jugendstil; a picture of it had stood on my grandmother's desk as I was growing up. This gesture of repatriation would have been regarded by my father as an act of rank superstition. And so, I suppose, it was. But it did seem right that some of him – however attenuated – should go back to where he had once felt both comfortable and troubled; and it did make me understand that he was dead. Such is the work of culture.

Notes

1 Sigmund Freud, *Moses and Monotheism* (1939) in *Standard Edition* 23, pp. 113–14; for the German from which I have translated somewhat freely, see Marie Bonaparte (ed.) (1950) *Gesammelte Werke*, London: Imago, 14, pp. 220–21.
2 This letter and all of the subsequent manuscript sources that I cite were passed on to me by my cousin Peter Silton when his mother, my father's older sister, died. How she came to have them I do not know.
3 On this cemetery see Maciej Lagiewski (1999) *Das Pantheon der Breslauer Juden*, Berlin: Nicolai.

References

Auden, W. H. (1995) "In Memory of Sigmund Freud", in *Auden: Poems*, selected by Edward Mendelson, New York and Toronto: Alfred A. Knopf, pp. 100–101.
Bonaparte, M. (ed.) (1950) *Gesammelte Werke*, 14, London: Imago, pp. 220–21.
Diggins, J. P. (1996) *Max Weber: Politics and the Spirit of Tragedy*, New York: Basic Books, p. 48.
Freud, S. (1900) "The Interpretation of Dreams", trans. James Strachey (1953), *Standard Edition*, Volumes 4–5, London: Hogarth Press, pp. 209–11, 216–17, 259.

—— (1901) "The Interpretation of Dreams", trans. James Strachey (1953), *Standard Edition*, Volume 5, London: Hogarth, pp. 426–29.

—— (1913) "Totem and Taboo", trans. James Strachey (1968), *Standard Edition*, Volume 13, London: Hogarth Press, pp. 147–48.

—— (1939) "Moses and Monotheism", trans. James Strachey (1964), *Standard Edition*, Volume 23, London: Hogarth Press, pp. 113–14.

Hine, D. (ed. and trans.) (2005) *Hesiod, Theogony, in Works of Hesiod and the Homeric Hymns*, Chicago: University of Chicago Press, pp. 59, 69–70, and more generally.

Meyer, J. P. (1979) *Max Weber and German Politics*, New York: Arno Press, pp. 23.

Scholem, G. (1976) *On Jews and Judaism In Crisis: Selected Essays*, New York: Schocken, pp. 3, 61–70, and more generally.

Part III

The father in theory

INTRODUCTION
Arnold Richards

When did the Father die? If what we have in mind is the Father as Law in the Lacanian sense, then in my view the father as authority died at the Sorbonne in May 1968, the year David Galbraith (Starr, 1995) has called "the year that refuses to die." That year is often cited as the marker dividing modernism and postmodernism. The sit-in at the Sorbonne was preceded by an April "dress rehearsal" at the Paris Cinémathèque, at which a group of film enthusiasts, including the directors Godard, Truffaut, Chabrol and Berri, invaded the building to protest the ousting of Henri Langlois by the Gaullist cultural establishment and its Minister of Culture, André Malraux. Daniel Cohn-Bendit, a protester who became known as Danny the Red, was the first to enter the building through a broken window. This was his dress rehearsal for his subsequent role in the May events. There is a story (which I believe to be apocryphal) to the effect that Lacan spirited Danny the Red from France to Germany in the trunk of a car, thus making Lacan a hero of the new left.

On April 23, 1968, even before the events in Paris, a group of Columbia University students began their sit-in to protest both the war in Vietnam and the building of a gym with a special entrance for the black neighborhood. Some readers will remember the descriptions of the students in the university president's office smoking his cigars, drinking his sherry, and leaving his office a mess.

I was a candidate at the New York Psychoanalytic Institute at the time, and I remember the blow-by-blow account I received from one of my patients, a graduate student at Columbia who had participated in the protests. He described the brutal crackdown by the police. A colleague who also was a candidate at the same institute had an analysand who was among the 150 students who participated in the sit-in. The patient was said to have climbed out of the window each day to attend his daily analytic session. He made his own rules about which Law of which Father he would follow.

In October 1964, a group of civil rights protestors took over Sproul Hall at the University of California and remained there until the police forcibly removed and arrested 800 of them. The event sparked the Berkeley Free Speech movement – "free" meaning in this case defiance of the Father. In that rebellion, Mario Savio played the same role that Danny the Red would play in Paris almost four years later. It is noteworthy that just as Cohn-Bendit went on to become a bureaucrat functionary of the EU, Savio also had a respectable career during the years that followed his revolutionary days as an orator in Sproul Plaza, which was renamed in his honor after his death in 1994.

A lag followed between the erasure of the Law of the Father in the culture and the subsequent death of the authoritarian father in psychoanalytic theory and practice. The Father was central for Freud. As Christine Anzieu-Premmereur points out (see Chapter 6) Freud was named after his paternal grandfather and was born when his father was mourning his own father. Freud began his self-analysis after his father died. The role that Freud's self-analysis played in the discovery of psychoanalysis has been documented most convincingly by Anzieu-Premmereur's own father, Didier Anzieu, in his biography, *Freud's Self Analysis* (1986). The father was featured prominently in many of Freud's cases, such as Little Hans, Dora, the Rat Man and, of course, Schreber. The father was one-third of the Oedipal triangle and one-half of the primal scene.

Clearly, Freud's father was the more important parental figure in his life, a personal inclination that I believe contributed to the centrality of the father in his theoretical work. George Mahl (1985) investigated the frequency with which Freud used "father" and "mother" in his psychological writings. Overall, he used "father" more frequently than he used "mother," a trend that began with the writings following his father's death and in documenting his self-analysis. Although eastern European Jewish family structure was matriarchal (the mother ran the household and the father studied), Austro-Hungarian family structure was patriarchal. Freud's wish for a more patriarchal father was part of his quest to assimilate into a patriarchal culture (A. K. Richards, 2007, personal communication). Evidence for this wish is the importance that Freud gave to the incident of the hat in the gutter.

When he was 14, his father told him about an incident from his own past. He was walking down the street in Freiberg when a Gentile told him he should walk in the gutter and then knocked Freud's father's hat off his head. When Freud asked his father about his reaction, his father answered that he had stepped into the gutter and picked up his hat. Freud was disappointed that his father acted as a non-aggressive, subservient man, quite the opposite of the Teutonic patriarch he desired.

Freud's father died in 1896. His self-analysis followed during the years 1897–1899. Mahl, in another contribution (1982), showed that Freud's self-analysis was more concerned with his relation to his father than to his mother and that his evolving psychology of family relations was father centered rather than mother centered. Although Freud continued for several years to focus on the father more than on the mother, this pattern changed in 1931 following the death of his mother, as evidenced by the publication of his paper on female sexuality during that year. Clearly, the death of his father affected him more than did the death of his mother, whose funeral he did not even attend. The difference in the impact made on Freud by his parents' deaths might be partly attributed to his respective age at each event, but I think it also seems to indicate the emotional valence that each parent had for Freud. After his father's death, Freud wrote to Fliess:

> I find it so difficult to put pen to paper at the moment that I have put off writing to you to thank you for the moving things you said in your letter. By one of the obscure routes behind the official consciousness, the old man's death affected me deeply. I valued him highly and understood him very well indeed and with his peculiar mixture of deep wisdom and imaginative lightheartedness, he meant a great deal in my life. By the time he died, his life had long been over, but at a death, the whole past stirs within me. I feel now as if I have [been] torn up by the roots.
>
> (1954, Letter 52, cited by Mahl, 1985, p. 107)

Writing later of his reaction to his father's death, he generalized the event as "the most important event, the most profound loss of a man's life" (1900, p. xxvi).

In 1936, Freud described his visit to the Acropolis with his brother. Sara Winter (1999) points out that even before Freud made the trip, which he commemorated in "A Disturbance of Memory on the Acropolis" (1936), "he was uncomfortably aware that he had," as he put it, "surpassed" his father, who could not read Sophocles' *Oedipus Tyrannus* in Greek as Freud could, thanks to his classical education. Both the awareness and the discomfort are relevant. Freud himself writes in the Acropolis paper: "Our father had been in business. He had no secondary education and Athens could not have meant much to him. Thus, what interfered with our enjoyment of the journey to Athens was a feeling of filial piety." On the other hand, Freud's reaction to his mother's death was calmer, "more curious" (Mahl, 1985, p. 108), but connected with deeper layers of his mind. In *Female Sexuality*, Freud wrote, "Everything in the sphere of this first attachment to the mother seemed to me so difficult to grasp in analysis – so grey with age – shadowy and almost impossible to revivify – that it was as if it had succumbed to an especially inexorable repression" (1931, p. 226).

Before pursuing the rise of psychoanalytic interest in the mother and the decline of interest in the father, which began in the 1930s, we should note the central place of the father in Freud's last contribution, *Moses and Monotheism*. As Rosine Jozef Perelberg reiterates in Chapter 7, the theme of Freud's *Moses* is the killing of the father, which was also the theme of *Totem and Taboo*, and of the *Future of an Illusion*. Perelberg observes the paradox that "the killing of the father is the requirement for the creation of the social order which from then on prohibits all killings" (see Chapter 7). Dead or alive, the father looms larger for Freud and for most of his male colleagues in personal and interpretational life, for the society and for the individual, than does the mother. In contrast, Arlene Kramer Richards (1999, 2003) has made the case that Freud's relationship with women/mothers/sisters was much less ambivalent than his relationship with men/fathers/brothers, supporting Perelberg's observation that the perverse, violent, incestuous father "possesses all the women and rules though violence" and is "killed in the founding myth." The dead father, killed metaphorically or actually, retains from its prehistoric roots a very active presence in our psyches and in our psychoanalytic psychology.

The re-emergence of the mother/woman in Freud's 1931 paper on female sexuality was a response to the contributions from women analysts that began in the 1920s with Melanie Klein and Karen Horney, later continued by Helene Deutsch and Anna Freud. The thrust of these contributions was to restore mothering and mothers to their important place in psychoanalysis and to temper Freud's emphasis on the significance of the father and the phallus in the construction of gender identity. These authors all drew on their own experiences with mothering and being mothered to advance psychoanalysis. Melanie Klein had a weak, ineffectual father and a strong mother, and her work accordingly granted equal time and significance to the breast as to the penis. Horney loved her mother and turned the tables on Freud by developing her theory of men's mothering envy. Helena Deutsch, on the other hand, hated her mother and offered a view of the narcissistic personality disorder that results from wounds inflicted by identification with the mother. Anna Freud stressed the patterning impact of the child's first relationship with its mother on all of the child's subsequent relationships. Although her father has been faulted for his phallocentric theories and his male-dominated psychoanalytic organization, he had salutary relationships with several key women – Sabina Speilrein, Marie Bonaparte, and Lou Andreas Salome. Furthermore, as Kramer Richards has written, Freud essentially gave his family business to his daughter.

In the decades following Freud's death, we have seen the decline of the phallus and the demise of the father in theories of pathogenesis. Winnicott wrote about the "good enough mother," not the "good enough father." Theories on patterns of mothering (Brody), stages of separation and individuation (Mahler), and attachment to the mother (Bowlby, Slade, et al.), represent the active center of psychoanalytic theoretical developmental discourse. In aggregate, these theories can be viewed as the "dead father syndrome" in that the father plays little role in them. Kohut's work is applicable in this regard, with his view that the unempathic parent was more often the mother than the father, permitting the inference that the unempathic part of self-psychology also relates more to the mother than to the father.

Similarly, attachment theory, as well as the work of Winnicott, figures the mother–infant dyad as the leitmotif of its presentations. But it is critical to pay attention to Herzog who in Chapter 8 reminds the reader of the detrimental impact of this asymmetry in theory, particularly of the potentially "parricidal effects" of "excluding the father's presence from this equation." All three contributors to Part III provide clinical material that supports this point.

Another psychoanalytic patricide occurred in Kansas and in New York during the 1950s and 1960s, as David Rappaport, the father/systematizer of metapsychology, was "slain" by his sons/students George Klein, Robert Holt, Donald Spense, Roy Schafer, et al., at the Menninger Clinic in Topeka and the NYU Psychoanalytic Research Center in New York City. These students advocated for the existence of two theories rather than one: separate, simultaneous conceptualizations of a near-clinical theory as well as a more abstract metapsychological version. Rangell and others have argued that their reformulation of psychoanalytic theory was driven by a need to revolt against Rappaport as their brilliant and authoritarian mentor, in order to carve out intellectual turf for themselves.

Initially a classical Freudian, Oedipal, father-centered analyst, Kohut also revolted against his "father," Freud, with the publication of *The Analysis of the Self* in 1972. Unlike the anti-metapsychologists, Kohut's self-psychology encompassed a metapsychology of its own; the theory of pathogenesis was the generational divide distinguishing his work from that of his predecessors. His paradigmatic paper "The Two Analyses of Mr. Z" (1979), apparently a disguised account of Kohut's own first analysis (by a classical Freudian, Viennese woman analyst in Chicago), described both this and his subsequent self-analysis from the analyst's point of view:

> Within the analytic setting, the patient complied with my expectations by presenting me with Oedipal issues. Outside the analytic setting, he acceded to my expectations by suppressing his symptoms (the masochistic fantasies) and by changing his behavior, which now took on the appearance of normality as defined by the maturity morality to which I then subscribed (he moved from narcissism to object love; i.e. he began to date girls).
>
> (Kohut, 1979, p. 12)

The Law of the Father clearly prevailed within the analysis and in the external factors delineating it, such as the "maturity morality." Self-analysis, however, provided space for an investigation of the maternal aspects of the psyche. In the clinical context, Kohut interprets the "patient's persistent attachment to the mother as a libidinal tie that he was unwilling to break" (1979, p. 12), but through self-analysis he uncovers the presence of a pathology greater than suggested by this initial analysis. The self-analysis following the clinical interpretation allowed Kohut to deal with the vicissitudes of his relationship to his mother, who had been deeply depressed (if not overtly psychotic) during his childhood. A similar emphasis on the pathogenic developmental effects of disturbed mothers is evident in the cases described in *The Psychology of the Self* (1978), edited by Arnold Goldberg.

The shift in the theory of psychoanalytic technique began in 1983, with the publication of Greenberg and Mitchell's *Object Relations in Psychoanalytic Theory*. It ushered in the ascendancy of the relational turn that took place in the decades that followed. Self-psychology represented a change in psychoanalytic technique brought about by and explored by the articulation of new transference configurations. This did not constitute a movement that directly opposed the model of the authoritarian analyst as such. Instead, with the relational turn, the analyst-as-father, distant and unquestionable, was superseded by the self-disclosing participant analyst in the analytic encounter.

Personal, political, cultural, and sociological factors led to the establishment of the new relational culture in psychoanalysis. Its progenitors were all psychologists who had been excluded from membership in the hegemonic establishment of the American Psychoanalytic Association. Their roots were in the NYU Post Doctoral Program and the William Alanson White Institute. The NYU program, started by Bernie Kalinkowitz, maintained strong leftist political commitments, while William Alanson White founders Erich Fromm, Karen Horney, and others stressed the importance of social and cultural influences in psychoanalysis. The relationalists clearly advocated one side of what they considered the drive/relational dichotomy, largely rejecting Oedipal dynamics. They aligned themselves with a broad spectrum of Freudian dissidents, including Melanie Klein, Donald Winnicott, Fairbairn, and even Kohut. Unlike Klein, Mahler, or Kernberg, however, the relationalists willingly altered the technique of analysis. Whereas Hartmann, for example, proposed changes in theory but not in technique (except for with children or highly disturbed patients), the relationalists deposed interpretation from its traditional position as the central engine of change, replacing it with a focus on self-disclosure.

All things change. However, what was here yesterday and not today returns anew. Greenberg first offered his own version of drive theory (safety and effectance pleasure). More recently he has revived Oedipal theory as well. A Mahlerian, Ernst Abelin, brought the father back into Mahler's developmental mother–child dyadic process, and other Mahlerians, such as John Ross, followed. Relationalists (Greenberg, Mills) have written about what they call "relational excess," which can be read as an inclination to return to a more classical interpretive technique. However, amidst these tides of theoretical change, it remains wise to take note of James Herzog's admonition to construct theory from the analytic material of the patient rather than fitting patients into some theoretical defined by the latest figure considered an authority.

So it goes: the father dies and is revived. The father can be absent, but the dead father is always alive, despite our theories about him. Like Green's dead mother (1986), he is both absent and present simultaneously. The field is dynamic; the sands shift as we struggle to understand ourselves better in order to help our patients understand themselves.

References

Anzieu, D. (1986) *Freud's Self Analysis*, London: Hogarth Press and the Institute of Psycho-Analysis.

Freud, S. (1900) "The Interpretation of Dreams", trans. James Strachey (1953), *Standard Edition*, Volumes 4–5, London: Hogarth Press.

—— (1931) "Female Sexuality", trans. James Strachey (1961), *Standard Edition, The Future of an Illusion, Civilization and its Discontents, and Other Works*, Volume 21, London: Hogarth Press.

—— (1936) "A Disturbance of Memory on the Acropolis", trans James Strachey (1964), *Standard Edition, New Introductory Lectures on Psycho-Analysis and Other Works*, Volume 22, London: Hogarth Press, pp. 239B–248.

Goldberg, A. (1978) *The Psychology of the Self: A Casebook*, New York: International Universities Press.

Green, A. (1986) "The Dead Mother", in *On Private Madness*, Original publication "La mére morte," in *Narcissisme de Vie, Narcissisme de Mort*, Paris: Éditions Minuit, pp. 222–53.

Greenberg, J. R. and Mitchell, S. A. (1983) *Object Relations in Psychoanalytic Theory*, Cambridge, MA: Harvard University Press.

Kohut, H. (1972) "Thoughts on Narcissism and Narcissistic Rage", in H. Kohut *The Search for the Self*, Madison, CT: International Universities Press, pp. 615–658.

—— (1979) "The Two Analyses of Mr Z", *International Journal of Psychoanalysis* 60: 3–27.

Mahl, G. F. (1982) "Father–Son Themes in Freud's Self-Analysis", in S. H. Cath, A. R. Giowitt and J. M. Ross (eds) *Father and Child: Developmental and Clinical Perspectives*, Oxford: Blackwell, pp. 33–64.

—— (1985) "Freud, Father, and Mother: Quantitative Aspects", *Psychoanalytic Psychology* 2: 99–113.

Masson, J. M. (ed.) (1985) *The Complete Letters of Sigmund Freud to Wilhelm Fliess, 1887–1904*, Cambridge, MA: Harvard University Press.

Richards, A. K. (1999) "Freud and Feminism: A Critical Appraisal", *Journal of the American Psychonanalytic Association* 47: 1213–38.

—— (2003) "Rage and Creativity: Second Wave Feminists and the Rejection of Freudian Theory", *Mind and Human Interaction* 13: 145–55.

Starr, P. (1995) *Logics of Failed Revolt: French Theory After May '68*, Stanford: Stanford University Press.

Winter, S. (1999) *Freud and the Institution of Psychoanalytic Knowledge*, Palo Alto: Stanford University Press.

Chapter 6

The dead father figure and the symbolization process

Christine Anzieu-Premmereur

Schlomo Sigmund Freud was born on May 6, 1856, named after his paternal grandfather who had died three months before. Sigmund was born when his father Jacob was mourning his own father. Identifying with his prestigious grandfather, Sigmund Freud developed intense creativity, as described by Alain de Mijolla in his paper on identification and family prehistory (1987). De Mijolla demonstrates the strong identifications with the Oedipal objects of the parents that can come about.

As an idealized figure, Rabbi Schlomo, the mythic grandfather for Sigmund, helped him differentiate from his own father Jacob. Sigmund himself became a patriarch, the founding father of psychoanalysis. Freud constructed the myth of the Father's murder as the origin of culture. The death of the father served to limit omnipotence. The "renunciation of instincts" was "the beginning of morality and justice," the "first form of social organization" (1939, p. 82).

According to Moses, described by Freud as the one who could contain his anger and restrain his actions, the son is supposed to initiate a new system of thought. Incest now forbidden, early anxieties can be mastered. The process of symbolization is thereby ushered in.

The turning from the mother to the father marks a change from sensuality to intellectuality, "since maternity is proved by the senses while paternity is a hypothesis." Instinctual renunciation and the intellectual operation that follows, open the door of thinking in the child who, by designating his father, forms an abstract representation.

Symbolization is the substitution of one object for another. This is the result of a process that requires the capacity to represent a missing object, as well as the ability to comprehend that a symbol is not the real object.

I will present clinical vignettes from my analytic practice with infants, children and adults to illustrate how a symbolic father figure is essential to the introduction of the process of symbolization.

Henry

At the age of four, when he was brought for treatment, Henry screamed at me, "I know how to write the word Shark. It's M.A.M.A!" Henry didn't speak until he was three, and that was after 18 months of parent–infant psychotherapy when the symbolic function was finally on its way. Playing gave Henry the ability to transform his chaotic feelings into words.

Eight months pregnant, Henry's mother came to New York from Europe on September 10, 2001. She unfortunately found herself near the World Trade Center on September 11. Convinced that she was in the midst of nuclear war at the time of the attacks on the building, she ran, passport in hand, and jumped into a boat to escape the area. She gave birth to her first child soon after this catastrophic moment, and having the baby at her breast was the only way she found to calm down. Henry never slept through the night without waking up many times, screaming for the breast. When the boy was 15 months old, the father asked his wife to stop the constant breastfeeding. Full of anxiety, the mother then weaned him in two days, after which the baby didn't seem to sleep at all. She consulted me after three months of severe sleep disturbance in the entire family.

Henry was 18 months old when I met him. He found a shark in my toy box, and started to play with it, attacking baby animals. It was a representation of his greed and aggression, and I interpreted his intense feeling of frustration after the weaning. At the end of this first meeting, he wouldn't leave the toy in my office, so I told the mother they could take the shark home and bring it back for sessions. In a few weeks, he started to sleep with the shark clutched in his hands. Being sleepless and disorganized, Henry was at risk of being unable to integrate a sense of himself or a stable representation of his mother. Later he was unable to achieve an adequate level of language development. He required speech therapy concurrent with his psychotherapy.

By the time his father got involved in the therapy, Henry was already two years old. He drew for the first time in his father's presence, making a picture of sunshine. I told the father that what Henry had drawn was a symbol for a father figure, something very important for his son! Henry's father then came to the sessions regularly after that and started playing with his son, offering himself as a role model for a male figure.

When Henry was four years old, he was still playing with sharks. One day he rushed into my office at the same time that his mother wanted to speak with me. She complained, "You always put somebody between you and me!" This sentence embeds her frustration at not being able to speak to me privately within the larger context of her frustrated desire to have a pure dyadic relationship. Son, father and analyst all function as an intrusive third. When alone with me, Henry exclaimed, "I know how to write the word 'Shark.' It's M.A.M.A!"

This wish to be able to write shows his new ability to symbolize his angry and hateful conflicts. The analytical work with this family gave the father the role the child needed him to play so that he could organize his feelings, develop his own desires and figure out his internal representations, from affects to symbols. The need for an external object, in this case the analyst, was important in order to help the boy to regulate his aggressive impulses.

The father, with authority, asked the mother to separate from the baby and to stop breastfeeding, since he thought the son wasn't developing well. The merger between mother and infant seemed to have been caused by mother's traumatic experience on September 11, as well as by a traumatic personal history which included a permanent state of mourning for her own mother figure.

A father is supposed to be there from the beginning, present both in the mother's mind as well as in life, somewhere in between the mother and the child. André Green wrote in "The Dead Mother" that "from the mother's side this is expressed in her desire for the father, of which a child is the realization. On the side of the child, everything that introduces the anticipation of a third person, each time the mother is not wholly present and her devotion to the child is neither total nor absolute, will be, retrospectively, attributable to the father" (Green, 1980, p. 147).

In their work on insomnia, the French psychoanalysts Denise Braunschweig and Michel Fain (1971) wrote about the mother's internal world as she cares for her baby while thinking about the father – the child's father, and her own father. This dreamlike experience gives the baby a sense of a distance from the mother and allows room for a third person. That distance also protects the mother from her own erotic feelings as she takes care of the baby's body. Her fantasy about the father provides the baby with a protective shield that is essential for its psyche.

The two authors called this moment in the baby's life the "censorship of the lover." The mother turns away from the child to return to an erotic life with the father. She builds two representations of her infant, "the baby of the day," the child affiliated with the father, and "the baby of the night," the fruit of an incestuous fantasy about her own father. This discontinuity in the mother's libidinal cathexis gives the child space for his own fantasies and dreams, and opens a space for the third.

According to Braunschweig and Fain (1975), the baby develops a capacity for representation and the regulation of excitement precisely when it is left alone by the parental couple making love. In addition, they postulate a bisexual identification with the absent couple, stressing the role of the baby's identification with the father's penis in the constitution of the representational world. This is consistent with Lacan's (1949) theory of the Name of the Father (when the mother's absence indicates her desire for the father). To this formulation they add the importance of the identification with both parents. This allows the child to shift from active to passive.

In their view, a total desexualization of the mother's relation to the child would involve the castration of the father. The baby feels a discontinuity in the mother's cathexis and comes to distinguish day from night. The child forms an identification with the father – with the real father during the day and with the father who is the mother's incestuous object at night. When the mother does not regard the child as her incestuous object, he learns to include the third in the love triangle. The mother becomes the messenger who carries the castration threat by the real father. This message is colored by the father's fantasy of the child as well as by his fatherly concern.

Symbolization can be seen as the result of a process that involves the capacity for representing an object that is absent. One can understand this as a mechanism (defense) against the depressive feelings that emerge after the loss of an object. In this way symbolization helps build the capacity for fantasy and can establish a psychic space.

Symbolization means mediation between a subject and an object, between the internal world and external reality. This process works through the experience of loss. This is a movement from being to having, from "I am the breast" to "I have the breast," from narcissism to object cathexis.

The "Fort-Da" (Oo-Aa) game with the reel played by Freud's 18-month-old grandson Ernst (1920) can be viewed as a model of the symbolization process: the absence of the mother was symbolized by acting and speaking. Internal play with the object kept on the inside allowed it to be expelled. This process helped Ernst to contain anxieties caused by his separation from mother.

Symbols are mediators between the intrapsychic world and the intersubjective space. The correlation between the missing object, the mother, and the symbolic signifier, the "Oo-Aa" shows the child's access to the dialectical interplay between the need for satisfaction and desire. The mother can help with vital needs, but the child nonetheless experiences a lack in himself that he has to communicate. The use of signifiers, of language, shows the movement towards symbolism. And symbolization fosters the capacity for sublimation and creativity.

A third object is required for opening the space for symbolization. The role of the third is essential, and one can see the use of the frame in the analytic setting as the necessary third in the process of symbolizing. The relationship between patient and analyst is mediated through the frame, which represents the prohibition of incest and introduces the "third" between the two. It is close to Donald Winnicott's (1953) intermediate space of experience, a space that allows for the symbolization process and stimulates functioning in the preconscious area. The use of metaphors can be taken as proof of this functioning, as can play in child analysis. The psychoanalytic process is the unending work of binding representations and affects, thereby making room for displacement and movement.

The enthusiastic experience at being the one who creates something new, along with the dialectical differentiation between inside and outside, between keeping and losing, generates a way to face the fear of the unlimited maternal space. Psychic bisexuality plays an important role here.

The theme of verticality is a good example of the father's role, not just as a phallic representation, but also as a path from the mother's body to the social world. A marble block by Bernini at the Villa Borghese in Rome represents Aeneas, fleeing Troy, with his son Ascanius (or "Julo" for whom Julius Caesar was named) carrying his father Anchises on his shoulders. A muscular male body carries the older and the younger generations with a vertical movement that gives the sense of a wish for the future. This beautiful and powerful sculpture is a representation of the Father as the organizer, the one who transmits the capacity for creativity.

John

John was a sweet little boy, 13 months old when I met him. He was unable to stand up. His body was stiff and rigid, with his back leaning up against his mother when she tried to quiet him down. It was impossible to remain face to face with him. His legs were weak, and his body seemed to be cut into two parts. The neurologist found no cause for this delay. He was able to sit up and move about by sliding on the floor with his left leg folded up. John sucked his thumb day and night, never signaling that he wanted food.

During the first session, when my eyes met his, he looked at me without reaction with a "flat look." But talking to him seemed to trigger terror: John looked afraid, eyes bulging, his mouth open wide. His parents did not help him to adapt to the session. I told him it was normal to be afraid of me, a stranger in an unknown place. He started moving about the room, looking at the toys. Finally he found his way to the mirror. He again looked terrified and started to scream. His parents were paralyzed. I told him, yet again, that he was afraid because I was looking at him. When he saw my face in the mirror, he felt abandoned. He looked at his mother and picked up a soft ball that he put in his mouth, completely filling it with the toy. He came back to the mirror and looked at me very seriously. I said, "Hello, welcome." His eyes became interested, looking straight into mine. I smiled. It was the beginning of our relationship. He began each subsequent session by looking at me in the mirror and waiting for my greeting, using this communication like a ritual.

John did not play. His parents were surprised when I asked about John's interest in toys. They realized he never played. Both parents reported their guilt over being unable to pay attention to their third baby. Both were in trouble with their own families. John's father was an illegitimate child, the first child of a man who had had many wives and other children, but didn't recognize him officially as his first son. This man had just died, and John's father discovered that he would inherit nothing from him. He said he hated his father at the time that his own son was born. He gave his son the first name of his paternal grandfather.

While reporting his difficult story, the father was looking at his son. He saw that John was having trouble moving a big toy truck. His father stood him up on the truck. Gazing intensely at his father, John pushed himself on the truck in front of the mirror and screamed for joy. At long last in a vertical position, supported by his father, John enjoyed phallic narcissistic pleasure. Looking at his father looking at him in the mirror, he allowed him to integrate a sense of having a unity and an identity.

At the next session John had totally stopped putting his thumb into his mouth. He asked for food and was no longer stiff and rigid. He was able to settle in his parents' arms with tenderness. While looking at me in front of the mirror, John desperately wanted to put my pencil into his mouth. Somewhat later his father's pencil became a transitional object. A few weeks after that, he started to babble.

John's changes reassured his mother. She talked about her own depression. She discovered during the sessions that her son could be sensitive to her absence. She then played hide-and-seek with him. It was the start of a new game. John pointed his finger in the direction of the window, looking at his mother, waiting for her to describe the outside world. When the father was not present during the session, I talked about his being at work, and I described him. Trying to fathom the missing father, John developed a new capacity for playing and soon thereafter started to speak.

According to Lacan, a symbolic capacity is said to develop prior to the mirror stage. The genesis of subjectivity resides in the child's seeing his self-same image in the mirror, in a dialectical encounter with the specular image. The mirror represents the role of the Other in the constitution of psychic functioning.

John didn't have self-awareness. The interactive affective communication with his depressed mother failed to give him a sense of himself, and his father, who projected onto him his hatred toward his own father, did not intervene to support his son's identification. John not only did not see himself in the mirror, but in looking into the mirror he had an experience of terror at losing the bond with his parents. John had a significant developmental delay and didn't have the capacity for pre-symbolic functioning. When he looked into my eyes looking at him, putting a toy into his mouth as a link with the lost object, he returned to the mirror to look at me, not at himself. It was only when his father intervened to help him to stand up on the truck that John found narcissistic pleasure at seeing himself his own reflection.

For Jacques Lacan (1949), the identification process has two steps. The first is the imaginary identification. In the mirror the child is dependent on the other's image, asking for sameness. This allows him a sense of bodily unity. The child waits for the mother to look at him to support his image. After this symbolic identification begins with the child's wish to be in the future, like the idealized parent. This is the nucleus of the Ego Ideal. In John's story, there was no room for symbolic identification. His parents couldn't share an idealization of a father figure with him. His mother didn't communicate the importance of the father as an important figure whom she loved and in whom she took phallic pleasure. As Janine Chasseguet-Smirgel wrote (1976), the Ego Ideal is a booster for development. It is a wish for a future satisfaction that is unobtainable in the present.

Donald Winnicott (1953) sees the father's value in the fact that he provides "the first glimpse for the child of integration and of personal wholeness" (p. 193). The strength of such an environment for the growing child lies in the father's imperviousness to his hate and aggression. The child's aggressive impulses, envy, and jealousy must be integrated. Idealization of the father is an important growth-promoting step as a defensive function.

By choosing for his son's first name the name of his idealized grandfather, John's father was looking for a relationship with an imaginary good father figure who could erase his humiliating relation with his real father. Since the mother also had a very difficult relationship with her own parents and complained about male figures, John was included in a pathological scenario in which he was unable to integrate a capacity for representation. The real father is an important third in the infant's life, but so are the other fathers whom the mother holds in mind. In addition to her partner, her own father and other father figures function as significant thirds as well.

During the mirror stage, the child differentiates himself from the mother, but it is only after the Oedipal periods that he can construct himself as a subject with sexual identity and desire. In both situations he will ask himself about his mother, "Who is the other for the mother? What is her desire?"

The movement from the mother to the father opens the way for the child to discover others, their differences, in gender, in generation, the introduction to thirdness, moves him away from the dyadic system. When those steps are troubled, the child cannot discover himself as a subject and will have to search for the meaning of his own life. The father is a reference that allows the child to move from infantile and narcissistic omnipotence toward an identity as a subject who can supply meaning and live in a social world.

Ovid's *Narcissus* provides an excellent example of the consequence to development of the missing third. Narcissus' father, Cephisus, was a river. He raped the nymph Liriope, who gave birth to Narcissus. She never forgave Cephisus. Narcissus had a biological father, but not a symbolic one, since his mother lived as if his father didn't exist. She never gave the child access to a father figure. Having no desire as a result, the son wandered about the country. With no "other" in mind, a regressive motion overtook his libido. Falling in love with his own reflection mirrored by the water, he fell into the river and died, close to the origin of his forbidden father.

The father is not a symbolic equivalent to the mother. He is the figure of otherness. Thinking of the father requires confrontation with the connection to the mother and to a previous generation, a chain of thought that leads to the dead father.

Freud's story of the first father, violent, jealous, and murdered by his own sons, is also the representation of the origin of hate of the symbolic father that emerged from the mourning process, with all its ambivalence, guilt, and idealization that the sons elaborated. Fatherhood is linked with sexuality and death. The father figure makes the infantile psyche cope with the feeling of emptiness when separated from the mother and confronted with loneliness, death, and the limits of time.

During child analysis, it is interesting to attend to the moment when a young child able to learn about time and schedule, starts to ask questions about death while dealing with transitions and separation. The father that the parents hold in mind is the one who helps the child manage the persistent conflict between the search for security and radical innovation. The tradition of innovation must be transmitted to the next generation. The child then becomes creative. The role of the psychoanalyst in both child and adult treatments is to create a space for the thirdness. One can see the reconstruction of the role of the father through the frame: time and limits, rules, what is forbidden, what is allowed and the sameness of the setting, are vehicles for the installation of order and a place for difference. An exchange through transference–countertransference makes a common world of meanings and signifiers available. The analytic frame can stand for the mother's love as well as for the father's forbidding and founding role. The setting pushes the patient toward a renunciation of action in favor of a move toward mental functioning. It offers the possibility for mourning narcissistic infantile omnipotence.

The woman in her late twenties

A woman in her late twenties is in the second year of her analysis. She is a very inhibited, smart woman who cannot find a real job. She was the baby girl closest to her mother, using a bottle and sleeping with the mother until the age of 12. She struggles with my reluctance to change the schedule of sessions, always asking for a switch at the last minute. I recently asked her about the presence of her father in her life. She reports a dream:

> The man in charge of the office where I work, a patriarch to whom all the women want to be close, takes me by the shoulder and initiates me into my new job. I don't see very well because there is something wrong with my eyes. He shows me that my first name has been printed on heavy columns that are around the room. I feel the emergence of my "Self."

She relates her wish to change her first name, the one her mother chose without telling the father, who had already given another name to the administration. It reminded me of the Egyptian sculptures of characters whose bodies are covered with writings about their names and filiations. In the dream, she feels as if she is becoming herself with her real name, taking a step toward better symbolic functioning, through identification with a father figure.

Psychoanalysis does not bury the father. Instead, it enlivens him, more as an authority than as a power. The father figure is promoted in an analysis through the role of the third that the analyst plays while maintaining a strict frame. Both as a superego figure and as the ego ideal's support, the father is the source of the child's capacity for representation, for language, and for thought.

References

Braunschweig, D. and Fain, M. (1971) *Eros et Anteros*, Paris: Payot.

Braunschweig, D. and Fain, M. (1975) *La Nuit, Le Jour*, Paris: PUF.

Chasseguet-Smirgel, J. (1976) "Some Thoughts on the Ego Ideal: A Contribution to the Study of the 'Illness of Ideality' ", *Psychoanalytic Quarterly* 45: 345–73.

Chasseguet-Smirgel, J. (1986) "From the Archaic Matrix of the Oedipus Complex to the Fully Developed Oedipus Complex", in *Sexuality and Mind: The Role of the Father as the Mother in the Psyche*, New York: New York University Press, pp. 74–91.

de Mijolla, A. (1987) "Unconscious Identification Fantasies and Family Prehistory", *International Journal of Psycho-Analysis* 68: 397–403.

Freud, S. (1913) "Totem and Taboo", trans. James Strachey (1955) *Standard Edition*, Volume 13, London: Hogarth Press.

——— (1920) "Beyond the Pleasure Principle", trans. James Strachey (1961), *Standard Edition*, Volume 18, London: Hogarth Press.

——— (1939) "Moses and Monotheism", trans. James Strachey (1964), *Standard Edition*, Volume 23, London: Hogarth Press. (Original work published in 1939.)

Green, A. (1996) "The Dead mother", in A. Green *On Private Madness*, London: Karnac, pp. 142–64.

Lacan, J. (1949) "The Mirror Stage as Formative of the Function of the I", in *Ecrits, a Selection* (1977), New York: W.W. Norton and Company.

Ovid. (2004) *Metamorphoses*, Harmondsworth: Penguin.

Winnicott, D. W. (1953) "Transitional Objects and Transitional Phenomena: A Study of the First Not-Me Possession", *International Journal of Psychoanalysis* 34: 89–97.

Chapter 7

The dead father and the sacrifice of sexuality[1]

Rosine Jozef Perelberg

The theme of the killing of the father permeates Freud's writings, from *Totem and Taboo* (1913) to *Moses and Monotheism* (1939). Freud oscillates between hypothesizing, on the one hand, that this was a real event that took place in the distant past, was repressed yet preserved in the unconscious, and, on the other hand, regarding it as a myth. He thus presents a paradox: the killing of the father is the requirement for the creation of the social order that from then on prohibits all killings (Godelier, 1996). The father, however, has to be killed only metaphorically in that the exclusion of the father lies at the origin of so many psychopathologies, ranging from violence to the psychoses and the perversions. Jacques Hassoun has proposed a distinction between the murdered father and the dead father. The passage from one to the other inaugurates both the law and genealogy (1996, p. 17). I suggest that if the Oedipus *story* represents the former – the story of the murdered father – the Oedipus *complex* represents the latter, the dead father. The shift from the murdered to the dead father represents the attempt to regulate desire and institutes the sacrifice of sexuality. From then on certain categories of kin are excluded from the field of sexual exchanges. This exclusion constitutes the crucial marker of the beginnings of culture.[2] The regulation and sacrifice of sexuality is thus a critical indicator of the passage from nature to culture.

The primordial father, according to Lacan, is the father before the incest taboo, before the appearance of the law, social structures and culture (Lacan, 2005; see also Rosolato, 1969; Stoloff, 2007). Throughout the first period of Freud's work the father is perverse and incestuous; he possesses all the women and rules through violence. It is this violent and incestuous father who is killed in the founding myth. On September 21, 1897, Freud writes to Fliess about his surprise that in every one of his cases (including himself) the father should be accused of perversion. It is only in the second phase of his work that Freud identifies the unconscious nature of the universal, forbidden desires contained in his patients' accounts (Masson, 1985).

Totem and Taboo

In *Totem and Taboo* (1913) Freud described the primal parricide committed by the original horde that killed and devoured their father, who had possessed all the women and ruled through terror. In that the sons both hated and loved their father, his murder was followed by remorse and guilt. Moreover, although the brothers had been able to get together in order to kill their father, they were now faced with a situation in which each of them wanted all the women for himself. In order to prevent their own destruction, they instituted the law of incest, forbidding themselves sexual access to their mother and sisters. This prohibition inaugurated exogamy and reciprocity and represents the origin of the foundation of society.

The killing of the father brings the realization that this *renunciation* needs to take place if society is to survive. It is the basis of the social contract. The unconscious nucleus of all religions becomes the "parental complex" with the stress on ambivalent feelings of love and hate toward the father. Freud states that this is the beginning of society, culture and religion. Many years later, when he wrote about Moses, Freud would indeed state: "Religions might have been invented as antidotes to man's murderous desires" (1939, p. 188).

The dead father, however, was more powerful than he had been while alive. He became the possessor of the phallus:

> The dead father became stronger than the living one had been – for events took the course we so often see them follow in human affairs to this day. What had up to then been prevented by his actual existence was thenceforward prohibited by the sons themselves, in accordance with the psychological procedure so familiar to us in psycho-analysis under the name of "deferred obedience". They revoked their deed by forbidding the killing of the totem, the substitute for their father; and they renounced its fruits by resigning their claim to the women who had now been set free.
>
> (Freud, 1913, p. 144)

The phallus

As a social anthropologist I link this myth, present in Freud's work, with a notion present in so many traditional societies, namely that the individual only becomes a full person when dead and transformed into a (phallic) ancestor (Perelberg, 1998; see, for instance, the beliefs of the Tallensi of Ghana, in Fortes, 1969). In my reading of the anthropological literature I have also noticed, and wondered why, the phallus appears as an important symbol in many funerary rituals. What does it represent in these contexts? Bacchofen has suggested that the funeral rite "glorifies nature as a whole, with its two-fold life and death giving principle . . . That is why the symbols of life are so frequent in the tomb" (1967, p. 39). This may also account for the fact that the theme of sexuality and fertility dominates the symbolism of funerals (e.g. amongst the Lugbara, in Middleton, 1960; the Trobriand Islanders, in Malinowski, 1948; and the Kashi, in Parry, 1980). In 1998 I suggested that what is emphasized in the context of these rites is both separation and integration, part and whole, masculinity and femininity, and life and death. I would further suggest that it is the finite, limited quality of the facts of culture and the restrictions on sexuality that are, ultimately, denied in the symbol of the phallus. From this perspective the phallus is not only a signifier of a power structure but also of universal fears, beliefs, and wished for states of completeness and plenitude.[3] What the symbol expresses is the absence of what has been renounced. It is interesting to think of the traditional groups in the British Psychoanalytic Society as totemic. The Kleinians, Freudians and Independents represent the totemic ancestors that legitimize one's thinking and transform an "individual" into a "person."[4]

Moses and Monotheism

Moses and Monotheism represents the culmination of Freud's work on the father, and articulates his view of the role of god in the monotheistic religions, especially Judaism and Catholicism:

> Under the influence of external factors into which we need not enter here and which are also in part insufficiently known, it came about that the matriarchal social order was succeeded by the patriarchal one – which, of course, involved a revolution in the juridical conditions that had so far prevailed. . . . But this turning from the mother to the father points in addition to a victory of intellectuality over sensuality – that is, an advance in civilization, since maternity is proved by the evidence of the senses while paternity is a hypothesis, based on an inference and a premise. Taking sides in this way with a thought-process in preference to a sense perception has proved to be a momentous step.
>
> (Freud, 1939, p. 113)

In this text Freud does not regard the maternal function in a similar way to the paternal function. He does not consider the role of the mother in the process of helping the child to symbolize. However, Freud did consider this function in other texts, as I have previously discussed (e.g. Perelberg, 1998, 2007). He is now stressing the irreducibility of the father to the realm of the senses, underscoring that the father, like the monotheistic god, is invisible and hidden. He is the mystery linked to the mother's absences (see also Braunschweig and Fain, 1975; Botella and Botella, 1991; Stoloff, 2007). Moreover, monotheism also emphasizes the existence of a law that is universal and thus opposed to the narcissistic universe. What is at stake is "the invention of the concept of father that stresses its legislative function" (Stoloff, 2007, p. 100). It is the culmination of Freud's path in the creation and conceptualization of the dead father and its function in the creation and maintenance of the law. Rosolato understands this distinction in terms of the narcissistic father (of *Totem and Taboo*) and the symbolic father, more fully presented in *Moses and Monotheism*, the symbolic enabling the establishment of the law against incest and exogamy. "Each individual renounced his ideal of acquiring his father's position for himself and of possessing his mother and sisters" (1969, pp. 36–58).

Freud suggested that the catastrophe of the Oedipus complex represents the victory of the human order over the individual, instituting the sacrifice of sexuality among certain categories of kin. His writings are therefore about the creation of this order and how it becomes separate from biology (see also Mitchell, 1974, 1982; Kohon, 1999). Through the Oedipus complex, the individual enters the symbolic order by establishing the differences between the sexes and the generations. The fulfilment of incestuous sexual desires would bring about the collapse of kinship systems.

In psychoanalytic terms, the acceptance of an order based on the incest taboo, the differentiation between genders and generations, introduces the individual to an experience of renunciation and mourning (Cosnier, 1990). This is the source of identifications and thus of the foundation of psychic reality. As Lévi-Strauss has suggested, together with the incest taboo, and as a corollary of it, it is precisely this differentiation that inserts the person into an exogamous system of exchange (1969).[5] The origin of society, according to Freud, requires that mankind exercise control over its sexuality and desire, excluding both force and violence.

I would like to turn now to examples in my clinical practice that illustrate configurations that emerged when the father was not present as the symbolic third (the dead father), the father having in fact been eliminated. In both cases this was linked to the relationship with a mother that was experienced as perverse, where the mothers were said to make use of their sons as extensions of themselves and as vehicles for the fulfilment of their own desires.[6] Both sons were frightened of their mothers.

Robert

Robert's first contact with me was via a letter telling me the story of his life. He enclosed a self-portrait, painted many years earlier. Although he was an artist, he had felt unable to paint during the previous ten years. He came from an artistic, upper middle class Italian family with eight children, from whom he had taken flight. His father and sister were successful artists. His mother had also been successful prior to a series of psychotic breakdowns that had caused her to be hospitalized several times. She had been violent toward her children in their childhood, and they had grown up feeling terrified of her. As a child he was often frightened of her, and on several occasions experienced her as wanting to kill him. The father was absent and ineffectual and the account of childhood scenes seemed to be totally dominated by the mother's presence. In reading his well-written and engrossing letter, I had an inkling of a position that Robert wanted to keep me in. Had he told the story in my presence, it might have allowed for some exchange between us. Instead I was to read what he had written outside any actual interaction between us. Robert wrote of some of his violent encounters. His relationship with his girlfriend broke down after an escalation of his violence toward her. He had also made two serious suicide attempts. What engaged me most about his long and detailed letter was his contact with his experience of despair and his profound battle against feelings of hopelessness.

Robert then phoned me, and we arranged an initial consultation. A handsome man in his early thirties, Robert entered the room full of seductive sexual vitality, but also barely able to disguise his fear of me. I had the immediate thought that he felt confused about this encounter and that he might experience it as a scene of seduction. Indeed, for the first half of the session Robert proceeded to tell me about various intense affairs with older women that he had only managed to sustain for brief periods of time. I thought that it was important to address his confusion at the outset. I immediately let him know that I thought he was puzzled about what I expected from him. He calmed down visibly, relaxing in the chair. He was then able to tell me about his great pain at not being able to paint for such a long time. He described the life full of violent encounters that he had led since he had stopped painting. He expressed his anxiety and uncertainty about the future and his belief that he might one day kill himself in order to put an end to his torment.

An account of a violent episode emerged at that consultation. On a recent visit to Italy, he had been waiting for a woman to finish a phone conversation in a telephone box [booth]. She took longer than he could wait. He suddenly saw himself attacking and destroying the telephone box, hurting the woman in the process. The woman fled in terror, and he himself was utterly terrified by the extent of his violence. We began treatment the next week. Robert brought the following dream to his first session:

There was a beautiful house, the most beautiful house one could imagine, surrounded by lush gardens and filled with works of art and famous paintings. It was very spacious, one room leading to another. However, it was surrounded by impenetrable glass and one could only admire it from the outside.

This dream and the associations which preceded and followed it became paradigmatic of the many layers of Robert's analysis. My experience of his letter immediately came to mind, with his wish to be admired like this beautiful house filled with works of art that left him as well as the other on the outside. There was no live communication between inside and outside, between his inner world and the external. Everything was either locked in or out. This was a dream we repeatedly came back to during our work together. The house also represented the body of a mother whom he experienced as ungiving and impenetrable. Any contact had to be the result of a violent penetration (the episode of the telephone box). He had, in the same way, experienced her as intruding into him both psychically (with her psychotic episodes) and physically (the many incidents of physical violence). Finally, the dream represented his fear that whatever he produced would be trapped inside her. It was his terror of what the body and the mind of his psychotic mother contained that constituted the core of what we were to explore in his analysis.

Robert's first dream provided a map to which we turned to understand a great deal about the unfolding of the analytic relationship. Robert's implicit demand was that I admire him, without attempting to enter into too much contact with him. He came to the sessions full of vivid dreams and thoughts, associations and interpretations. He worked very hard both in the sessions and outside them on his many thoughts, experiences and impressions. His fundamental requirement was that I should simply admire him and his work, without intervening. I was left outside the house. The interesting point of technique for me in my work with Robert was that this is what I basically did for quite some time, aware that I was doing so. My interpretations and comments, especially at the beginning, were indeed sparse although I felt intensely present with him in the sessions. I was aware that interaction was unbearable for him and that unbearable interactions had led to violence.

Slowly, very slowly Robert's fear of relating to me shifted. It was possible to have a different way of interacting with him in the sessions, a sense of a dialogue that could more easily be put into words that he could tolerate. Until recently he had had a promiscuous sexual life, consistently being involved with several – older – women at the same time. These represented his attempts to experience himself as constantly participating in an uninterrupted primal scene that he could control (enter and leave), while at the same time he could exclude himself from any intimate relationship.

Some 18 months into analysis Robert entered a relationship with a girlfriend; and two years after the beginning of his analysis Robert started painting again. The conflict he had been struggling with was given vivid expression when he wanted to give me the first painting he was able to paint after such a long time. His utter surprise at my refusal to accept it allowed him to believe fully, perhaps for the first time, that our work together was for his. benefit. He started to participate in exhibitions and competitions, and he won a prestigious prize in Italy.

Karl – negation of the dead father[7]

My second clinical example is Karl, a violent young man about whom I have written extensively. In a session in which he had started to talk more about his childhood, Karl made a slip and said, "The problem with my stepfather is that he cannot bear the thought that he was not present when I was conceived. There were only me and my mother, he was not there." He then stopped, surprised at himself at what he had said. Karl was thus expressing his belief that he was present at his own conception, from which his (step)-father was excluded. This left him experiencing himself as living in a world in which only he and his mother existed from the beginning, a world in which he felt treated as an extension of her desires. Karl believed that his mother supported his beliefs and that she too stressed his biological father's absence from his conception.

He felt enclosed in a world created by his mother or by the analyst, where he experienced any questions about his father as being blocked. This was a very violent young man, and in the transference, over the course of an analysis that lasted for many years, we understood that his violence was an attempt to resist his mother's desire to have exclusive possession of him. Karl stated that he indeed had never really thought of himself as having a biological father. He said that he was in contact with his paternal grandmother, but he had never linked her to his biological father. It was as if she was on the side of his mother's family too. In that same session Karl said that he felt that he had just reached an understanding that was going to change his life.

Conclusion

The analyses of the patients discussed in this chapter concern a battle for survival in a relationship which they seem to believe involves only themselves and their mothers. Their father has been eliminated. They also express archaic modes of relating to the object. Robert's experience of this primary object was that of impenetrability. Contact was marked by violence and intrusion in a way that left him feeling confused. His solution was either to distance himself from the object, or to be constantly involved with it, in promiscuous sexuality where he could have the phantasy of constant participation in the primal scene. Karl's violence was paradoxically a way of separating himself from the object. He experienced his mother as sexually available to him, and violence was a way of separating from her. Both patients expressed, in different ways, a decathexis of representations. Their relationship with their internal objects seemed to be faintly represented and had to be acted out. Each analysis contained a search for a mental space where they could explore, think about and transform the relationships with their internal objects.

The collapse of the third and its consequences for the destiny of sexual desire and identifications has been explored. As Green reminds us, in this volume and elsewhere, thirdness is a requirement for meaning and understanding to take place (2004).

The acceptance of an order which involves a differentiation between the sexes and the generations introduces the individual to an experience of renunciation and mourning. One notes that Freud's book that marks the birth of psychoanalysis, *The Interpretation of Dreams* (1900), was published after the death of his own father, as Freud himself indicates in the Preface to his second edition:

> For this book has a further subjective significance for me personally – a significance which I only grasped after I had completed it. It was, I found, a portion of my own self-analysis, my reaction to my father's death – that is to say, to the most important event, the most poignant loss, of a man's life.
>
> (p. xiv)

If there be a work of mourning present in the writing of the book, it also expresses the experience of liberation, as Freud implies in his own words: "A physician will often be in a position to notice how a son's grief at the loss of his father cannot suppress his satisfaction at having at length won his freedom" (pp. 255–56).

Freud's mythical account of the killing of the narcissistic father and the institution of the dead father is an account of the creation of a social order based on the incest taboo and the system of exchange.[8] The individual must renounce his own parents, take them as sources of identification, develop his own sense of temporality and history and thus acquire an individual "project." The counterpart to this is that the parents must also renounce the possession of their children's sexuality. This would indicate a distinction between those who have been able to inaugurate their own individual project and those patients who have become immobilized in another's temporality and desire, as happened with Karl and Robert.

Notes

1 My title was inspired by Maurice Godelier (1996), although my view differs from his, as I will explain.
2 Recently Godelier has challenged Freud and Lévi-Strauss's assumptions that link incest and exogamy (2004). Jack Goody (2005), however, has pointed out that Godelier's book does not challenge the assumption that the incest taboo is universal in that in every society there is a category of people who are excluded from the field of sexual exchange.
3 An example of a phallic symbol that is linked to funerary rituals among the Asmat of Papua can be found in the Metropolitan Museum in New York. The Asmat, the most famous cannibalistic tribe of Papua, celebrated death with feasts and rituals that both commemorated the dead and incited the living to avenge them. The Mbis, a pole which represents the ancestors and which is the main carved object

of Asmat culture, has sacred value and is used to ask for the protection of the ancestors. It bears the carving of a respected person from the village who has passed away, as a family portrait. It had the shape of a canoe with an exaggerated prow that incorporated ancestral figures and a phallic symbol. My hypothesis is that phallic symbols are present in funerary rituals because at those occasions there is an attempt to re-create a social order which is "complete" and contains a promise of eternity. Leach (1971) suggested that religious ideology uses the promise of rebirth in order to negate the finality of death. This idea stresses the way in which "irreversibility" is disguised as "repetition."

4 See my distinctions between the notion of the "individual" and the "person" (Perelberg, 1980).

5 This is very well expressed in Lévi-Strauss's words:

> To this very day mankind has always dreamed of seizing and fixing that fleeting moment when it was permissible to believe that the law of exchange could be evaded, that one could gain without losing, enjoy without sharing. At either end of the earth and at both extremes of time, the Sumerian myth of the golden age and the Andaman myth of the future life correspond, the former placing the end of primitive happiness at a time when the confusion of languages made words into common property, the latter describing the bliss of the hereafter as a heaven where women will no longer be exchanged, i.e., removing to an equally unattainable past or future the joys, eternally denied to social man, a world in which one might *keep to oneself*.
>
> (Lévi-Strauss, 1969, pp. 496–7)

6 Braunschweig and Fain (1975) have suggested a distinction between the day mother and the night mother, which relates to the capacity to separate the mother's sexuality in relation to her child from her role of father's lover (*la censure de l'amante*).

7 This example has been more fully discussed in Perelberg (1999a, 1999b).

8 Perhaps it will be appropriate here to return to the work by Godelier that inspired the title of this chapter. Godelier perceives the process of disjunction between desire and reproduction that took place in the development of human sexuality as a consequence of the loss of oestrus in the woman that led to a process of independence of sexual relations from reproduction (1996, pp. 27–28). Desire and the potential for a generalized sexual exchange that from then on became possible represented a threat to society and the reproduction of social relationships. There was thus a contradiction between sexuality and society. The sacrifice of sexuality that then takes place is a sacrifice of the potential of the generalized sexual exchange and is the result of a repression of the asocial character of sexuality itself. Godelier emphasizes a sociological type of explanation for the sacrifice of sexuality. Society subordinates desire to the social order and places reproductive sexuality under societal control. If in some ways this is similar to Freud's suggestion that the interests of the individual are put at the service of the species, Freud's discovery is that it is the Oedipal, incestuous desires that need to be sacrificed. If I wish to retain Godelier's notion of sacrifice, I am, at the same time, linking it centrally to the notion that it is the sacrifice of the incestuous desires.

References

Bacchofen, J. J. (1967) *Myth, Religion and Mother Right*, London: Routledge and Kegan Paul.

Botella, C. and Botella S. (1991) *La Figurabilité Psychique*, Paris et Lausanne: Delachaux et Niestle.

Braunschweig, D. and Fain, M. (1975) *La Nuit, Le Jour*, Paris: PUF.

Cosnier, J. (1990) "Les Vicissitudes de l'Identité", in A.-M. Alléon et al. (eds) *Devenir "Adulte"?*, Paris: PUF.

Fortes, M. (1969) *The Web of Kinship Among the Tallensi*, Oxford: Oxford University Press.

Freud, S. (1900) "The Interpretation of Dreams", trans. James Strachey (1953) *Standard Edition*, Volumes 4–5, London: Hogarth Press.

—— (1913) "Totem and Taboo", trans. James Strachey (1955), *Standard Edition*, Volume 13, London: Hogarth Press, pp. vii–162.

—— (1930 [1929]) "Civilization and Its Discontents", trans. James Strachey (1961), *Standard Edition*, Volume 21, London: Hogarth Press.

—— (1939) "Moses and Monotheism", trans. James Strachey (1964), *Standard Edition*, Volume 23, London: Hogarth Press, pp. 1–138.

Godelier, M. (1996) "Meurtre du Père ou Sacrifice de la Sexualité", in M. Godelier and J. Hassoun (eds) *Meurtre du Père; Sacrifice de la Sexualité: Approches Anthropologiques et Psychanalytiques*, Paris: Arcanes.

—— (2004) *Metamorphoses de la Parenté*, Paris: Fayard.

Goody, J. (2005) *New Left Review* 36: 1127–39.

Green, A. (2004) "Thirdness and Psychoanalytic Concepts", *Psychoanalytic Quarterly* 73: 99–135.

Hassoun, J. (1996) "Du Père de la Théorie Analytique", in M. Godelier and J. Hassoun (eds) *Meurtre du Père; Sacrifice de la Sexualité: Approches Anthropologiques et Psychanalytiques*, Paris: Arcanes.

Kohon, G. (1999) *No Lost Certainties to be Recovered*, London: Karnac.

Lacan, J. (2005) *Des Noms-Du-Père*, Paris: du Seuil.

Leach, E. (1971) *Rethinking Anthropology*, London: Athlone Press.

Lévi-Strauss, C. (1969) *The Elementary Structures of Kinship and Marriage*, Boston: Beacon Press.

Malinowski, B. (1948) "Baloma: The Spirits of Dead", in B. Malinowski *Magic, Science and Religion*, London: Faber and West.

Masson, J. M. (ed.) (1985) *The Complete Letters of Sigmund Freud to Wilhem Fliess 1887–1904*, London and Cambridge, MA: Belknap Press.

Middleton, J. (1960) *Lugbara Religion*, Oxford: Oxford University Press.

Mitchell, J. (1974) *Psychoanalysis and Feminism*, Harmondsworth: Penguin.

—— (1982) " 'Introduction' I", in J. Mitchell and J. Rose (eds) *Feminine Sexuality*, London: Macmillan.

Parry, J. P. (1980) "Ghosts, Greed and Sin: The Occupational Identity of the Benares Funeral Priests", *Man* 15(1): 88–111.

Perelberg, R. J. (1980) "Umbanda and Psychoanalysis as Two Different Ways of Interpreting Mental Illness", *British Journal of Medical Psychology* 53: 323–32.

—— (1998) "Introduction III", in J. Raphael-Leff and R. J. Perelberg (eds) *Female Experience: Three Generations of Women Psychoanalysts on Work with Women*, London: Routledge.

—— (1999a) "A Core Phantasy in Violence", in R. J. Perelberg (ed.) *Psychoanalytic Understanding of Violence and Suicide*, London: Routledge.

—— (1999b) "The Interplay Between Identification and Identity in the Analysis of a Violent Young Man", *International Journal of Psychoanalysis* 80: 31–45.

—— (2007) "Space and Time in Psychoanalytic Listening", paper presented to the English Speaking Conference Weekend, October 2006, *International Journal of Psychoanalysis* 88: 1473–90.

Rosolato, G. (1969) *Essais sur le Symbolique*, Paris: Gallimard.

Stoloff, J.-C. (2007) *La Function Paternelle*, Paris: Editions in Press.

Chapter 8

Constructing and deconstructing the conglomerate

Thoughts about the father in life, in death, and in theory

James M. Herzog

> Perhaps there is a distance that is the optimum distance for seeing one's father, farther than across the supper table or across the room, somewhere in the middle distance: he is dwarfed by trees or the sweep of a hill, but his features are still visible, his body language still distinct. Well, that is a distance I never found. He was never dwarfed by the landscape – the fields, the buildings, the white pine windbreak were as much my father as if he had grown them and shed them like a husk.
>
> (Jane Smiley, *A Thousand Acres*, 1991)

The father is encountered in the psychoanalytic Spielraum (analytic space) as a representation of self with another and of self with two others, the parents. How are these representations related to actual experience and how are they tutored by fantasy, developmental history and actual family configurations? Are there templates present in the psyche for a masculine parent and a feminine parent? Is their relationship also of crucial import in the developing mind of a child? I shall try to explore these questions by presenting material from two analyses.

The two cases are as follows. The first is the analysis of a young man whom I saw beginning when he was almost 29. His father was never present after his birth having developed a fatal illness which he gave to his wife who herself gave up caring for my patient when he was six months of age. The second analysis is of a girl who began treatment at the age of four. She is the daughter of two lesbian mothers, both of whom for compelling historical reasons detested men. Her father was an anonymous sperm donor. The actual life circumstance of these two analysands allow us to examine the fate of paternal representations, both self with father and self with father and mother together, when no father has actually been present. Important questions related to the father's actual presence, or absence, aliveness or deadness, the ways in which a paternal figure might be conveyed from the mind of the mother, the nature of both dyadic and triadic representations in development and in the psychic inscape, and the relationship of what I have called the level of video-taped reality to the level of interrogative reality, and the domain of personal meaning can thus be explored.

The first case

> Children make fictions of their fathers, reinventing them according to their childish needs. The reality of a father is a weight few sons can bear.
>
> (Salman Rushdie, *The Moor's Last Sigh*, 1995)

Isaac was referred to me by his previous analyst when he began his graduate studies. His earlier treatment had extended over many years and was characterized by a familial quality, his analyst being friendly with his extended family and not involved interpretively with him. Isaac had been born in South America. His father was a right-wing bisexual diplomat and his mother a left-wing French student. Father contracted AIDS that he gave to the mother who became severely depressed and then committed suicide. The parents had separated before his birth and divorced when Isaac was less than six months. Father died soon thereafter. Isaac was sent to live with a maternal uncle in Paris who was then 17 years old.

In our work a mode soon declared itself which seemed very noteworthy. Referring to his childhood in France, Isaac told me about various events involving people, mostly in the analytic community, whom I knew there. This appeared to reflect the fact that his uncle and analyst moved in the same circles, but I was struck by the meaning or the multiple meanings which attached to my acquaintance with the characters in his life. Was I supposed to know them; was I not to know them? I did not comment on my knowledge, yet I felt that an important dynamic had been joined.

For a number of months, Isaac told me about his obsession with a woman named Florence Klein. She was a meteorologist, and he first saw her on television giving the weather report each evening when he was about six and vacationing in Cagnes sur Mer with his uncle. Isaac found her irresistible. She was so beautiful, her voice had a soft, southern accent, and he told me that she might even be Jewish. He used to think of her all of the time. He tried to tell Madame X, his previous analyst, about this wonderful woman. His recollection was that she did not want to hear it and countered with stories of the Lebovicis in Cannes and the Lévi-Strausses in the Luberon. He developed the notion that he should not speak about Florence Klein, and so she went underground. I thought that this possibly Jewish woman from the south might be a representation of his mother. I kept this thought to myself. In later years, when he returned to the south of France, she was no longer on the television. He developed an uneasy notion that she had been the victim of foul play, perhaps a murder. Occasionally it occurred to him that the right-wing politician Jacques LePin might be involved in her disappearance or death. Sometimes he wondered whether one of the Parisian analysts of whom Madame X disapproved so vehemently might have done her in. Again, I wondered to myself if this man from the right might be a representation of the paternal murderer. We were to learn that he thought of Florence every day for many years. After his initial attempt to discuss her with his analyst, he never spoke about her again. I had actually seen Florence Klein on television in the south of France. I wondered whether it would be helpful to share this with Isaac. I decided that I always could share this information at a later date and that now my job was just to listen and, if possible, to hear.

Here is an hour in the second year of Isaac's analysis. We have been meeting five times a week for 14 months. Mostly Isaac uses the couch. On this day, he brings his guitar, sits in a chair and begins to sing a song by a little known pop group, which, remarkably, I recognize. I say nothing. I listen intently as this is the first time that Isaac has brought his guitar or sung during a session. The song describes an ill-fated love of a couple from different life circumstances, much like his own parents, destined to go down together.

I don't catch all of the words at first, and I ask him, as the music is hauntingly beautiful, if this is like his own compositions. I think to myself that this does not sound at all like the anguished final screams of a sow strangling on her own blood after her throat has been cut, a way that he described the music he wrote in Paris. I then think again about how I actually know this music. My daughter has given me this very CD as a gift. This feels like a curious coincidence. Is it similar to my knowing Florence Klein?

Isaac looks at me strangely and says, "It depends on what you mean. This is a song written by the group that recorded it. But it could be my own composition." The band's name reminds me of a pre-revolutionary Russian intellectual group and its possible connection to his father's side of the family; but fortunately I don't say this as Isaac proceeds to tell me that this vocal group is from the West Coast, and that if I would like, he'd bring me their CD. Again I observe that I distance myself with my association, when I actually already know this group and this song.

"Does my singing stump you?" he asks, as I am silent for a moment. I respond by saying that I was very moved by the lyrics. He then says, "But did you notice that the music is in fact quite upbeat and almost sexual?" I ask if he will say more and he makes a gesture as if to say "Well, did you notice?"

I now say, "I don't know if I would have made that observation; but when you point it out, I can hear it."

Isaac puts down his guitar and now goes to the couch. He begins to speak. "I wanted to play that song for you. I assumed that it would be completely unknown to you. By your reaction, I think that you confirmed that fact. When a person hears new music, if he is open to it, it is like something penetrates and makes a space inside of your mind, which has never been there before. Do you know what I mean?" I was struck by this reference to penetration and to the making of a new psychic space. I thought that this might be some reference to a masculine force.

I said, "That sounds extremely interesting. Would you say more?"

Isaac then says, "I don't believe that words have this effect. It is beyond words. That is why I wanted to sing to you. Perhaps I am wrong, and you do not understand what I was trying to convey." Now, I felt very uneasy. I understood that my not sharing what I knew had to do with a reluctance to penetrate. I was conscious of not wanting to be the AIDS-disseminating husband, father, but was I also reluctant to be the co-creator of an inner, contemplative space? I wanted to understand, but I was far from sure that I did. It was as if I sensed an opportunity and did not know how to actualize it. I remembered the conspiracy of silence forged by the grandparents, the uncle and Madame X. Was I now a part of that tribe, that cabal?

I said, "It feels as though you are telling me something very important, and I sense what it is, but I do not yet know how to formulate it." I then found myself humming the tune, and I repeated one of the lines. I considered substituting the name "Florence" for the name of the woman in the song, remembering his discussion of the weather woman of his youth. But then, fortunately, rejected that too facile alteration before actually voicing it.

Isaac laughs a little and says, "I don't know if we are alike or very different, but that is what music is like for me. I am not so alone if I can hear a melody, and it is even better if I can remember the words." I felt quite unsure about my humming and actually singing the words, but relatively comfortable with my more active stance. I had been able to maintain, with the help of melody and lyric, a connection to Isaac as he was telling me about what could penetrate him and me, and open up hitherto unopened psychic space. I was glad that I had been able to think about my own dilemma in regard to recognizing and participating, and I resolved to continue listening. Not to my surprise and, with a sense of all rightness, I could now remember that the lyrics were about class difference and about sexual intercourse. I thought that Isaac was probably singing to me about his parents, about whom he had said quite literally hardly a word.

I felt increasingly interested in the possibility that we were establishing access to his representational world. I was also curious that the mode we were utilizing seemed to require that I continuously process the relevance of what I knew in relation to what Isaac was sharing with me. I also knew that I was experiencing a kind of split. As with Florence Klein, what Isaac was telling me about was at least phenotypically not unknown to me. What was the meaning of this overlap, that my daughter had given me this very music, that Isaac wanted it to be new to me, to open up a mental space which had not hitherto been there? Could it be said that the countertransference, which I was experiencing but unable to formulate, was the vehicle by which I would either presume, or far better, actually learn what Isaac's inscape featured? What was this dichotomy between presumption and actually finding out? It seemed very curious. I was becoming aware that I had no idea what the South America of Isaac's mind was actually about. This gave partial meaning to this apparent dichotomy between presumption and listening in order to find out.

Yet, something else was also in play. Was this the transference or was there a better way of conceptualizing the enactment, which I felt to be an invitation? Isaac wanted me to know that at the same time he did not know. I was being continuously invited to populate his intrapsychic space, to create it and to fill it, while I had thought that my job was actually to find out what was there. This was how the father was encountered, constructed and deconstructed in our work. We overlapped, yet I needed to hear the music inside of Isaac's mind as he developed, composed, fathered and unfathered, in a representational world that featured his being with the father, albeit ambivalently.

The second case

> In the eyes: dream. The brow as if it could feel
> something far off. Around the lips, a great
> freshness-seductive, although there is no smile.
> (Rilke, *Portrait of My Father as a Young Man*, 1938)

Tilda entered analysis at the age of four. Her parents Rosa and Milly were concerned that she seemed moody, would often appear to be withdrawn and look as though she were depressed. Sometimes she would become unexpectedly quarrelsome and pugilistic, "almost as if she were an unpleasant man," I was told. Tilda was the product of Rosa's egg, had gestated in Milly's womb, and sperm had been provided by a donor from a California bank. Four other embryos were frozen and available for future sibling production. Both mothers were physicians and the sperm donor was alleged to be a doctor too. Neither mother's work was in the mental health area, although each had female friends with good analytic experiences.

The pregnancy and the delivery were uncomplicated, and all three members of the family were thought to be healthy. There was a family history of bipolar disorder on Rosa's side, and this was mentioned as a diagnostic concern. Neither Rosa nor Milly had ever been in psychiatric treatment. At the time that Tilda came to see me, both were 40 years old. Her parents told me that they had grudgingly decided on a male analyst for their daughter. They said that they preferred a world without disturbing and disturbed men in it, but recognized that their daughter should have some male contact. Perhaps, given that I was a psychoanalyst, a profession of mostly women, meant that I was not really very masculine. I felt a combination of curiosity about the mothers' stance, some annoyance about their characterization of my gender, and great empathy for whatever lay behind their attitude toward masculinity.

I assumed that it was not pleasant, and I wondered how all of this had impacted Tilda's inner world.

Tilda was a natural born player, as most children are. Quickly, we began to enter the "Bat family," sometimes also called the "Brat family," composed of two mothers, a little girl and a "quarrelly prowler." I wondered about the prowler, as he was the least well-defined member of the ensemble. Tilda said, "Keep your eyes open and you will learn more." This seemed like good advice and I made a note to myself that I might expect to see more about the prowler, rather than to hear more about him. I wondered why this thought about a sensory modality had been highlighted in my mind. Tilda told me that the quarrelly prowler was made to stay outside. He actually lived in a doghouse and was not allowed to come in. The reason for this was that he was boisterous, rough, smelled bad and was totally lacking in refinement or social grace. I wondered if this were an approximate description of what I had called a father's disruptive attunement as contrasted with a mother's gentler homeostatic attunement – a father engaged in rough and tumble play, thereby helping his child with the organization and modulation of aggressive drive and fantasy.

As the play progressed, we were enormously occupied with the household which now consisted of Gilda, Hilda and Wilda. Wilda seemed to be the child, but as everyone looked alike and all of the names sounded alike, it was really hard to say. Wilda wanted to play doctor with her doctor. This did not mean that she wanted to examine his body or have both of them take off their clothes, but rather that she wanted to look at her doctor's face with a magnifying glass. Tilda, who first defined what playing doctor would not be, told me that Wilda would surely be disappointed because, of course, the doctor would not agree to such an inspection. She could look with the naked eye, but not with a lens. Moreover, she told me that everyone already knew that the doctor looked like the prowler. I was, of course, very interested in this. "How did they look alike?" I wondered.

"Look in the mirror, silly," was Tilda's response. "See your mustache, see all that hair growing out of your face. That's what the prowler has too, something prickly and sticking out on his face." I am clean-shaven and thought that the need for a magnifying glass was now more apparent.

"Mommy Rosa always tells Mommy Milly how soft her face is. Mine is too. Once Uncle Rob came over and he hugged me. His face felt different. He didn't smell like my Mommies. Wilda would hug you to feel your face. I told her that you are a doctor, not the prowler. I told her that she wasn't allowed to hug the doctor. Wilda is so foolish. I don't think she has even been born yet." So Wilda wanted to get really close to the doctor to see, to feel and to smell something about him that was different from Hilda and Gilda, and which he shared with the prowler.

Uncle Rob was Milly's brother and lived in California. He had visited only once, when Tilda was two. She had a vivid memory of this visit. There had been some strife between brother and sister during this visit, and, as we were to learn much later, Milly had said to her brother that she didn't want him prowling around their family, coming east every two years as was his practice. Thus the identity of the prowler was born as well as Tilda's idea, which emerged after much play, that their quarrel was the way that babies were made. Tilda believed that she must have issued forth from his visit two years prior to her birth, and that a new baby, Wilda, might now be en route. She also concluded that a man's pokey face and different scent were part of the necessary admixture.

As the analysis continued, we became ever more interested in the quarrel between Rob and Milly. Every time Tilda spoke of it, she would become somewhat flushed. In the play, Wilda, the unborn sibling, longed for such an occurrence that would result from the prowler visiting Gilda or Hilda or both of them. I thought that we were encountering Tilda's "knowledge" that there were other California fathered embryos and that passion was required to transmute them into actual babies. Thus Wilda, the unborn protagonist, in her very name, described what was needed in order to make a child.

I thought that Tilda in this phase of her analytic work was conveying that in her fantasy life procreation required passion and biological difference, a soft face and a pokey one. That the quarrel stood for intercourse and that Wilda was the outcome of such a union, albeit held in reserve in a way that mirrored actual reality. Was this a representation of self-with-father as well as a complex statement about biological origins and their connection to passion between the procreators? As the analysis unfolded, Tilda was increasingly preoccupied with questions about her analyst's presence or absence, power or lack thereof, and deadness or aliveness. This became even more pronounced when her mothers decided to have another child. They explained to Tilda that a stored fertilized embryo would now be thawed and implanted and that she had begun life in a similar fashion. In the analysis, Tilda told me that this might be scientifically the case, but that it was certainly not true in the realm of her feelings. It was and would to continue to be our job to maintain a safe place for what she felt, for what was essential and true for her.

Analysis provides a space for a child of any age not to have to be entirely alone with what goes on inside. As is so often the case, the greatest aloneness is with those thoughts, fears and fantasies that involve the parents or, in the child's mind, must be kept from the parents in order to protect them. Rosa and Milly allowed Tilda to have such a safe enough play space. In this and many other respects, they were and are truly good parents. Yet, Tilda has a dilemma. How is she to represent self-with-father and self-with mother-and-father-together, given her mothers' active demeaning of all things masculine and given the total lack of maleness in her surround. Curiously, Tilda actively works on ways to enliven, to resurrect, to construct and to reconstruct such a representation. Her transference to the analyst contains both elements; his countertransference contains absence, non-aliveness and availability, presence, as well as functional and anatomical referents to his paternity. Again, there is a way in which the identification of the missing but essential male, the father is conducted in biological terms. Facial hair and smell demarcate something essentially masculine or paternal.

Conclusion

This chapter has attempted to present analytic material that reveals the ways in which the father is accessed in the Spielraum in three modalities: the analysand's material, conscious and unconscious, the transference/countertransference experience, and in various enactments that are enfolded in both of the above and that involve the ways in which the analyst provides insight, interpretation, or other forms of "penetration" that help to create and to maintain an internal play space. Further, it has focused on the circumstances of his doing so and on the circumstances when he did not or could not, often in ways that were particularly noteworthy as they evolved in the process. With Isaac, I particularly focused on the ways in which the analyst knew more than he could share, how I understood this, and how it might have been related both historically to Isaac's experience, and in the analysis to the pace and the manner in which the aliveness or the deadness of the paternal representation might be gauged as a fixed or fluctuating entity. With Tilda, the emphasis has been on the ways in which she needed both to ban and to desire the aliveness of a male parent in order to be reborn, to thaw and thus to be fully enlivened herself. She created the simultaneous aliveness and deadness of the analyst, the transference father. It was my job to respect her mothers' pain and preference, while affording a space in which Wilda could preserve her internal reality even in the face of an external reality that she needed both to accept and simultaneously to reject. I would like to suggest that all of these happenings are ways in which the father is created, re-created, killed or acknowledged as either missing, longed for, present or necessarily absent and dead within the analysand's inscape and concomitantly within the analytic Spielraum. I have also tried to emphasize that the relationship between actual presence and internal representation is complex and neither is as simple as one of actual interaction or of maternal endowment. As is almost always the case, the idiographic supersedes the nomothetic. The analyst is well advised to make his theory from the material and analytic experience of his patient rather than to fit his patient into an existing theoretical structure.

My own thinking as a child analyst and as an observer of young children accompanied by research into their evolving psychic structures using play interviews has led me to believe that paternal representations are constructed by the young child early in development both as self-with-father depictions and as self-with-mother-and-father-together depictions. These depictions are always in "trialogue" with self-with-mother depictions. All representations are continuously reworked, reconstructed by every subsequent fantasy, interaction or event. My research has focused on families in which there is actually a mother and a father present. Always, the nature of their affective and sexual relationship is a factor in the libidinal, aggressive and narcissistic availability of each parent to the child and is also a factor in the evolving representation. Only overwhelming trauma short circuits this process of continuous reworking by eliminating the metaphoric capacity of the play process (Modell, 2003). Is the actual death of the father to be conceptualized as the ultimate way in which representational mobility and motility is "ceilinged" as in Freud's postulation in *Totem and Taboo* (1913)? And what happens if there is overwhelming strife in the parental relationship or *desetayage* as Braunshweig and Fain (1981) have noted? And what of the situation in which semen has been donated, but an actual father has never existed?

In my own theorizing, I have drawn on Spinoza's conception of the developmental and integrative satisfaction deriving from greater regulation. Damasio (2003) has utilized this perspective, applying it to both the neuropsychological and intrapsychic. Implicit in this concept is the existence of dissatisfaction and an aversive quality that accompanies lesser regulation. I have conjectured about the ways in which the father assumes the role of regulator of internal drives while the mother assumes the role of internal regulator of physiological states, together culminating in the internalized patterns by which mother and father together function as co-regulators of evolving and continuously changing self states. Murderous tensions within the psyches of either parent, or between them if unmodulated are, of course, decisive factors in the ways in which evolving or devolving forces predominate in the dynamic structure that the child comes to develop. Such tensions lead to either greater or lesser capacities for regulation and result in recognizable affective vulnerabilities. This is the origin of the term conglomerate as applied to self structure and its development (temporally and idiographically tied to a recent geological expedition to Patagonia by this chapter's author). It is immediately clear that this level of abstraction favors the nomethetic over the idiographic and as such is hardly suitable for clinical analytic work. Here too, in my theorizing, one sees how meaning is built upon patterns of regulation. Biology comes first, serving as the necessary Anlagen, foundation, for what is to become elaborated as psychology.

In thinking on what is perhaps a level of maximal abstraction about the relationship of material experienced and analyzed within an analytic setting, I have pondered the pivotal question of the essential deceitfulness of the dyad. Developmentally, in the absence of triadic reality, the self is continuously impinged upon by the unintegrated pain of the interactive partner, and this asymmetric representation becomes a feature of subsequent development. Is it not completely clear that the transferential and theoretical propensities of the analyst qualify as just such a burden presented by the interactive partner in an analysis? If there are two interactive partners, then the possibility exists that the parentogenic alliance will be able to titrate and even to contain unintegrated pain. Theories of development that emphasize the maternal–infant unit and exclude the father's presence from this equation introduce parricidal effects (directly linked to and arising from unmodulated murderous tensions) and simultaneously deprive the evolving self structure of an essential aspect of its internal mobility, e.g. its playfulness, from the very beginning. It is as if the triad insures both unlimited representational possibility and the necessary structure in which this very unlimitedness can be held and tolerated. It is an historical as well as a pragmatic feature of the analytic situation that it features an asymmetric dyad that favors the emergence of certain patterns of relating, regressing, formulating and finally constructing a coherent narrative. A number of analytic authors included in this volume have struggled, often rather awkwardly, with ways of conceptualizing triadic reality within the analytic space. It is as if the operative term in most analytic nosologies, the ways to make the dyadic triadic, are the most convoluted to conceptualize. I think that our patients teach us a great deal about the ways in which triadic reality is created. They work hard to continue this process in our offices. Murderous feelings toward the father, the stuff of myth and reality, as well as similar feelings toward the mother, are present in all of us, including in psychoanalytic theorists of one school or another, especially when they defend their turf against insidious attacks from proponents of another. Yet both in our patients and in ourselves, an equally prevalent current exists in which the realities of biology are echoed in the aspirations of psychology. Here, even in the presence of murderous impulses, an attempt is made to preserve the components of the conglomerate self, self-with-mother, self-with-father and self-with-mother-and-father-together. It is an endlessly interesting learning experience for each analyst to see how this struggle is waged. This struggle is both pro life and under the tutelage of processes which favor dissolution. Constructing and deconstructing the conglomerate proceeds as long as life does, influenced by external reality, opportunity, loss and setback. Psychoanalytic theory needs to take cognizance of this ongoing process of construction and deconstruction in that it occurs in our offices at all times and in myriad ways. I would also like to suggest that psychoanalytic technique is immeasurably enriched when the father is not banned, when the dyadic becomes triadic, when the analyst has an actual consultant, and when the biological model of triadic reality is approximated in the analytic treatment sphere as well as in efforts to conceptualize the mind at work, while also conceptualizing what facilitates or impedes its ongoing play.

Was du ererbt von deinen Vatern hast, erwirb es um es Zu besitzen.

(Goethe, *Faust*)

References

Braunschweig, D. and Fain, M. (1981) "Bloc-Notes et Lanternes Magiques", in *Revue Française Psychoanalyse* 45: 105–226.

Damasio, A. (2003) *Looking for Spinoza: Joy, Sorrow, and the Feeling Brain*, New York: Harcourt.

Freud, S. (1913) "Totem and Taboo", trans. James Strachey (1955), *Standard Edition*, Volume 13, London: Hogarth Press.

Modell, A. H. (2003) *Imagination and the Meaningful Brain*, Cambridge, MA: MIT Press.

Rilke, R. M. (1938) "Portrait of My Father as a Young Man" [Jugendbildnis Meines Vaters], in *Translations from the Poetry of Rainer Maria Rilke*, trans. M. D. Herter, Norton, New York: W. W. Norton.

Rushdie, S. (1995) *The Moor's Last Sigh*, New York: Pantheon Books (original work published in Great Britain, 1995, by Jonathan Cape, London).

Smiley, J. (1991) *A Thousand Acres*, New York: Ballantine Publishing Group.

Part IV

Father culture

INTRODUCTION
John P. Muller

We see in the vast body of Freud's writing that the primary domain of the "dead Father" is culture, not the individual case history. By this I mean that the reference to the dead Father is not primarily to someone's own dead father, but rather to the mythical Father of the "primal horde," a sort of postlapsarian Adamic figure whose ruthless power holds his women and children for his own enjoyment. In Freud's myth of psychosocial genesis, the primal Father's paradise ends through the disobedience of the sons when they violently revolt, with irreversible social consequences for the group.

In *Totem and Taboo*, after the Father of the primal horde is murdered, the other side of the ambivalence of the sons emerges: "After they had got rid of him, had satisfied their hatred and had put into effect their wish to identify themselves with him, the affection which had all this time been pushed under was bound to make itself felt." How did the affection manifest itself? "It did so in the form of remorse. A sense of guilt made its appearance, which in this instance coincided with the remorse felt by the whole group. The dead father became stronger than the living one had ever been" (Freud, 1913, p. 143). What is at stake here is the socializing function of the dead Father, that which enables individuals to live as members of a group with a shared language, laws, and ideals. Freud shows, according to Lacan, how "this murder is the fertile moment of the debt by which the subject binds himself for life to the Law." The Law structures human desire through its symbolic articulation of constraints, in particular the prohibition against parricide and incest. For this reason Lacan refers to the dead Father as "the symbolic Father," when he states that "the symbolic Father, insofar as he signifies this Law, is truly the dead Father" (2004, p. 189). This point was made earlier in this volume by Green when he quotes Freud in *Moses and Monotheism* on the paternal function: "But this turning from the mother to the father points, in addition, to a victory of intellectuality over sensuality that is an advance in civilization, since maternity is proved by the evidence of the senses while paternity is a hypothesis based on an inference and a premise" (Freud, 1939, p. 114). Knowledge of paternity requires symbolization, symbolizing the father. For thousands of years before the use of DNA testing, paternity was a function of what Lacan called "The Name-of-the-Father," that is, the father as named by the mother, and therefore an object of belief: the father's name was held in mind as an object of belief in the mother's speech.

For Freud and Lacan, therefore, the dead Father is very much alive in anchoring the symbolic order and thereby impacting members of the social group. In this volume, however, others assert that *this* Father is dead in contemporary culture. If *this* Father is dead, we may wonder if Freud and Lacan are dead too – dead in their relevance to our world, dead insofar as their ideas misrepresent the current actuality – dead, that is, in their authority, their verbal authority to speak to us with relevance and truth.

The verbal authority of the symbolic Father is at issue in each of the chapters that follow. In Chapter 9, Tayler succinctly poses the issue of verbal authority for pedagogy as he reviews the relationship between Latin and English in Elizabethan England: "Divided and distinguished linguistic worlds – that of Mother Tongue and that of the Father Tongue". Learning Latin was not simply learning another language, for "to learn Latin is to learn the Father Tongue, constituting a ritual initiation into the tribal lingo of adulthood". The Mother Tongue, we could say, is the language of the unconscious, to be socialized by the language of the Father Tongue, taught with the voice of paternal authority, in whose view "the child . . . lived almost irredeemably inside his id-like center of self-absorption and self-aggrandizement". Tayler shows us how this arduous pedagogy backed up its verbal authority with corporal punishment. But the era of "a manuscript-print culture based on patriarchal order and degree," requiring the knowledge of Latin to navigate legal, religious, and pedagogical frameworks, is over: "The Father is dead, survived only by the Mother Tongue," with one consequence that "our system of secondary education does not exhibit much in the way of order and degree". The death of the Father, the Father Tongue, and the authority of Latin texts is accompanied by the death of the verbal authority of the teacher as well as the authority of language in general. Tayler reports how a lecturer in theology at Georgetown University reacted to student e-mails demanding immediate answers: "It's a real fine balance to accommodate what they need and at the same time maintain a level of legitimacy as an instructor" who is "institutionally authorized to make demands on them". If even the Jesuits are doubting their pedagogical authority, then God save us all!

In Chapter 10, Crapanzano shows us how paternal verbal authority has become congealed in the "frozen discourse" of "the dead but living father" in the families of Harkis, those Algerians residing in France who had been supporters of the French army during the Algerian war for independence. Suffering persecution and discrimination from all sides, these families transmit their trauma through the silence of the fathers or in the rote renditions of their histories. These fathers exhibit a living-dead existence which their children suffer, for "stronger even than the dead father is the *living*-dead father. By the living-dead father I mean more than a symbolic father, a symbolic alive or a symbolic dead father. I refer to a father who experiences himself, and is experienced by his issue, and others around him, as dead but alive, alive but dead". Their frozen discourse is marked by lifeless repetition, unresponsiveness to changes in context, and therefore constraining in its effects on the listener and leading nowhere.

Crapanzano examines the notion of frozen discourse in relation to the Third, conceived as "a regulatory function in any social encounter" and "embodied in authoritative figures like gods, totems, and fathers". He thereby offers a semiotic approach to the familial transmission of trauma: "Here I want to ask how the living-dead/the dead-living father, as a faulted symbolic embodiment of the Third, affects the modes of discourse of his children". By invoking the notion of the Third, Crapanzano provides an important opening by explicitly placing the dead Father in relation to trauma, semiotics, and socialization.

In Chapter 11, Kristeva focuses on the role of the dead Father in Christianity. She re-reads Freud's paper, "A Child is Being Beaten," in a novel manner by elaborating differences between sons and daughters in how they unconsciously deal with desire and prohibition in relation to fathers. She begins by telling us of the killing of her own father in a Bulgarian hospital a few months before the Berlin Wall came down. She then goes on to develop the position that Christianity, in presenting us with the image of the Crucifixion, shows us the murder of the Father, insofar as the Son is identified with the Father, so that the suffering and death of the Son is the death of the Father. She states that this is "the essential nuclear fantasy of Christianity: 'A father is beaten to death' ". And again: "The 'father beaten to death' appears to me to be a logical necessity in the Christian construction of the desiring subject". The image of the suffering and murdered Father is the unconscious pivot around which boys and girls differentially deal with forbidden desires toward the Father. One outcome of these vicissitudes of desire is an enhanced capacity for sublimation through language and thought, "the capacity *infinitely to represent and name*".

In Kristeva's earlier reflections on possible unconscious meanings of the dead Christ (see her chapter, "Holbein's Dead Christ," 1989), she notes "our all-too-human identification with the dead Son" (p. 117). To now assert that the dead Son is the dead Father with whom we identify is a surprising conflation of the Trinity, which, since at least the fourth century, has been an explicit part of the Christian tradition. Pelikan, for example, states: "The climax of the doctrinal development of the early church was the dogma of the Trinity" (1971, p. 172). Kristeva appeals to this tradition when she states that "although Christ is the *Son*, according to Saint Paul, it is as the *Father* that he is put to death". She refers here to Paul's letter to the Ephesians (Chapter 4, verse 9) in a quote, in her words, regarding the "descent of the Father himself, after the Passion, to the deepest recesses of the earth." In the *Oxford Annotated Bible* (the Revised Standard Version) the cited passage in context (verses 7–10) reads: "But grace was given to each of us according to the measure of Christ's gift. Therefore it is said [Paul now paraphrases Psalm 68, verse 18], 'When he ascended on high he led a host of captives, and he gave gifts to men.' (In saying, 'He ascended,' what does it mean but that he had also descended into the lower parts of the earth? He who descended is he who also ascended far above all the heavens, that he might fill all things") (p. 1418). Paul uses "he" here to refer to Christ (the Messiah). The gifts given all aim at "knowledge of the Son of God" (verse 13) and earlier in this passage Paul exhorts the Ephesians "to maintain the unity of the Spirit in the bond of peace. There is one body and one Spirit, just as you were called to the one hope that belongs to your call, one Lord, one faith, one baptism, one God and Father of us all, who is above all and through all and in all" (verses 3–6). The tension in Paul's text is between unity of membership and diversity of gifts, between unity of God and an inchoate Trinity of Father, Son, and Spirit. There is not an identity of Father and Son, and strenuous theological discussion has attempted to clarify the notion of three Persons and one divine substance for more than 1500 years (Rahner, 1997).

When Kristeva writes of the Son that "from the perspective of the Trinity it is not possible that his suffering to death not also be that of the Father", she is (perhaps knowingly) stating the central doctrine of Monarchianism, one of the many currents of thought grappling with the status of Christ as divine and yet also human that roiled the theological waters from the second to the sixth centuries and which tradition eventually saw as unorthodox for "driving out the Paraclete [the Spirit] and crucifying the Father," and, more explicitly: "According to Hippolytus, Noetus reasoned thus: 'I am under necessity, since one [God] is acknowledged, to make this One the subject of suffering. For Christ was God, and suffered on account of us, being himself the Father, that he might be able to save us.' This was, Hippolytus responded, a 'rash and audacious dogma [that] the Father is himself Christ, himself the Son, himself was born, himself suffered, himself raised himself" (Pelikan, 1971, p. 180). Kristeva could perhaps argue that the chief tenet of Monarchianism, the identity of Father and Son, having been over time repressed by orthodoxy, returns in the unconscious fantasy of the killing of the Father, but she does not do so. Such an argument would have to labor over the territory covered by many Patristic scholars, including Pelikan, in which other tenets of belief regarding the Son were also repressed by the eventual orthodox canon; and what of the return of their repressed? In any case, for the past one thousand years or more, when a crucifix is displayed, it is unlikely that a Christian sees the dead Father. The mystery of the Passion for Christians is not the murder of the Father but rather the killing of the Father's Son, somehow in accordance with the "will" of the Father and as vehicle for the gifts of the Spirit. But perhaps what is at issue here is the Father's "issue" (to use Crapanzano's term), the Father's progeny, the murder of the Father's work in the world and thereby the killing of the Father's future relevance by the killing of the Son. This surely must have been the challenge to the faith of believers at the sight of Christ's dead body.

Kristeva judiciously tells us that she is not a believer ("I am an atheist", yet: "Whether we are believers or non-believers, we are all affected by the cultural-religious environment in which we move". She does not clarify what the nature of "belief" might be for those who are "believers," but this is fair enough, since this is not a paper on the nature of belief. She does, however, go on to use the word "belief" when she states that the range of her reflection includes the psychic effects on "believers" of two different kinds of "belief": "belief" in the sense of accepting as "historical" fact Freud's hypothesis of how civilization began through the murder of the mythical Father of the primal horde; and "belief" in the sense of accepting, the way Christians do, of Christ as a genuinely "historical" person whose "murder" they "commemorate" as indeed quite real. The reader will, I hope, see that these are two different kinds of "believing." No one today believes in the existence of Freud's primal Father, but taking it as a founding myth, one can treat Freud's text as offering a paradigm, a model, for thinking about the relation between aggression and guilt, desire and limit. The Christian who believes in the existence of the dead and resurrected Christ is engaged at a wholly different level of his or her existence. Belief in Christ changes how one lives; it includes semiotic indicators of forms of address, it is ritualized in public ceremony and private devotional practice, it joins one to a community of believers anchored in a shared tradition. Belief in Freud's primal Father, if it had such effects, would be considered mad. I am not prepared to declare all believing Christians delusional – many may be, of course, but not because of belief in Christ.

The dead Father in Kristeva's chapter bears on the eclipse of the Third. Not only is the Father–Son distinction collapsed "through the suffering of the Father, incarnate as his Son to be beaten to death", but the resulting "murder of the Father" is presented as experienced unconsciously in a dyadic relation with the subject. Kristeva writes of "our immersion in paternal passion", of how Christianity places "the fantasy of the father beaten to death at the summit of the evangelical narrative, so that it calls out for our identification", and that "it is through the thought and speech I create around the *father beaten to death* that I become this Other's *chosen one*". The dyadic relation to the murdered Father has pervasive effects: "The superman father is humanized, even feminized by the suffering he undergoes; and because of this he is at once my ideal love object and my double, an ideal ego. A complicit 'us' is formed by and in the father's passion. From here on we shall share love, guilt and punishment together. For my unconscious, such a father is not only positioned as an agent of the prohibition and the punishment it entails, but he is also the forbidden love object suffering from prohibition and punishment *like me*". In the context of Trinitarian thought, what has been eclipsed in this narcissistic/imaginary dyadic relation to the beaten Father–Son is the Spirit, the Third to the Father and Son, what in semiotic terms is their interpretant and their mediating relation.

The American philosopher and semiotician Charles Sanders Peirce offers an approach to thinking about the Trinity based on the triadic structure of the sign (Brent, 1993, p. 332). In Peirce's notion of the sign, there are three necessary components: the *sign* with its determined qualities, which is determined at least in part by the *object* it stands for in some respect, and the *interpretant* of the sign, a complex of feelings, actions, and thoughts produced by the sign in the receiver which brings new knowledge of the object of the sign (Muller, 1996). The interpretant is not simply the verbal interpretation of the sign's meaning – the interpretant is lived; we are living interpretants of one another as signs (Muller, 2005). In this framework, the Son is the sign of the Father and stands for the Father in some respect *quoad nos*, in relation to us in time, and is determined by the Father to be the sort of sign the Son is. The Father remains as the object of the sign in His infinite unknowability. The Spirit is the interpretant of the Son as sign of the Father, bringing new knowledge of the Father as object of the Son as sign. The Spirit as interpretant addresses the relation between sign and object, the relation between Son and Father, as their Third, that intermediate space in which human efforts in time elaborate a discourse about what is essentially unrepresentable, for, as Lacan tells us, God is in the Real.

When Kristeva addresses the issue of sublimation, she grapples with the issue of the murder of the sign. What is the status of a dead representation (Tayler and Crapanzano also ask this), what is the function of a murdered sign, what relation might it have to: (1) its object, in this case the Father; and (2) its interpretant, which in this case would be the effort to speak to this relation in an affectively alive manner. From this perspective, Kristeva's consideration of Christianity's effect on art and language as the resurrection of the murdered sign in sublimation is compelling. It is as if the killing of the Son, the murder of the sign, leads to the erasure of the Word-made-flesh, opening a vast nameless abyss that calls out for naming. The murder of the Word-made-flesh leads to the resurrection of this human flesh made word, the translation of bodily states into signs, the resumption of our work in the world. It is here that we may perhaps find the way toward a triadic perspective, here where the creative Spirit "blows where it will."

References

Brent, J. (1993) *Charles Sanders Peirce: A Life*, Bloomington: Indiana University Press.

Freud (1913) "Totem and Taboo", trans. James Strachey (1955), *Standard Edition*, Volume 13, London: Hogarth Press.

—— (1939) "Moses and Monotheism", trans. James Strachey (1964), *Standard Edition*, Volume 23, London: Hogarth Press.

Kristeva, J. (1987) "Holbein's Dead Christ", in J. Kristeva *Black Sun: Depression and Melancholia*, trans. L. Roudiez (1989), New York: Columbia University Press, pp. 105–38.

Lacan, J. (1966) *Ecrits: Selection*, trans. B. Fink (2004), New York: Norton.

Muller, J. (1996) *Beyond the Psychoanalytic Dyad: Developmental Semiotics in Freud, Peirce, and Lacan*, New York: Routledge.

—— (2005) "Approaches to the Semiotics of Thought and Feeling in Bion's Work", *Canadian Journal of Psychoanalysis* 13: 31–56.

Oxford Annotated Bible (Revised Standard Version) H. May and B. Metzger (eds) (1965) New York: Oxford University Press.

Pelikan, J. (1971) *The Christian Tradition: A History of the Development of Doctrine. Vol. 1: The Emergence of the Catholic Tradition (100–600)*, Chicago: University of Chicago Press.

Rahner, K. (1967) *The Trinity*, trans. J. Donceel (1997), New York: Crossroad.

Chapter 9

A little pedagogy, then and now

Edward W. Tayler

As a professor of sixteenth-century poetry, I am an interloper here. It is true that I have, as it happens, a dead father and plan to be one myself in just about a lifetime, but obviously this kind of mundane personal experience, for the moment incomplete, does not qualify me for an august volume on the Dead Father. I have had to settle, as a teacher of language and literature, for a dead tongue (that's t-o-n-g-u-e), a dead-father tongue. Not a dead father, then, but only a father-tongue, though a paternal language about as dead as they come. And, as my title advertises, a little pedagogy, then and now; if I were bold enough to borrow from Robert Frost, my title would be "playing for mortal stakes."

A few of you may remember the voice of the older pedagogy as it sounds in Ben Jonson: "Language most shewes a man: speake that I may see thee. . . . No glasse renders a mans forme, or likenesse, so true as his speech" (Tayler, 1967, p. 123). And as most of you know, Heidegger holds precisely the contrary, namely that it is language that speaks man, "for, strictly, it is the language that speaks" (Heidegger, 1971, p. 216), which may be the voice behind the murmurings of the current pedagogy: according to Lacan the "world of words creates the world of things" (he himself, rather more grandly, likes to think of himself as a "poem that is being written" by language, Lacan, 1977: English Preface) and, according to one of his epigoni, people – including students, though I do not think this particular francophiliac had them in mind – are "rhetorical effects." The linguistic turn of the twentieth century has, then, saved man from Foucauldian obliteration by allowing him to live a little, dolled up in words. To declare my own allegiance (necessarily in words), I quote the poet Robert Frost, who wanted his students, above all else, "to make free, to make free, and outrageous if you want, outrageous connections" (Hewlett, 1964, pp. 177–78). The phrasing puts me in mind, anachronistically perhaps, of Dr Johnson's description of the kind of wit found in the poetry that I study and teach: it consists in the "discovery of occult resemblances in things apparently unlike," the yoking of "heterogeneous ideas . . . by violence together" (Tayler, 1967, p. 420). In brief, the making of outrageous connections!

In the sixteenth and seventeenth centuries the system of education, inaugurated by Erasmus and the leading pedagogues of the time, received its impetus from the new *studia humanitatis* and focused on the trivium of grammar, rhetoric, and logic. The aim of this trivial education, like that of the older rhetorical *paideia*, was to teach speaking, writing, and thinking. It produced not only a Gilbert, a Harvey, a Copernicus, a Galileo, a Newton; in England alone this trivial training also provided the foundation for the literary achievements of Edmund Spenser, John Donne, Ben Jonson, John Milton, and William Shakespeare. It even enabled Jonson, educated at Westminster under William Camden, to condescend to his friend and colleague from Stratford-upon-Avon – as a man of "small *Latine*, and lesse Greeke" (Tayler, 1967, p. 93). Shakespeare has the melancholy Jaques in *As You Like It* describe how the "whining schoolboy with his satchel/And shining morning face" crept "like snail/Unwillingly" to school (2.7, 11–13), first of all to Petty School, where he learned the rudiments of reading, writing, arithmetic – and for the security of the state and the sake of his soul the fundamentals of the Anglican faith. These he learned in what the Protestant Reformers called The Mother Tongue. Upon the occasion of their confirmation, according to the authors of the *Prayer-Book of Queen Elizabeth* (1559), the boys must answer "wyth their owne mouthe, and wyth theyr awne consent . . . what their godfathers and godmothers promised for that in Baptisme." "It is thought good," I am quoting again, "that none hereafter shalbe co[n]firmed but suche as ca[n] saie in their *mother tongue* [my emphasis] the articles of faith, the Lordes praier, and the x Commaundmentes" (as quoted in Baldwin, 1943, p. 218). These catechisms and vows may be viewed, for my purposes here, as a prepubescent ritual of initiation into the Queen's Anglican Church-State, solemnly presided over by *god*parents and ecclesiastical fathers – not by the natural parents. The ritual is conducted, moreover, and conducted expressly and explicitly, not in Latin but in English, which is to say, and with more than metaphorical force, the "mother tongue" of the boy.

At the age of seven the child of ambitious parents advanced from Petty School to Grammar School, where the grammar in question was not English but Latin, as indeed were the readings, the written exercises, and just about everything else (Baldwin, 1944, p. 218). The translator of Montaigne and tutor to the Earl of Southampton, John Florio, tartly observed that English can get you no farther than Dover. Which is only one of the reasons why Roger Ascham, the tutor of Queen Elizabeth, can declare unequivocally in his influential *The Schoolmaster* (1570) that "all men covet to have their children speak Latin" (Ryan, 1967, p. 17). Latin provided access to the international republic of letters, and it could become the means, as well, to material success in Elizabethan letters and life. And even during those transitional years, as England and Europe moved from an oral toward a print culture, Latin retained the aura of magical power that attaches to a language that seems to be the exclusive property of some more privileged segment of society. Jack Cade, the illiterate rebel in the second part of *Henry the Sixth* (4.7, 35–36), knows just so much when he threatens to kill the good Lord Say because he has "most traitorously corrupted the youth of the Realm in erecting a Grammar School." Grammar school not only spelled success; it could even, as was the case with Ben Jonson, allow you to kill your man and yet escape death by hanging, simply by repeating what was called the "neck-verse" in Latin.[1] It was the international language of men of learning that carried with it something almost sacramental from its hieratic associations during the medieval period.

Except on religious holidays the whining schoolboy crept to school at six o'clock in the summer, seven in the winter, six days a week, every week of the year. Mornings in the lower forms were devoted primarily to Latin grammar, the afternoons to classical literature and literary exercises. Denominate and memorize the major tropes and schemes in Cicero's *De Oratore*, translate into English the portion where we learn that true eloquence requires more than rhetorical theory, promptly translate the English back into Latin, and compare with the original; memorize and scrutinize lines from Ovid's *Metamorphoses*, turn them into English prose, thence back into Latin verse, compare with the originals, anatomize the rhetorical schemes, the poetical tropes (Baldwin, 1944, p. 318). From eleven o'clock to one o'clock, however, the schoolboy had plenty of time to eat lunch, con his lessons, and play – king of the grammar mountain, for example: the historian Stow records in 1598 that the "arguing of Schoole boyes about the principles of Grammer, hath been continued even till our time: for I my selfe [have] seene . . . schollers of divers Grammer schooles repayre . . . upon a banke boorded about under a tree, some one Scholler stepped up, and there hath apposed and answered, till he were by some better scholler overcome and put downe." Playing may be for mortal stakes: as Montaigne observes, Alexander played chess as though it were for the world: "and so," adds Stow, "proceeding from this to questions in Grammar, they usually fall from words to blowes, with their Satchels full of bookes many times in great heaps that they troubled the streets and passengers" (as quoted in Clark, 1948, pp. 48–49). But then, at one o'clock, it was back to grammar school – conjugating, scanning, declining, conning – until five or five-thirty in the afternoon. Six days a week, all year long, learning and playing and living Latinity. To misappropriate the words of Sir Thomas Browne, the Elizabethan schoolboy is that "true *Amphibium*, whose nature is disposed to live, not onely like other creatures [in their own element], but in divided and distinguished [linguistic] worlds" (see Martin, 1964, p. 33).

In this patriarchal culture, governed by absolute monarchs and imperious aristocrats, schoolboys did not pine away from lack of good advice from tyrannical fathers, despotic guardians, authoritarian ecclesiastics, and homiletic authors. This from the popular *Youths Behaviour*:

> During the time that thou shoud'st study . . ., it is not fit to make a noise,
> or read so loud that thou be'st understood by others that study. . . .
> Hearing thy Master, or likewise the Preacher; wriggle not thy selfe, as
> seeming unable to containe thy selfe within thy skinne, making shew to be
> the knowing, and sufficient, to the misprice of others.
>
> (as quoted in Clark, 1948, p. 51)

Contain thyself within thy skin. Always good advice. Boys all over England
worked out of William Lily's Latin grammar, to which was appended Lily's
rules of manners and morals, here quoted in the translation of William Haine
(the little boys got their advice in Latin):

> Little youth who art my scholar, and desirest to be taught, come hither,
> conceive well these sayings in thy mind. . . . When thou shalt see me, thy
> master, salute me, and all thy school-fellows in order. And see that thou
> sit where I will [have] thee to sit and stay in thy place, unless thou beest
> commanded to go thence. And as every one is more excellent in the gift
> of learning, so he shall sit in a more excellent place.
>
> (as quoted in Clark, 1948, pp. 51–52)

The pupil must salute the master, then his fellows, but not at random, rather
"in order" and in degree, just as the "more excellent" scholar shall occupy the
"more excellent place."

Shakespeare glosses this schoolroom microcosm of the Elizabethan layer-
cake world in Ulysses' famous speech on order and degree in *Troilus and
Cressida*: "Take but degree away, untune that string, / And look what
discord follows." "Strength should be lord of imbecility, / And the rude
son should strike the father dead." "How could communities, / Degrees in
schools, and brotherhoods in cities . . ., [?] But by degree, stand in authen-
tic place" (1.3, 103–09)? Indeed, only by degree and place. "All men covet
to have their children speak Latin," and all men covet to have their children learn order and degree along with the Latin (the Elizabethans spoke
much of order much as modern academics of power – they didn't have
much).

Here's William Lily again: "Sometimes Virgil wisheth to embrace thee,
sometimes Terence himself, sometimes withal the work of Cicero wisheth
thee." The phrasing implies an endearing, indeed intimate, relationship
with the dead who yet live to "wish," "embrace," and talk to thee, my
child (as quoted in Clark, 1948, p. 53). Just so Montaigne, taught Latin as his
first language by a tutor because his father "coveted" to have his child "speak
Latin" even before grammar school; there is Montaigne in his Tower, reading
his Seneca and Vergil for pleasure and instruction, precisely as Horace would
have wished. There is Machiavelli, dressed in formal robes for the evening,
sitting down, so he imagined, to converse with Tacitus, Livy, and Lucan.

Divided and distinguished linguistic worlds – that of The Mother Tongue and that of The Father Tongue.

Although Virgil wisheth to embrace the young scholar, the Protestant Reformers knew from Augustine, as well as from Scripture, that Rousseau and Wordsworth would prove to be utterly mistaken in their view of childhood innocence. Significantly enough, Ascham opens his treatise with an account of how disturbed William Cecil, then Elizabeth's chief secretary and known for his "discretion" and learning, was on hearing that "divers scholars of Eton, be run away from the school for fear of beating" (Ryan, 1967, p. 6). But despite the Cecils and the Aschams, the barbaric practices of caning and flogging persisted into the twentieth century. The child, the Reformers knew for sure, lived almost irredeemably inside his id-like center of self-absorption and self-aggrandizement, quite incapable of employing what Sir Philip Sidney called "our erected wit" to govern "our infected will," to say nothing of the raging appetites (then a term of psychological art) of adolescence. The end, then, of learning, concludes Milton in his tractate *Of Education*, "is to repair the ruines of our first Parents by regaining to know God aright" (Patterson, 1931, 4.277). In brief, education must do what it can to mitigate the effects of the Fall (the early meaning of "ruin") from the Garden of Eden. John Dewey need not apply.

Scripture witnesses that "Foolishness is tied in the heart of a child, but the rod of discipline shall drive it away," and that "the rod and correction give wisedome, but the child set at libertie maketh his mother ashamed." Of the influential educator Richard Mulcaster, High Master of St. Paul's School from 1596–1608, Thomas Fuller writes:

> *Atropos* might be persuaded to pity, as soon as he to pardon, where he found just fault. The prayers of cockering Mothers prevailed with him as much as the requests of indulgent Fathers . . ., though it may truly be said (and safely for one out of his school) that others have taught as much learning with fewer lashes.
>
> (as quoted in Clark, 1948, p. 61)

As Fuller's parenthetical comment "(and safely for one out of his school)" implies, Mulcaster was, as High Master, the ultimate authority in his domain. Dr Alexander Gil the Elder, who succeeded Mulcaster, was a "very ingeniose person," though not without "moodes and humours, as particularly his whipping fits." He had flogged, among countless others, a boy named Duncombe, who later became a colonel of dragoons and fought like the man he was at Edgehill. Returning to his old school he had imprudently (if he was indeed the culprit) "throwen a stone in the window." The schoolboys (and I must take this to be crucially important) promptly sallied out – their loyalty to the flogger and not to the victim – and the colonel was "taken pissing against the wall." "He had," according to Aubrey (John Aubrey, seventeenth-century gossip columnist), "his sword by his side, but the boyes surprized him." Duncombe, Aubrey adds, "would have cutt the doctor, but he never went abroad but to church, and then his army [the schoolboys, referred to as "little myrmidons"] went with him. [Duncombe] complained to the councill, but it became ridicule, and so his revenge sank." Aubrey also tells us that the estimable Dr Triplet returned to pay his humble respects to Dr Gill – and Aubrey provides this laconic summary: "Dr. Triplet came to give his Master a Visit, and He whip't him" (Dick, 1957, p. 298). Amusing anecdotes, sadistic practices.

This was the grammar school – St Paul's and Stratford-upon-Avon – that educated John Milton and William Shakespeare. Many years later Milton complains in *Areopagitica* that it does not profit to come to manhood "over it is to be a boy at school, if we have only scapt the ferular, to come under the fescu of an *Imprimatur*" (Patterson, 1931, 4.324). A pretty piece of sarcasm fully appreciable only by adult males, for we have Aubrey to witness that Milton's first wife "oftimes heard his Nephews beaten and cry" (Dick, 1957, p. 201) as their uncle-poet-teacher used the ferular to help them grasp the principles of true Latinity. The world of the child conserves such cultural memories as these in dateless rhyme: "Readin' and writin' and 'rithmetic/ Taught to the tune of the hick'ry stick." Ben Jonson sums up the situation in his "Conversations" with William Drummond when, in castigating an amateur poet and professional headmaster of Warwick, Jonson expresses his contempt for the "pure Pedantique Schoolmaster sweeping his living from the Posteriors of little children" (Tayler, 1967, p. 87).

The ritual pattern seems obvious enough. Going to grammar school does not separate the literate from the illiterate; many men and rather more women than some of you might surmise were superbly eloquent and literate in The Mother Tongue. Rather, grammar school separates the girls from the boys, and then makes men of the boys. It is what Father Walter J. Ong, S.J., has called a puberty rite (Ong, 1959, pp. 103–24; see also Kerrigan, 1980, pp. 261–308, for a more thorough, learned, and Lacanian view). Ong means, presumably, that to learn Latin is to learn The Father Tongue, constituting a ritual initiation into the tribal lingo of adulthood. The boy, segregated from females and placed in the hands, not of a teacher but a school*master*, must undergo trials, must endure exacting ordeals, must surmount difficult tasks, must experience pain (though not, usually, mutilation), and must come to identify (those loyal, "little myrmidons") with his taskmasters. In Shakespeare's day, as in Milton's, Latin is being spoken by thousands upon thousands, and had been spoken by many more thousands over a period of well over a thousand years – but it is being spoken, magically if you will, only by those who can write and read it. Learning Latin is not just picking up a language, it is learning The Father Tongue: it is becoming a man in a manuscript-print culture based on patriarchal order and degree.

Unlike those early grammar schools, our own secondary education does not, needless to say, require mastery of The Father Tongue. The Father Tongue is dead, survived only by The Mother Tongue, breathing her last gasp in courses of expository composition. This does not mean that the Father, actual or symbolic, is dead, though it may well prove to be the demise of the schoolmaster; for in those days, to state the necessary tautology, the school-master was the schoolmaster – not the father, not the buddy, not the comrade, not the bunkie, not a person whom you "hang out with" – but the school-master. And, again it is needless to say, our system of secondary education does not exhibit much in the way of order and degree. In addition to the well-documented American antipathy to intellectuals and their "pointy-headed" intellectualism, there are the zephyrs of egalitarianism that periodically waft through the halls of academe, as when, only a few years back, a group of newly elected PhiBetes realized only in the nick of time that it would be elitist – therefore objectionable and unjustifiable – to accept the PhiBetaKappa keys they had just been awarded. And those pesky headlines always seem to be everywhere: *The New York Times* (2006, March 29), "America's Techno-logical Future at Risk," and "Teaching at Risk," *The Teaching Commission*, headed by Louis Gerstner, Jr. A slightly earlier op.ed. piece in *The New York Times* (2005, September 6) points out that "American taxpayers," as the writer quaintly refers to parents, have been hearing for years that "their children lag behind the children of Britain, France, Germany, and Japan." To this familiar list, to which presumably we have become inured, the writer breathlessly adds: "Poland, Ireland, and the Czech Republic." Also in *The Times*, even more recently, the reporter Jonathan D. Glater quotes Michael Kessler, an assistant dean and lecturer in theology at Georgetown, who querulously complains of importunate e-mails from students that say, "I want to know this and you need to tell me right now." Kessler adds, with more tolerance than we would be likely to expect from those great unflagging floggers, the redoubtable Mulcaster or the indefatigable Gil – poor Kessler adds that, "It's a real fine balance to accommodate what they need and at the same time maintain a level of legitimacy as an instructor[,] someone who is institutionally authorized to make demands on them, and not the other way around." Indeed.

I myself could glimpse all this coming when I was a graduate student and instructor of writing at Stanford University in the mid- to late 1950s. Several of my fellow teaching assistants made a self-conscious effort to "democra-tize," so the jargon went, "the writing process," which in this case meant teaching the students on what was referred to as A First-Name Basis, a pedagogical strategy unheard of at the time, at least by me. My Stanford colleagues, you see, wanted to be comrades, friends, buddies, with their stu-dents: uncomfortable with the role of schoolmaster (there were notable exceptions, of course), they wanted to be pals with their students, which puts me in mind again, if you will excuse the transition, of Robert Frost. Frost, during the course of an informal poetry reading (*Amherst Alumni News*,

Fall 1962), found himself rambling on about his days as a teacher, opining "that love and need are one," that "they must be one, in marriage or in teaching. . . . And the thing," he added, "must be for mortal stakes, you know." My Stanford colleagues, the ones alluded to earlier, did not know. Language speaks TAs, not all of them to be sure; and the ones being spoken perhaps naturally want to speak to their "rhetorical effects" on a first-name basis. Frost went on to say, and I to repeat, that as a teacher he tried to get the students "to make free, to make free, and outrageous if you want, outrageous connections." He then, in one of his habitual advertisements for himself, luckily happened to recall an occasion on which he himself had managed to come up with just such a brilliant and "outrageous connection." "It was right here in Amherst," he remembered complacently, "that I introduced my friend Carl Sandburg once. I was on the platform with him, and all I said was that, of course, Carl wrote free verse; and as for me, for me I said very particularly, just for me, I said, I'd as soon write free verse as play tennis with the net down." That's the "kind of thing that's always made me happy," Frost reported, with what may strike you as unseemly glee, "when I had a connection like that. And that's what I want [the students] to have. . . . And that," he adds, "means the most subversive thing in the world it could be; you don't know where it might land you, you know. It bothers Carl still, and," continues Frost, his sense of mischief verging on malice, "Carl wrote an essay to prove that you could play better tennis with the net down. And the *Atlantic Monthly* printed it. Our relations have never been the same," Frost concluded, with what must have sounded like mock sadness (Hewlett, 1964, pp. 176–78).

The pedagogy hasn't been the same either, for at least one of the same reasons: you can't play for mortal stakes with the net down. The devolution of the paternal function, the change in the representation of the Father that I have sought to describe, has brought the net down in the classroom too. That softened boundary between student and teacher complicates the pedagogical task on both sides, devaluing education itself. As Anzieu-Premmereur shows earlier (Chapter 6), maintaining the frame of psychoanalysis allows the analyst to function as the third, as the Father in the treatment. (See also Green, Chapter 1.) Holding the Father's place is essential to the development of both language and thought. With the net down in an educational setting, with no place held for the Professor/Father, both language and thought are, in important ways, sacrificed.

Note

1 On September 22, 1598, two days after the premier of his second surviving full-length play, *Every Man in His Humour*, Jonson was imprisoned at Newgate for the killing of Gabriel Spenser, a 22-year-old actor with whom he had previously collaborated. (Their respective roles as contributing writer and lead actor in the

controversial work *Isle of Dogs*, whose scandalous content was objectionable to both the Queen and her Privy Council, caused the two men to be imprisoned together for a period of nearly two months starting in August of 1597.) The nature of the altercation, at this point, is hard to determine, as is the role each played in the incident. In his later accounts of the experience, Jonson insisted that Spenser had challenged him to a duel and had been the first to strike – with a sword that was ten inches longer than his own, no less – thereby injuring him in the arm. At that point, Jonson struck back, inflicting a mortal wound on Spenser's right side, causing him to die on the spot. The jury's assessment of the situation, however, characterized Jonson as the aggressor, finding that he had "made an assault with force and arms against" Spenser, and that he "feloniously struck and beat" him, noting that the fatal wound was one inch wide and six inches deep. (In retrospect, both accounts are plausible; neither man was a stranger to violent outbursts, and each had previously killed a man over similarly trivial altercations.) On October 6, Jonson was arraigned, confessed, and was convicted of manslaughter. Knowing that he was, in his own words, "almost at the Gallowes," he pleaded "benefit of clergy," an archaic custom originally designed to ensure that any clergyman accused of a crime had the right to be heard in the bishop's court. Dating from the early Middle Ages, a time when literacy rates were astonishingly low outside the clergy, it was little more than a legal loophole in Jonson's time; under the plea, any first offender who could translate on sight a passage from the Latin Bible was entitled to have the charges against him dropped. Johnson translated the so-called "neck verse" (Psalm 51), and, as such, was saved from hanging. As an alternative punishment, the court confiscated all that Jonson owned, including property, and branded him at the base of the thumb with the letter T, for Tyburn, the site where he would have been hanged. The brand served to identify him as a felon for future cases; no man was permitted to plead benefit of clergy more than once in his life (Riggs, D. [1989] *Ben Jonson: A Life*, Cambridge, MA: Harvard University Press).

References

Baldwin, T. W. (1943) *William Shakspere's Petty School*, Urbana, IL: University of Illinois Press.

—— (1944) *William Shakspere's Small Latine and Lesse Greeke* (2 vols), Urbana, IL: University of Illinois Press.

Browne, T. [Sir] (1964) *Religio Medici and Other Works*, L. C. Martin (ed.), Oxford: Clarendon Press.

Clark, D. L. (1948) *John Milton at St. Paul's School*, New York: Columbia University Press.

Dick, O. L. (ed.) (1957) *Aubrey's Brief Lives*, Ann Arbor, MI: University of Michigan Press.

Heidegger, M. (1971) *Poetry, Language, Thought*, trans. Albert Hofstadter, New York: Perennial/Harper and Row.

Hewlett, H. (ed.) (1964) *In Other Words*, Amherst, MA: Amherst College Press.

Kerrigan, W. W. (1980) "The Articulation of the Ego in the English Renaissance", in J. Smith (ed.) *The Literary Freud*, New Haven: Yale University Press.

Lacan, J. (1977) *Four Fundamental Concepts of Psychoanalysis*, J.-A. Miller (ed.), trans. Alan Sheridan, New York: Norton.

Ong, W. J. (1959) "Latin Language Study as a Renaissance Puberty Rite", *Studies in Philology* 56: 103–24.

Patterson, F. A. (ed.) (1931) *The Works of John Milton*, Vol. 4, New York: Columbia University Press.

Ryan, L. V. (ed.) (1967) *The Schoolmaster* (1570) by Roger Ascham, Ithaca, NY: Cornell University Press.

Tayler, E. W. (ed.) (1967) *Literary Criticism of Seventeenth-Century England*, New York: Alfred A. Knopf.

Chapter 10

The dead but living father, the living but dead father

Vincent Crapanzano

My theme is frozen discourse, what the French would call *discours figé*, and the dead but living father. By frozen discourse I mean a discourse that is repetitive, though not obsessively or compulsively so, insistent, constricting, and lifeless, though it may be injected with emotion which stems, however, less from its referents in their immediacy than as a reaction to its stale recitation. Though incited by the particular context in which it occurs, it is not responsive, certainly not creatively responsive, to that context. It so frames its subject matter, indeed the speakers and their interlocutors and their diegetic – in-text – counterparts such that there is little room for escape from the picture it draws, the story it tells, and the way it constructs speakers and interlocutors.[1] Turned in on itself, on its reproduction, frozen discourse seems to lead nowhere. It is, I am sure, familiar both in your practice and everyday life.

I will also be concerned with the passage of a wound – I prefer not to use the word trauma since it is so encrusted with banality – that passes from generation to generation; with the rhetoric, the protective rhetoric, of pain; with bearing witness to that which strictly speaking has never been witnessed; with absence; and with the melancholy that arises from failed or faulted communication. Haunting my thinking is the presence, the absence, of a dead father as somehow responsible for the phenomena I am considering. I do not wish, however, to reduce responsibility for these phenomena to a dead father, such causal reduction would itself be deadening. The dead fathers I am considering are not, however, dead, or at least the effects of their death long preceded their actual demise. I would like to change Freud's famous epigraph: "the dead father became stronger than the living one had been." I would like instead to say, at least with reference to my subjects, that stronger even than the dead father is the *living*-dead father. By the living-dead father I mean more than a symbolic father, a symbolic alive or a symbolic dead father. I refer to a father who experiences himself, and is experienced by his issue, and others around him, as dead but alive, alive but dead.

The subjects of my talk are the Harkis – those Algerians, numbering around 250,000, who sided with the French during the Algerian War of Independence, which lasted from 1954 to 1962.[2] Strictly speaking "Harki" (from the Arabic for movement, military movement) refers to those Algerian civilians of Arab or Berber descent who served as auxiliary troops for the French, but the term is often used loosely for any Algerians who served with the French military or police forces. The Harkis have been called history's forgotten; for, until recently, they have been ignored by both scholars and the press and have lived, for the most part, in abject silence. Although some of the Harkis sided with the French because they believed that Algeria would be better off under them than independent or because they and their fathers had served in the French army, most of them, poor, illiterate peasants, did so to survive in a war-torn, impoverished country. Many had suffered at the hands of the FLN, the militant and often brutal Front de Libération Nationale, which led Algeria to independence.

Despite warnings of likely bloodshed from French officers who had fought alongside the Harkis, de Gaulle's government ordered their demobilization after the signing of the Treaty of Evian on March 18, 1962, and sent them, unarmed, back to their villages. In the ensuing months, between 70,000 and 150,000 Harkis were tortured, mutilated, and killed by the Algerian population at large.[3] I myself heard stories of Harkis whose throats were cut in front of their wives and children, and there have been reports of others who were impaled, roasted live, or even forced to eat chunks of their own flesh. One man I interviewed was thrown, after being tortured, into a dry well where he was kept for eleven months, fed couscous mixed with sand and blood when he was fed at all.[4] He was never given a change of clothing nor was the well cleaned and his excrement removed.

Overwhelmed by the arrival in 1962 of more than a million *pieds-noirs*, or Algerians of European origin, de Gaulle's government did almost nothing to halt the bloodbath. As little sympathy as the General had for the *pieds-noirs*, he had even less for the Algerians themselves. Almost 50,000 Harkis did manage, however, to escape to France by the end of September, 1962. By 1967 another 60,000 had arrived.

Once in France most Harkis were incarcerated in camps, like Rivesaltes near Perpignan, forced to live in miserable conditions, subjected to abusive discipline and constant humiliation, and offered, if any, the lowliest of jobs. Fourteen thousand families were eventually moved to remote forestry villages where they worked on an enormous reforestration project. Those who could find work outside the camps and villages left as soon as they could. Many of those who remained, some for more than 16 years, until the last of the camps were closed in 1978, suffered the pathologies associated with abjection: identity loss, depression, bouts of violence, suicide, and, among the men, alcoholism. The women lived in a sort of double purdah: that imposed by tradition and that stemming from the fear of venturing out into a "threatening" world they could not understand. Children not only suffered discrimination at school but lived under their father's silent and often violent regime. They understood neither why they were treated as they were, nor did their fathers (or mothers) tell them what they had gone through. But, despite their parents' silence, the children came to know, if only by indirection, the Harkis' story and experienced, at a step removed, their parents' confusion and ambivalence. Educated, they became their parents' cultural brokers.

Today, though there are still concentrations of Harkis in the south of France and in the industrial north, Harki families are scattered across France. They, and to a lesser extent their children and grandchildren, have remained a population *à part*. Condemned as traitors by the Algerians, abandoned by the French, anxious not to be identified with Algerian immigrant workers, who reject them in any case, they have lost their bearings, their country, but not their dignity and pride. Those who escaped found themselves in a country where they were treated as half-citizens (though they have the rights of any French citizen), mistrusted, marginalized, and often subject to virulent racism. They did not speak up; they did not write. For the most part they lost themselves in their despair. The Harki writer Zahia Rahmani (2003, p. 20) refers to them as "*soldatsmorts.*" Yet, their children have assumed the wounds they suffered and articulate their identity in terms of those wounds. They share, if vicariously and not without ambivalence and regret, their parents' sense of having been betrayed, abandoned, and humiliated. Unlike most of their parents, many have taken an activist stance, forming political associations, lobbying for the recognition of the sacrifices their parents made for France, and demanding compensation for the losses their parents sustained and the pain and isolation they themselves suffered in the camps. In the last few years, they have begun publishing life histories, family memoirs, novels, and histories, all of which express their ambivalent loyalty to France.

I will focus this chapter on the children of the Harkis – specifically those children, both men and women, now in their forties, who spent their childhoods in the camps and forestry villages. They are sometimes called "the hinge generation." With rare exceptions, they all stress with very considerable emotion their fathers' silence about their war experiences. They cast their fathers as victims, broken men, devalued, dishonored, emasculated, lost in themselves. They remember them sitting alone or in groups, leaning against a tree or wall, ruminating. Some speak of their fathers' depression, their drinking, their drunken rages, which were often directed against them and their mothers. They were often beaten. Rarely did they want me to meet their fathers. "They won't talk to you," they said. "They didn't talk to us. They're old. Why bother them? Why bring up a painful past." Those who did introduce me to their parents tended to be very protective. They would urge their fathers to repeat what seemed to me to be set narratives: fragmentary reminiscences with little narrative elaboration and even less introspection. Seldom did they say "I remember" and go on to recount something that had happened to them in particular. Like other Harkis I met, they tended to dwell less on what they had experienced in Algeria and more on their abandonment by the French and their incarceration in the camps. It was as though they expected less from the Algerians than from the French. What they wanted from the French was recognition and compensation. What they wanted even more, though they admitted, cynically, that it would never happen, was an apology from the French. Still they expressed their loyalty to France. Those who had them proudly showed me the citations and medals they had been awarded.

When I asked Harki fathers about why they did not want to talk about the past or why they had not talked to their children about it, they almost invariably said, "Why bother? The past is the past. It was written." (By "written" they meant it was in God's hands.) And then they would add, protectively, "Why should we burden our children with what we went through?" At such moments, they spoke to me as an older man, a father, who would understand. Otherwise, I was immediately cast, as I was by the children, as someone who would reveal to a larger public what they had undergone. They were serving as witnesses.

Like their fathers' deadened and deadening stories, the children of the Harkis were also consumed by their narratives, but unlike their fathers' narratives, theirs were not all-consuming. Though at some level they infused their daily lives, they were a story apart. It was a monologue that once triggered was oblivious to contextual convention and constraint. A young Harki was stopped by the police for drunken driving. He refused to take a breath-test and locked himself in his car. When the police finally forced him out of the car, he started fighting with them, claiming they had no respect for the Harkis and went on – at least he tried to go on – to tell them how his grandfather, who was rotting away in a former forestry hamlet, had sacrificed himself for France. Another was refused a subsidized apartment, which was then given to an immigrant worker. He told me and a friend of his, a *pied-noir*, who supported the Harki cause, that he had been refused the apartment because he was a Harki and went on to tell us, that is until we stopped him, how the Harki had been betrayed by the French. His story, a set recitation, had little to do with his complaint. In fact, we discovered, when he had calmed down, that he had been refused the apartment because he and his wife's earnings exceeded the limit for subsidy. Such occasions aside, Harki children, at least the activists and those they recruit, tell their stories to one another at private gatherings, political protests, and commemorations.

In my experience, there is a marked difference between the narratives told by men and women of the children's generation. Both express outrage. Both keen their mistreatment, how they have been dishonored, how they have suffered from racial prejudice, how the government has done little for them, how the government has done more for immigrant laborers from North Africa, how the French would prefer if they disappeared. "We are their bad conscience," they like to say, not without a show of contorted pride. Almost always, sometime in the interviews, they assert their loyalty to France. For the most part they vote for the right, but not the extreme, right. At least in the

South they dissociate themselves from Islamists. Most of them are only nom-inally Muslim, though their aged fathers now spend much of their time at the local mosques if there should happen to be any nearby.

For the most part, the men's stories are less personal, less developed, less emotional, more fragmentary, legalistic, and political than those of the women. They are centered on the Harki cause. The men take pleasure in their bureaucratic manipulations and political machinations: each success is a conquest. They spoke to me in monotones, soberly, avoiding painful memor-ies. When they did speak of such memories, they did not center them on their families, on the shame of their fathers, as much as they did on life in the camps, schools, and reformatories. They spoke of being seated apart at school, of arbitrary punishments, and of being beaten by their teachers. In a way they were emulating their father's style, but coupled with French discre-tion. At least among the more educated, they punctuated their observations with summary moral conclusions so cultivated in French schools. With the exception of those few who had had psychotherapy, they were not particularly introspective. When some event (less often my probing) drew them out of themselves – out of their frozen discourse – they experienced so deep a wound, so intense an emotional outbreak that they seemed on the verge of losing control.

Belkacem, a builder in his late forties, an activist, took me to the abandoned forestry hamlet in the Montagnes Noires, north of Carcassone, where, along with his mother and sisters, he had spent his childhood. About 25 kilometers from the nearest village, with a population of a couple hundred, it was certainly the most isolated place I had ever been in France. "When they sent us here, they claimed it was to integrate us into French society," Belkacem told me bitterly as we approached the hamlet. It consisted of stone huts that reminded me of pigsties above which stood a robin's egg blue blockhouse where the commandant and his wife had lived. They were notorious for their abusive discipline and their robbing the Harkis of the pittance they earned. "It's now the commandant's hunting lodge," Belkacem observed cynically. "When they shut down the camp, he was able to buy it was for 6000 francs."

With the exception of a couple of German hippie squatters, the village was deserted. Shaking his head sadly, Belkacem looked at the abandoned cars and the stacks of old tires that lay at the entrance to the hamlet. With tears in his eyes, he showed me the hut where he had lived, the school he attended, the one well, the field where he had played soccer. "I make this trip twice a year," he told me at lunch. "It is my memory, my pain." He explained that his mother had been sent to the forestry camp, where she and her children had nothing to do, as a punishment because, as she spoke French, she had interceded on behalf of other Harkis at the camp where they had first been sent. It was the most infamous of the camps – for the infirm, the insane, alcoholics, and widows. Belkacem told me how, after Independence, the FLN had slit his father's throat in front of his mother. Without ever saying that he had also seen his father's throat slit – he would have been three or four at the time – he said he could never forget it.

In the car, on the long drive back, Belkacem, who had been drinking heavily at lunch, sat silently, ruminating. Finally, he said, "Were it not for my mother, I would kill myself. She is a strong woman who says we always have to look ahead. I can't do that to her. But she is old. I don't know what I'd do." He stopped himself. Later, after receiving a business call on his cell phone, he told me about a protest he was helping to organize and, forgetting that he had already told me about them, he went on to tell me about other protests he had been in.

Women – the activists – tend to express themselves personally, in terms of their own experiences and those of their parents (insofar as they know them). Many are quite independent, several are leaders of Harki associations, and most are only nominally Muslim. Many have feminist leanings, though they are generally subservient to their husbands and at times their sons. They stress the importance of their children's education. Though the majority appear to be married to Harkis, some are married to French or other North Africans. One woman who had been so badly abused by her husband that she fled and managed to raise her three daughters on her own, told me proudly that all three had married or were living with European men.

The women with whom I spoke showed far more interest in what happened to their parents than did the men. For them their particular stories are exemplary. It is noteworthy that the novels and memoirs written by Harki women generally take the form of a quest: to learn their father's story.[5] Though they are as capable as the men in describing how the Harkis as a group have been wronged, they tend to respond to their mistreatment as a personal effrontery. With rare exceptions they cried at some point in my interviews. Though I do not want to minimize their pain, I sometimes felt that their tears were generated less from immediate memory than mediated by their discourse, its rhetoric. Several of the women I interviewed seemed to use their stories as a way to generate emotions and were occasionally carried away by them.

Celestine Rolland was one of these. An activist and feminist in her late forties, she is passionately articulate. Born in Algeria, she and her family came to France in 1967 when she was nine and were billeted in a Harki camp near Aix-en-Province. Unlike Harki children, Celestine attended the lycée, and passed her baccalaureate. Today she is married to a former foreign legionnaire, a quiet man, who is proud of her activism.

Celestine took an immediate interest in my research. Our first interview lasted more than four hours. I asked few questions. Celestine spent the first 20 minutes describing how she came to have a French name. Her mother, an orphan, was raised by her paternal uncle and aunt, who married her off to an older man when she was 13. At the age of 14, she had a daughter, Celestine. "My mother did not want to stay with him," Celestine explained, "because she was traumatized. She told me that for days she lay on the floor weeping. Though she had lived in misery at her aunt's house, she wanted to be with her family. She told her husband, 'I want to be with my relatives or I'll kill myself.' He was not an abusive man; he never beat her. He gave her her freedom." He must have been an exceptional man, for, though by Muslim law he had the right to keep the baby, he let her keep Celestine. Two months later, Celestine's mother was married again, this time to an older cousin, who drank and beat her. It is this man Celestine calls father. He had been a Harki courier, not a fighter or torturer. After Independence, he was arrested by the Algerians, tortured, and imprisoned for five years until the International Red Cross managed to get him released and sent him and his family to France. Celestine stressed her mother's suffering. She had also been a courier and was continually insulted during the years of her husband's incarceration. "People would spit at her," Celestine said angrily.

When Celestine was 16, she was informed that her papers were not in order and that if they were not regulated within six weeks she would be deported. She was terrified. "Where will they send me?" she asked the gendarme who had brought the order.

"To Algeria," he said.

"But where in Algeria? It's a big place. I have no family there.

"That's not my affair," he said.

Celestine was virtually reenacting the occasion. And then, dramatically, she switched emotional registers as she went on mechanically to describe in excessive detail the bureaucratic entanglement she found herself in. It turned out that when her stepfather came to France, he neglected to include her among his children. Thus, as she bore the name of her real father, she had no legal status as a Harki child. She cried as she told me this. She was panicked; her family was panicked. "The arrival of gendarmes always terrifies us." Finally a camp administrator and his wife intervened and arranged for her naturalization. ("I thought I was already French but they had to make me French again – what I was to begin with.") As the administrator prepared the papers, he told Celestine that she could change her name if she wanted to. "It hurt me not to have the same name as my brothers and sisters. You are nothing. You are not configured. You are not part of the family. You have no bonds (attaches). A little girl, you don't know who you are." Celestine was despairing and quickly changed the direction of her story, announcing that she didn't know who had paid for her naturalization.

Calm again, Celestine went on: "I revolted. Why me? I should have the same name as my father. I suffered enormously from the difference. My 'father' had made it clear from the time I was two or three that he didn't want me to call him father. Still I wanted to be accepted, to be treated as a family. . . . I said yes. I'll change my name. . . . I'll change my name because I'm no one's daughter. I want to be some one." Celestine took the most French name she could think of. "After all, I'm in France; it's my land (*terre*)." I could sense her anguished, embarrassed ambivalence. Though a Harki activist, she had chosen a French name.

It was at this point that Celestine told me about her "father's" imprisonment. She didn't tell me how she knew, but I imagine she had learned it from her mother; for at other times she said her father didn't like to talk about the past. She then complained that no one paid attention to the suffering of Harki wives and daughters, and, then with relief, she launched into the prêt-à-porter Harki story I had heard so often. It struck me that this fixed tale protected Celestine from the feelings her own story had evoked by displacing the particular with the general. Her rage became outrage. As an activist, she could act on the outrage – in protests. Several hours later, as the interview was coming to an end, she gave me a highly emotional blow-by-blow account of a recent protest in the Senate, which concluded with her calling to the other Harkis there to join hands and sing the *Marseillaise* as they were forced out of the Senate by the Garde Nationale.

I don't want to reduce Celestine's pain or Belkacem's or that of any other Harki, to mere rhetoric, though, as I have argued elsewhere, pain is perhaps our strongest indexical, for it unquestionably determines the context in which it occurs or evokes as painful and thereby prescribes a certain etiquette – in everyday life and in therapy (Crapanzano, 1992, pp. 229–38). Certainly the Harkis use their pain to elicit sympathy but this pain serves also as a ground for political action, dramatically in protests. While such protests may serve to alleviate some of the pain, converting, as I have suggested, rage into outrage, it also serves to intensify that pain and the rage with which it is associated. Pain – wound, trauma – cannot simply be reduced to intra-psychic processes, for, minimally, insofar as they index their contexts of occurrence and expression, they implicate that pain and that pain is implicated – circularly – in those contexts. Put no doubt too simply, the wounds the Harkis suffered and passed on to their children are supported, if not encouraged, by the political action that seeks relief from that pain.

Having said this, I now want to discuss the wound and its (unwitting) legacy to the progeny of the wounded. Though I shall focus on the Harkis, I believe that what I have to say has ever-increasing relevance to a world in which millions live in the refugee camps that are sprouting up around the world. I begin with several quotations from Rahmani's extraordinary novel, *Moze*, which recounts poetically her quest to come to terms with her father's death. A veteran of World War II, a Harki, a man who would not talk, Moze committed suicide after attending an Armistice Day ceremony in Paris. Rahmani (2003, p. 19) writes:

> Moze had died before his death.
>
> His tears, they're his death that groans. Standing, the night, outdoors, inside, alone or with us, an ailment, an affection, of tears. A death that endures.
>
> He was only this outburst without voice. A groan, like the deaf with an open mouth.
>
> This unsustainable look, this extreme figure of guilt – I want to rid myself of it, I don't, however, want to render it innocent. What can one do with this error. That which I bear, which is not mine and which I cannot forgive. How to escape alone a shouldered guilt? This life given in the cradle. Moze's error, I have to say is my flesh and my custom.

Impassioned, Rahmani captures, nonetheless, the expressive silence of the Harki and its seemingly inescapable effect on their children. It is the effect of the dead but alive father who exhibits in silence, and rage, the effects of his wounds; the dead father who through his silence, his enraged silence, cannot reveal the nature of those wounds. Wounded, the dead father, however knotted by conflicting and intolerable experiences, knows at some level what those experiences were. He can regret, he can justify, he can self-righteously blame the French, and indeed the Algerians, for what they had done to him. However overwhelmed by what Flaubert calls "the dark immensity of history" and others simply destiny, he has to assume some responsibility.

But the children can take no responsibility for what they inherited from the cradle on. They are doubly wounded. They have suffered the effects of their father's wounds – a silent but emotional transfer – without knowing what they were. They cannot resurrect them in their particularity because they never knew or experienced them in their particularity. They cannot even repress them in their particularity, though no doubt they repress some of their effects. They are tortured by an absence: an unknown they can never know but only imagine. They have – perhaps – to defend themselves against their fantasies if only because those fantasies index an absence. Some, the women in particular, strive to know. Others either deny any interest or simply take action for their cause. What they all have – the seekers, the deniers, and the activists – is a generalized story, one that contains, to be effective, fragments of particular stories (hence, the importance of witnessing) but is in its generality removed from the particular, from that which can be possessed and transmitted in its particularity. Their story can never, I believe, satisfy their desire, their curiosity, indeed their wish to forget. Nor can it protect them from the fantasies – the what if – that accompany that story. That story can only memorialize what they do not know and may in fact not want to know as it memorializes what they do know and may not want to know. It can, as such, only be a frozen – lifeless – discourse.

In a number of papers (Crapanzano, 1992, Chapters 3 and 4, 1998) I have argued that negotiations of interpersonal relations and their relevant contexts makes reference to what I have called the Third. (See also Green, Chapter 1.) The Third is a function whose functionality is stable, but whose parameters are unstable, except in the most conventional of encounters, since the parameters shift with the witting or usually unwitting appeals to it by all the parties to the encounter. I have suggested that this Third authorizes various pragmatic or indexical maneuvers that define the encounter, its relevant context, its personnel, its modes of communication, how that communication is to be taken, the appropriate etiquette, and thereby fitting interpretive strategies and their transgressive possibility. I have argued further that this function may be conceptualized as, for example, Law, Grammar, Convention, or Tradition and embodied in authoritative figures like gods, totems, and fathers.[6] I stress fathers here. In its abstraction my use of the Third, as a regulatory function in any social encounter, is logically prior to the Third as it occurs in psychoanalytic thinking. I am particularly interested in how its conceptualization and incarnation defines relationships and communicative styles and expectations. In my reading of Schreber's *Memoirs of My Nervous Illness* (1998) I stressed the interlocutory collapse that arises from a faulted Third. Schreber often became one with his real or fantasized interlocutors. Here I want to ask how the living-dead/the dead-living father, as a faulted symbolic embodiment of the Third, affects the modes of discourse of his children. I suggest that the split between living and dead is not only reflected in the children's ambivalent relationship to their fathers and other authorities (including their mothers, so evident in Belkacem's relationship to his mother), but also in the division between the frozen – the deadened – discourse of their history and the live discourse of their everyday lives. The division is porous, and both discourses are implicated in each other in ways that have to be teased out in each case. In melancholic fashion Rahmani (2003, p. 24) offers if not a way out, then a possible transformation of that deadened and deadening discourse.

> *Je suis parole de mort faisant serment non pas de mort, mais faisant serment avec la mort comme parole. Moze m'a offert la sienne.*

> I am the word of death making an oath not of death but making an oath with *death* as the word. Moze offered me his.

Rahmani does not specify here what Moze offered her. The French is ambiguous. Death or the word or both. Perhaps they cannot be separated: the father, dead or alive, from the word.

Notes

1 See Crapanzano (1996) for discussion and bibliography of the interplay between author, interlocutor, diegetic narrator and narratee, and diegetic characters.
2 For bibliography, see Moumen (2003).
3 All statistics concerning the Harkis are very approximate since there are no official records or, if there are, they are unavailable.
4 The ingestion of blood is forbidden to Muslims.
5 See, for example, Besnaci-Lancou (2003), Kemoum (2003), Kerchouche (2003), and Rahmani (2003).
6 Technically speaking, insofar as the Third authorizes various pragmatic or indexical – that is, contextualizing – maneuvers, it "figures" the metapragmatic constraints of the exchange.

References

Besnaci-Lancou, F. (2003) *Fille de Harki*, Paris: Editions de l'Atelier.

Crapanzano, V. (1992) "Glossing Emotions", in V. Crapanzano *Hermes'Dilemma and Hamlet's Desire: On the Epistemology of Interpretation*, Cambridge, MA: Harvard University Press, pp. 229–38.

—— (1996) " 'Self'-Centering Narratives", in M. Silverstein and G. Urban (eds) *Natural Histories of Discourse*, Chicago: University of Chicago Press, pp. 106–27.

—— (1998) " 'Lacking Now Is Only the Leading Idea, That Is – We, the Rays, Have No Thoughts: Interlocutory Collapse', in Daniel Paul Schreber's *Memoirs of My Nervous Illness*", *Critical Inquiry* 24(3): 737–67.

Kemoum, H. (2003) *Mohand le Harki*, Paris: Anne Carrière.

Kerchouche, D. (2003) *Mon Père, ce Harki*, Paris: Seuil.

Moumen, A. (2003) *Enter Histoire et Mèmoire: Les Rapatriés D'Algérie*, Nice: Jacques Gandini.

Rahmani, Z. (2003) *Moze*, Paris: Sabine Wespieser.

Schreber, D. P. (1998) *Memoirs of My Nervous Illness*, New York: NYRB Classics.

Chapter 11

A father is beaten to death

Julia Kristeva

> The "Christian" – he who for two thousand years has passed as a Christian – is simply a psychological self-delusion. Closely examined, it appears that, despite all his "faith", he has ruled only by his instincts – and what instincts!"
>
> (Nietzsche, *The Antichrist*, 1895)

The "dead father" is a clinical experience that I've often encountered with analysands in various forms that resonate with my countertransference. My personal experience of this was especially strong when I lost my own father under dramatic circumstances in September 1989. He died in my native Bulgaria, two months before the fall of the Berlin Wall, murdered in a supposedly socialist hospital where experiments were performed on elderly patients; family members were forbidden to visit for "fear of germs." Since bodies of practicing Christians who died were cremated to prevent religious gatherings, while mourning I could only talk about this through writing a novel.

I found myself writing, for the first time, what I called a "metaphysical detective novel." It is a genre in which I continue to work, combining philosophical, political, poetic and even psychoanalytical approaches. I entitled the first of these *The Old Man and the Wolves* (1994). My father's death drove me to see society as the criminal pact that Freud described: "Society was now based on complicity in the common crime" (1913). In addition, I felt a loss of inhibition that enabled me to unveil the repressed sadomasochism of the lovers surrounding the novel's "dead father."

The grief and melancholy I felt after my father's death, their working through and subsequent sublimation, underlie the reflection contained in this chapter. In it I share personal countertransferential connotations that vary according to sexual difference. In particular I examine the fantasy of the "father beaten to death," which I maintain lies at the foundation of the Christian faith.

A recently discovered Coptic manuscript, translated from Greek in the third or fourth century, represents Judas as having fulfilled the wishes of Jesus rather than betraying him. This breaks with the traditional notion that has fostered Christian anti-Semitism. The analyst has no need of such "proof" to understand that the putting to death of the body of Christ is not just an unfortunate accident due to some betrayal or because of the internal rivalry among the Jews. The "father beaten to death" appears to me to be a logical necessity in the Christian construction of the desiring subject in that it liberates this subject from *guilt* over the incestuous *love* of the father and for the father by its projection onto passion-suffering as the only possible path for sublimation. This logical necessity begins with a displacement of the *prohibition* of incest, or its abandonment, now transformed into punishment *by* and *of* the father. Passion is joined to suffering before finally allowing both the father's love and the love of the father in the "reconciliation" through something like Spinoza's "infinite intellectual love" or Freud's sublimation.

I should specify that I am an atheist. Yet I am convinced that psychoanalysis has the formidable privilege of being able to extend its thinking to the religious sphere where contemporary "clashes" still aggravate, if not condition, civilization's discontents. Whether believers or non-believers, we are all affected by the cultural-religious environment in which we move. My conviction is that a psychoanalytic focus could lead to important advances in this field, on which the future of psychoanalysis might even depend. I am afraid, however, that at the moment we are still very much behind in our capacity to analyze the newer variants of the crisis of civilization.

The father complex is a universal though modulated very differently through the history of different civilizations and religions. Today, confronted with the new methods of procreation described by Eric Laurent in Chapter 4, it becomes imperative to consider these varieties of father complexes, and with different kinds of dead fathers. As children of the Enlightenment, and as disciples of Freud, rushing to confirm the death of God, psychoanalysts have tended to be blind to the complexities and paradoxes that abound in the history of religion, especially as they pertain to the role of the father, both living and dead.

My intention is to propose a new reading of *Totem and Taboo* (1913) inflected by an interpretation of *A Child is Being Beaten*, in order to examine the guilt that underlies the murder of the father as the other side of the desire for him.

Freud: *A Child is Being Beaten* (S.E., vol. 17, 1919)

When Freud postulates the existence of "original fantasies"[1] in the unconscious, stemming either from the observation of certain events or from a "prehistoric truth" dating back to "the original time of the human family," he mentions only three: the primal scene, castration and seduction. The "a child is beaten" fantasy, introduced in 1919, seems to occupy a particular, privileged place between these "original fantasies" which structure the psychoanalytical interpretation of desire and the variety of individual sexual scenarios in which the singular eroticism of speaking subjects unfolds. Poised halfway between the "original" and the "individual," the mythic and the poetic, could the "a child is beaten" fantasy represent the beginning of individuation, that decisive time when the subject constitutes himself, starting with his *sexual choice*, and then as a *speaking identity*, in the ternary structure of oedipal kinship? I, male or female, excluded from the primal scene, look for my place between father and mother in order both to mark out my difference and to find my place among the ties, inseparably those of love and speaking, erotic and signifying.

Freud insisted on distinguishing between how the "a child is beaten" fantasy is played out for the little girl and the little boy. The young girl (and the woman) protects herself from her incestuous love for her father (first stage of the fantasy: "He loves me."), and from her defensive masochism (second stage of the fantasy: "No, he doesn't love me – he beats me."), by projecting it inversely onto another, preferably someone of the same sex as the coveted paternal object (third stage: "He's beating a boy."). Two questions arise here. How does this transfer occur, this delegation of feminine desire to *another object*, of the same or more frequently of the opposite sex, which shelters her as a desiring *subject*? What becomes of this *reversed delegation of desire*, which properly speaking is not repression? It is what I would call an introjection of the affection for the father and of the father: a redirection of the affect *to* the father, a *père-version* in French – from the Latin *versus* meaning "toward."

As I have commented elsewhere,[2] the little girl experiencing her first Oedipal stage with her mother, constructs a precocious alterity, a sensitive, preverbal presence, at one and the same time a pole of attraction and a pole of repulsion against which she will measure herself and from which she must separate. "You or me?" – such is her question from the outset. Unlike Narcissus, she cannot pose the question with the certainty of an Ego imbued with its own image. The little girl puts herself outside the bounds of arousal, nevertheless agitating, and protects herself against her passion. That passion is at first incestuous, then masochistic, concentrating on others: "He doesn't love you because he hits you." Who is this "you," this beaten second person who protects my desire that is guilty of loving and being loved?

Freud's interpretation is that the repressed, that follows desire, transforms paternal love into punishment of another person who is jealously hated. The prototype of this other beaten person is the mother, the little girl's humiliated rival, even in the best of patriarchal families. However, the ambivalent love of the little girl for her mother protects the envied matron and seeks other targets, thereby sheltering the loved/hated maternal object. Usually other children take the place of this beaten rival in the little girl's fantasy. But why this displacement and this masquerade?

The founder of psychoanalysis does not evoke a child's observations of other children frequently submitted to paternal punishment. His thinking suggests that it is the guilt internal to the voyeur's own repressed desire that creates the necessity for punishment, with or without observation of scenes of punishment. Where would this guilt-laden repression of the father's love, and love for the father, come from? A repression that finds its acme in the fantasy of punishment or even thrashing?

There is but a single compelling answer: It must be a repetition of the repression of incest that is both constitutive of the history of humanity and dictated by it. The foundation of the culture that characterizes our species, namely the repression of incest that underlies the original repression, necessarily engenders guilt as well as its corollary, masochism. This prehistoric guilt can lead to strong individual drives and incestuous overtones in the family, fostering a regression to pre-genital stages such as to oral-anal excitation (spanking), to masturbatory satisfaction, or to variants of the punishments – thrashings – that take the entire body for an erogenous zone.

I propose an addition to Freud's vision of this *endogenous masochism* determined by the *original repression of incest*. This very repression, pushing away incestuous desire, leads to a final *displacement of arousal*, this time not to another "object" ("a boy") but to the *medium of expression and communication itself*. Repression of incest leads to an investment of language and thought.

I am saying, therefore, that parallel to the fantasy that "another is beaten" which protects me from prohibited genital satisfaction and/or the incestuous desire to be loved and to love, I, the little girl, transfer the intensity of my desire to speaking and thought, to representation and to mental creativity. This transfer of libido onto language and intelligence is not a simple defense against guilty genital desires, for it moreover creates a new object of desire which becomes a new source of satisfaction that supplements erogenous pleasure. It is the capacity infinitely to represent and to name, to give words to genital and masochistic arousal itself. In this is the hope of finding partial substitutes to prohibited incest through symbolic work, but also of meriting this prohibited love, made guilty, to merit it by the extravagant capacity of sublimation. All humans possess that capacity, but the little girl works hard to excel at it better than anyone else.

So in addition to *masochistic perversity* ("I take pleasure in the fantasy of being beaten") is the *sublimatory jouissance* of the capacity to speak and to think *for and with* the beloved. From the beginning sublimation accompanies this perverse defense. Perversion acts as sublimation's double. This sublimatory movement re-emerges in the extreme in what I take to be the essential nuclear fantasy of Christianity: "A father is beaten to death."

The final fantasy "one beats a child" erases the representation of the masochistic scene "he beats ME" from the girl's conscience and replaces it by a double movement: on the one hand, the sadistic version of the fantasy "he beats HIM," and, on the other, a hypercritical moral conscience identified with the parental superego, in which the feminine superego takes root. The vigilance of the latter can reach a self-observation so extreme that it is akin to delirium.

The tension between this symbolic construction and excitability can engender the symptoms of the conflicted double personalities we call hysterics, a group largely composed of women. Yet this very conflict in a favorable familial context can be a strong stimulus to the development of women's symbolic creativity. On a backdrop of tamed masochism, however, the conflict is merely tempered.

The girl's strong identification with the paternal superego fused with the phallic function can work to the detriment of her feminine identifications. Causing the repression of the mother, who is reduced to castrated, sick femininity, can give rise to a virile mimetism that propels the feminine subject toward a glorification of spirituality. These all tend to reunite the little girl, and the woman she will become, with the symbolic father.

Nor does the little boy escape this sadomasochistic economy. The difference here is that his punishment fantasy, from the beginning, is experienced as passive: "I am loved by the father" (like a passive woman). To protect himself from this feminine position and the homosexuality it suggests, the boy superimposes his defensive fantasy "I'm beaten by the father" upon another fantasy that represses the father by inverting the sexual attributes of the punisher: "It's not *he* who beats me, it's SHE, a woman, the mother." This is the third stage of the male masochistic fantasy. This fantasy, culminating in the scenario of the man flagellated by a woman, protects the subject from the danger of the father's sadistic desire. It is against this desire that the son must protect himself at all cost, for it is this that persists both as an unconscious homosexual attraction and as the ultimate threat.

Although this masochistic fantasy of being beaten by a woman does not keep the man from occupying a feminine position given the nature of his passive role, it offers him a double benefit. "*That* doesn't happen between men, since I have sex with a woman. Even if I am in a passive feminine position, I haven't chosen a homosexual object. Moreover, the child beaten by his mother – who I now am – is not a passive woman, because this man suffering with the mother, that is to say me, feels as I suspected father to have felt, humiliated, always overshadowed by the power of maternal hysteria. Beaten, I join my father once again; we are united by these nuptials under the whip. After all is said and done, my man-beaten-by-a-woman masochism is the only compromise that makes me a man, perhaps belittled a bit, but who exists as I myself exist, solely through the feeling of suffering, of his suffering. My mother's husband/lover, is, of course, the man I've always desired with a fearful desire and whose sadism I no longer have reason to fear."

A father is beaten to death

Had you recognized me you would have known the Father.

(John, 14, 7–12)

Remember that for Freud the murder of the father is a foundational act, a historical reality in human civilization. In a similar way, for Christians, Christ is a historical figure and it is a real event that believers commemorate. I take these considerations into account, nevertheless distancing myself from them in what follows. I am only interested in the *psychic reality* that generates fantasies in the subject who does believe in such events, whether or not they actually occurred.

On another point: although Christ is the *Son*, according to Saint Paul, it is as the *Father* that he is put to death. From the perspective of the Trinity it is not possible that his suffering to death not also be that of the Father. What would happen intra-psychically if Jesus were not only a child or a beaten brother, but also a beaten father – beaten to death?

For the little girl, this situation means that the one she loves – the father as the object of maternal desire and as the phallic function that supports her access to representation, language and thought – finds himself in the position of the victim, similar to that of the boy subjected to the girl's sadistic fantasy. The fantasy of the "father beaten to death" could then be summarized as follows: "It's not me who's beaten; it's a boy who is beaten. Yet here is a beaten father. This father is therefore a sort of boy or brother or 'alter ego'."

By combining the son and the father, this scenario has the advantage of appeasing both the incestuous guilt that weighs on the desire for the Other (Sovereign Father) and of encouraging virile identification with this tortured man, but under the cover of the masochism promoted, even recommended by this double movement. "This beaten father and/or brother is my own kind, my alter ego, myself endowed with a male organ," says the girl or woman.

The path is thus paved in the unconscious for the Oedipal father, usually the agent of the Law and Prohibition now to be able to fuse with the subject of the guilty amorous passion that "I" am, as a girl loved by this same father. The superman father is humanized, even feminized by the suffering he undergoes; and because of this he is at once my ideal love object and my double, an ideal ego. A complicit "us" is formed by and in the father's passion. From here on we shall share love, guilt and punishment together. For my unconscious, such a father is not only positioned as an agent of the prohibition and the punishment it entails, but he is also the forbidden love object suffering from prohibition and punishment *like me*. I dedicate superego-like idealization to him, one that permeates my feeling of being a minor excluded from the primal scene to the point of actually resorbing this feeling. I thus return to the first phase of my Oedipal fantasy: "I love him and he loves me." Because of our immersion in paternal passion, this love expresses itself differently: "We are both in love, and guilty; we both deserve to be beaten to death. Only death will bring us together again."

It follows that for the unconscious, these father/daughter reunions *suspend the incest taboo* by the suffering of the two punished lovers, in such a way that this suffering necessarily will be experienced as a marriage. The suffering of the father beaten to death, sexualized under the whip of faith, this love without pity, is the paradise of masochism.

Masochism encourages sublimation by placing the fantasy of the father beaten to death at the summit of the evangelical narrative so that it calls out for our identification. Christianity does not content itself with reinforcing the prohibition of desire. It also paradoxically displaces them and opens up the path to their working through or sublimation.

The neurotic's desire is curbed and/or stimulated by the threats of judgment, condemnation and expiation, all of which mutilate that desire. However, being beaten as this son-father is beaten, the believer-subject's unconscious releases his desire from guilt's hold, enabling it to take form in what must be called sovereign, divine suffering. This is no longer the *guilty suffering* that results from *transgression*. It is rather suffering as the only way to *union* with this ideal that is the Father. This is suffering made new. Christic, it is not the flip side of the Law but the Law's suspension for the benefit of jouissance in idealized suffering. It is a jouissance in longing, in the essential failure to satisfy the desire for the father. The suffering-jouissance in that ambivalent longing is a reorientation of desire toward the father. (Remember the Latin "versus" from which is derived the French *vers le père* and hence *père-vers*.) The father beaten to death does not make suffering commonplace or banal. Nor does he authorize incest. By the glory and the grace of our suffering-together, of our com-passion, he adjusts and justifies it.

Moreover, the adoration of the beaten father leads to another fundamental consequence: beyond the surreptitiously accepted *incestuous link* with the father, it is *symbolic activity* itself that the subject is encouraged to sexualize through paternal passion.

To the extent that it is by thought and language that I connect with the beaten-to-death Other, it is indeed this *representation* of my frustrated desire that promotes the passion for the father, or the *Father as a figure of passion* that replaces the *Father of the Law*. The resexualization of the ideal father as the Man of Passion brings about an unprecedented resexualization of representation itself, of the very activity of fantasizing and of speaking. We know that while favoring compassion, the Passion of the Father of Pain invites me to enact my sadomasochistic drives, not only in everyday reality but also in acts of mortification and penance. Sadomasochistic drives are diverted beyond the reality of suffering to death to the kingdom of representation where language alone can move ahead to appropriate them. More than through my mere communication with the beaten-to-death Other, it is through the thought and speech I create around the *father beaten to death* that I become this Other's *chosen one*.

The activity of representing-speaking-thinking, attributed to the father in patrilinial societies and which connects me to him, now becomes the privileged realm of sadomasochistic pleasure, the "kingdom" indeed, where suffering opens out, justifies and appeases itself. *Sublimation* is this displacement (metonymy/metaphor) of pleasure starting with the body and culminating in representation. Perversion and sublimation are the opposite sides of this flexibility, if not of this fabulous suspension of the incest taboo induced by the beaten-to-death father.

A traversal of the death instinct?

Another essential moment of the fantasy "a father beaten to death" not only *frees* the death instinct as sadomasochistic aggression, but also confronts this drive in its profound and radical Freudian sense. This implies an undoing of ties, to living itself: *déliaison* as Green calls it. This is precisely what the Gospel narrative hints at when God the Father himself regains nothingness.

This "descent of the Father himself, after the Passion, to the deepest recesses of the earth"[3] is called *kenosis* in Greek, meaning "non-being," "nothingness," "inanity," "nullity;" but also "insane," "deceiving," (cf. the adjective *kenos* means "empty," "useless," "vain;" and the verb *kenoun*, "purge," "cut," "wipe out").[4] Beyond the beaten father's sadomasochism, we are confronted with *the suspension of the paternal function itself*, which is to say the canceling out of the capacity to represent or to symbolize that this function upholds in psychoanalytic theory. In theological terms, it is no more and no less than a matter of *the death of God*. In philosophical terms and in reference to the death instinct as a "carrying wave" of all drives, we can say: only "Thanatos is," as Deleuze (1967) wrote, meaning, "only nothingness is."

It is God himself who "suffers" in Christianity. This scandal, which theology is hesitant to confront, prefigures the modern notion that "God is dead." "God is dead." "God himself is dead" is a prodigious representation, one "which presents representation with the schism's deepest abyss."[5]

Christian theology seems barely to have mentioned the death of the Father, almost as though it prefers to deny the death of the symbolic function that it implies, given that Christ's resurrection is almost immediate. This *splicing* of this desired death, the emptying of the symbolic function (*kenosis*) on to its denial (*resurrection*) possesses tremendous therapeutic power! What a marvelous way to restore the capacity to think and to desire in an exploration that suffering pushes to the limit of sanity! Because the Father and the Mind are mortal, extinguished by the Man of Pain, who thinks up until the point of his suffering to death, they can be reborn and thought begin anew. Could this be the ultimate variant of liberty made possible by Christian suffering that Nietzsche had in mind when he observed that this abandonment to *kenosis* endows *human and divine* death on the cross with "this liberty, this sovereign detachment,/ which puts suffering/ beyond all resentment" (Nietzsche, *L'Antéchrist*, 40).

According to Green, human subjects are all the result of the long work of the negative: birth, weaning, separation and frustration. Christianity highlights the essential internal drama of becoming by presenting Christ at the heart of the split between Passion and Resurrection. In so doing, it endows itself with an immense cathartic, unconscious power. It represents in fact an advance in the understanding of the psychosexual variants of suffering that has otherwise required the development of the sciences, particularly the human sciences. Freud's psychoanalysis made a great leap forward in this direction. However, much of this long road has yet to be traversed.

In the scenario of the Father-beaten-to-death, *kenosis*, the nothingness, of the divine is a return to the fresh consciousness of a new beginning, the fantasy of resurrection. The sovereign suffering of *kenosis* is paradoxically a depassioning: *kenosis* de-eroticizes suffering. The internal necessity of the human mind to yearn for the Other, to desire the divine, to grasp for meaning, suddenly becomes empty, vain, useless, mad. The duality of desire as both an absolute and as nothingness takes Christianity to the limits of the religious, understood as a need to believe. The *kenosis* of the Father–Son is an encounter not with the religious, but with the *sacred*, if understood as thought of the unthinkable. Mystic Meister Eckhart said, "I ask God to leave me free of God." Perhaps Saint John of the Cross best expressed the presence of the impossible in the tension of desire and thought, the nothingness that punctuates the "vain pursuit"[6] proper to the need to believe. Isn't it the *sacred* to which modern knowledge aspires, when seeking not a new way to maintain the creation of meaning in the modern subject threatened by fragmentation, criminality and delirium? Isn't this the task of psychoanalytic interpretation? In my *Hatred and Forgiveness*, I suggest that interpretation is *for-giving*, not in the religious or sacred sense, but giving sense to what was non-sense, deciphering desire and/or hatred through the elucidation of transference in countertransference.

In the Christian model of the Dead Father, the believer introjects the Father's death through his identification with the Father–Son, finding resolution in *reconciliation*, the Christian version of the Jewish *alliance*. Spinoza, interpreting this ultimate mystery for modern man, writes in his *Ethics* V,[7] "God loves himself with intellectual love," translating what for the believer is a resorption of suffering into "the new body" of Christ "risen to heaven" at the right hand of the Father. Since "infinite intellectual love" coexists with an existential suffering that it is able to elucidate, Spinoza renames it "God" now transformed into joy. By having focused, on com-passion and nothingness (*kenosis*) as inseparable from "loving intelligence," the genius of Christianity provides an excellent counterweight to suffering in its sublimation and its working through by psychic and verbal activity. "I," suffering because desiring/thinking, loving/loved, am capable of *representing* my passion to myself; this *representation* is my resurrection. The mind, in love with passion, re-creates by means of loving intelligence in thoughts, narratives, paintings and music, the fruits of the tree of life.

To put it another way, Christianity at once avowed and denied the putting-to-death of the Father. This is the solution that it imposed on the universal "dead father" of the human condition. Christianity took hold of the Greco-Roman body. The beaten-to-death-Father died 2000 years ago through the passion of the Son, while post Counter-Reformation Catholicism resorbed the body of Antiquity rediscovered by the humanists, and pushed it to its limits in the Passion of Man. Painting, music and literature then developed these passions, radically shaking up the subject of monotheism.

The tension between desire and meaning, particular to the speaking being and commanding the sadomasochistic logic of human experience, is resolved in a way described by Nietzsche as a "self-delusion dominated by instincts." What follows is a summary of some of the features of this Christian heritage in modern culture and society:

- Christianity promotes a direct relationship with the Father, one comparable to the "primal identification," *direkte und unmittelbare* according to Freud (1923). This is the experience of faith, still present in derivative form in modern secular culture, especially in the sociological *need to believe*, particularly manifest in unpragmatic outbursts of behavior such as riots and revolutions so frequent in post-Catholic countries like France. These could be interpreted as so many sadomasochistic appeals to the loving Father.
- The subject renounces incest in order to rediscover the *desiring and desirable father* as a *loving and symbolic* father and to join him by introjecting the passion of the body as well as the *symbolic capacity* itself.
- This new beginning ("In the beginning there was the Word" (John 1: 1) is suffering. The speaking child must renounce his Oedipal desires and compensate for his guilt; the speaking child is a beaten child. (See Freud's "separation-frustration," Klein's "depressive position" and Lacan's "lack.")
- And yet, by relieving this infantile, incestuous, speaking and suffering humanity, through the suffering of the Father, incarnate as his Son to be beaten to death, Jesus shakes up the primary constituents of the human condition.
- The eroticization of suffering makes manifest the torment of the desiring body in the human family triangle. Incest with both parents, particularly with the father, is not just an unconscious desire. It becomes *preconscious*. The unconsciously encouraged father/daughter incest will stimulate the cultural and social dynamism of the Christian woman. The unconsciously encouraged fantasy of homosexual father/son love will tend to facilitate

a social bond based on political and warlike brotherhoods, though not
without the risk of abuse and permissiveness.

- The seam between *beaten-to-death* and *resurrection* could create a kind of
  double bind, but with an optimal Oedipal complex it could in contrast
  stimulate the sublimatory performance of the Ego. *For the girl*: "rebirth
  has never exceeded my powers," writes Colette. Detective novels, as well
  as psychoanalytic inquiry, not far from the logic of detective stories,
  could constitute the path of this kind of rebirth. *For the boy*: identification with the beaten-to-death Father and his resurrection represents
  the threat of passivization and feminization that generate anxiety, while
  on the contrary, the optimal working through of homosexuality opens
  up the possibility of thought, fertilized by the imagination.
- Both the heroism of Antiquity and the unlimited phallic power of
  monotheistic man appear to be untenable. Superman does not exist,
  sovereignty is only possible in the symbolic dimension, and this depends
  on the sadomasochism of desire.
- With regard to repression, there is no other way out of the *père-version*
  other than to transfer it to sublimation. Since the subject is inherently
  père-verse, he can only become a glorious body if he keeps to the ideal,
  while resexualizing it. And it is art, thought as art or art as thought, in all
  its variants that will be his element. Hence, perversion is in the process of
  being depenalized and depathologized in modern secular society.

As for the Death of the Father that crowns this sadomasochistic course, it
de-eroticizes incestuous passion and leaves open the possibility of another
kind of psychic experience, namely that of the abolition of the symbolic
and/or paternal power, bringing in its wake the risk of mental, social and even
biological disorganization with which we are confronted in the global era.
But the death of the father also confronts us with unknown possibilities
of freedom generated by the decline of religion – new variants of Spinoza's
"intellectual love" which for the philosopher would be of God. The love
relationship experienced in the *process of transference* is currently our modest
and difficult counterbalance. Through interpretation of transference and
countertransference, the Father is infinitely dying and resurrecting in me, if
and only if I am a subject in analysis.

Conclusion

Freud hypothesized that the prohibition of incest, on which human culture is
founded, begins with the discovery by the brothers that the father is an animal
to be killed. Of this Totem, only the Taboo has been preserved, in order to be
transformed into rules for the exchange of women, laws, names, language and
meaning. After the Holocaust, the Freudian approach was the only one that
emphasized the sadomasochistic desire for the law of the father that feeds

both the moral order and the dark *Eros* that underpins *père-version* and the sublimation of *homo religiosus*. The beginning of the third millennium, with the collapse of paternal and political authority and the massive return of the need to believe, reveals something else. The Dead Father, a necessary condition for the existence of *homo religiosus*, died on the cross 2000 years ago, but the promise of his resurrection is to be sought neither in the next world, nor in this. Then where and when? Freud, a man of the Enlightenment, began by making love lie down on the couch. In order to return to the love of the father and the mother, he gambled that the "I" is capable of going beyond its progenitors, beyond itself, and its loves, on the condition that it be subject to perpetual dissolution in analysis, in transference and countertransference. This presupposes that not only is there a Dead Father, but also figures of paternity and of loves, in the plural, in which the "I" takes pleasure, which the subject kills and resuscitates when it speaks, loves and thinks. I recently argued in a similar vein that the various "needs to believe" were just so many impassable *père-versions* of the speaking being, and that the *mère-versions* themselves, encouraged by feminism, the pill, and medicalized procreation, were no exception, and that the "clash of religions" could be elucidated by psychoanalytic attention.

We thought that "Big Mother" had replaced the Oedipal Father. This is not really the case. The Freudian analyst, whether a man or a woman, works with a new version of the "paternal function," neither totemic animal, nor Laïos/Oedipus, nor Abraham/Isaac. In the love–hate relationship of transference, the father is not only loved and hated and put to death and resuscitated, as the scriptures would have it. He is literally *atomized* and incorporated by the analysand; and this continuous dissolution–recomposition, for which the analyst stands as the guarantor, enables the analysis of drug addicts, of cases of somatization, of criminals, of borderlines. The subject of these "new maladies of the soul" develops a paradoxical identity, which reminds me of the Brownian motion of that drip painting of Jackson Pollock called *One* (One, Number 31, 1950).[8] Where has the One gone? Am I the same One when I analyze and when I am analyzed? Yes, but my identity is undecidable, without a fixed centre and without morbid repetition; I am rather a kind of serial music, an improvised dance that is nevertheless supported by an underpinning and an open order.

Such is the secret, the troubling fascination of European and American culture imbued by 2000 years of Christianity. Psychoanalysis is perhaps the best-prepared mode of thought available today to attempt to interpret its hold, as well as the grip of other world religions. Psychoanalysis offers a space for reflection in which the effort of clarification takes precedence over the deadly confrontation between a tendency to *regression* on the one hand and the explosion of the *death drives* on the other. Both together now threaten global humanity.

Notes

1 *Urfantasien*, cf. "Un cas de paranoïa", *A case of paranoïa*, 1915, SE, t. 14.
2 J. Kristeva, (2000) "The Sense and Non-Sense of Revolt, *Œdipus again*", p. 65 *sq* and in *The Extraneousness of the Phallus*, p. 94 *sq.*; (2004) "The Two-faced Œdipus", p. 406 *sq.*
3 Paul, Epître aux Ephésiens, IV: 9.
4 cf. J. Kristeva, (1989) "Holbein's Dead Christ", in *Black- Sun*, p. 105 *sq.*
5 Hegel, *Lessons on the Philosophy of Religion*, III.
6 Chant entre l'âme et l'Epoux.
7 Proposition XXXVI.
8 Museum of Modern Art, NYC.

References

Deleuze, G. (1967) "La Vénus à la fourrure", in *Présentation de Sacher Masoch*, Paris: Minuit, p. 100.
Freud, S. (1913) "Totem and Taboo", trans. James Strachey (1955), *Standard Edition*, Volume 13, London: Hogarth Press.
—— (1919) "A Child is Being Beaten: An Infantile Neurosis and Other Works", trans. James Strachey (1955), *Standard Edition*, Volume 17, London: Hogarth Press.
—— (1923) "The Ego and the Id", trans. James Strachey (1961) S*tandard Edition*, Volume 19, London: Hogarth Press.
Kristeva, J. (1989) "Holbein's Dead Christ", in J. Kristeva *Black Sun*, New York: Columbia University Press, p. 105 *sq.*
—— (1994) *The Old Man and the Wolves*, trans. B. Bray, New York: Columbia University Press.
—— (2000) "The Sense and Non-Sense of Revolt 'Œdipus again' ", in J. Kristeva *The Extraneousness of the Phallus*, New York: Columbia University Press, p. 65 *sq*, 94 *sq.*
—— (2004) "The Two-faced Œdipus", in J. Kristeva *Colette (European Perspectives)*, trans. J.-M. Todd, New York: Columbia University Press, p. 406 *sq.*
Nietzsche, F. (1895) *The Antichrist*, trans. R. J Hollingdale (1968), Harmondsworth: Penguin, p. 161.

Epilogue

Helen C. Meyers

This book is an extraordinarily rich volume, rich in its diversity as well as in its originality. I feel quite privileged to have been asked to write an epilogue referring to ideas stimulated by it. There are many different ways to approach this task: as a summary, as an abstract of what the different contributors have in common or how they differ; or how these contributions relate to the authors' other work and how they relate to each other. Further, one could explore how they do or do not relate to classic Freudian theory, to current ego psychology, or to any other psychoanalytic theory in current use. I am particularly pleased with the selection of authors in this volume. For many years now I have been interested in studying and teaching different psychoanalytic approaches, differentiating them as well as correlating them, trying to integrate them into one overarching usable psychoanalytic theory. This involves, of course, a thorough knowledge of each approach both theoretically and clinically. I have included ego psychology, self-psychology, developmental theory, and intersubjectivity from the United States; and, from England, Kleinian and post-Kleinian, Bionian and Winnicottian contributions.

The French have been less well known in the United States. This volume, in addition to some North American and British thinkers, provides some of those less known to American readers. French theoretical contributions by contemporary Lacanians like Eric Laurent as well as some of Lacan's former pupils such as André Green and his followers, Aisenstein, Kristeva, Urribarri and Perelberg, appear here. They dramatically help to round out our knowledge.

I would like in particular to consider three concepts, all addressed by the authors in their different ways: "the dead father" and the paternal role; the use of the negative; and "thirdness." I will try to compare, to differentiate, and to integrate their usage.

Why was the topic of the "dead father" chosen for this psychoanalytic inquiry? Are we referring to the impact of the real death of a real father, or the internalized image of a dead father, the image representing the father metaphorically killed by his offspring, the well-known image of the primal horde? It appears that all of the contributors to this volume, whatever else they are interested in, are concerned with the internal image of a dead father, although, interestingly, they also tend to bring in the actual death of a real father. The internal image of the dead father appears to be both important and even essential for normal psychological development, but it can also become the basis for pathology. For example, according to Freudian theory, in healthy development the father has to be eliminated by the son for him to resolve his Oedipal complex and for the dead father to become the superego. In André Green's theory the father image likewise must be killed for normal development to take place. His idea takes off from, and is inspired by, his original, well-known concept of the "dead mother," where the real mother can be alive alongside a dead internalized or metaphoric mother image; and the internal mother image can be alive when the real mother is dead. It is important to understand here that the internal "dead" mother or father representations, the superego in the ego-psychological terms, is more powerful in its impact than the actual real parent ever was. Similar to Green, most of the French authors also assume that normal development requires a transition from the real external father to the internalized dead or lost father. According to Aisenstein, for instance, if this unconscious intermediate step to the internalized dead father is omitted, the aggression contained and controlled in this process may instead be expressed directly in somatization rather than in a more complex neurosis. This can be viewed in developmental theory as a process on a preverbal level or prefantasy level. Furthermore, according to other authors such as Perelberg, the elimination of this intermediate step that binds the aggression may instead loosen this aggression and lead to direct expression of overt aggression or violence. That is, such patients may hurt themselves in suicidal gestures or, through traumatic action, hurt others. Several contributors describe their work with non-neurotic patients, adding an important step in our psychoanalytic understanding.

I found fascinating Kristeva's commentary on the unconscious killing of the father in her discussion of the development of Christianity. While I always thought of Christianity as the basic religion of forgiveness, being mediated by the all-important good mother, in Kristeva's chapter, to my surprise, she stresses the basic role of the killing of the son who stands for the father. She thus sees it as a murderous religion where the killing of the father is basic to normal development. Thus, in what would appear as a contradiction, the killing of the father seems to be necessary or essential for psychic development. At the same time, the potentially damaging effects of the unconscious killing of the father have been stressed by these authors, illustrated in their work with borderline and psychotically violent patients. Another example of this damaging effect is described by Crapanzano in his work with the Harki Algerians. The Harkis maintained their loyalty to the French during the Algerian War of Independence. After the war they were reviled by both fellow Algerians and the French. Unfortunately they became a severely isolated social group. The whole experience, repressed and not worked through, resulted finally in what the Crapanzano describes as a "frozen discourse" among them, a rigid narrative that interfered with further development. It yielded no resolution of developmental conflicts when looked at from an ego psychological point of view. This "frozen discourse" consisted of simple repetitions of a story rather than any attempt at emotional understanding and conflict resolution. This developmental arrest impeded the group's ability to relate in a meaningful way. It was only with an enormous effort that Crapanzano was able to get the younger generation past beyond this defensive pattern. This pattern was basically a "denial" of their parents' experience, represented by an unchangeable internal image of a dead father in the second generation's inner world. Again translated into the language of ego psychology, we would refer to this as a developmental arrest or a fixation. When the image of the dead father was given up and changed to a more alive image, the empty "frozen discourse" was given up as well. This work then enabled the second generation to move on and ego development to be resumed.

Now, why this concern with the dead father? One reason is that, thanks to André Green and Margaret Mahler, psychoanalysts have paid a great deal of attention to the impact of the dead mother. However, very little has been written about the impact of the dead father, even though Freud was always concerned about the relationship with father. He considered the father's loss to be the most traumatic event in a man's life. Now we return to father again. Why now? – It's about time and it's about us. – A new war has been started, and fathers are getting killed. It also is the one hundred and fiftieth anniversary of the birth of the father of our theory, Sigmund Freud. And then there is this notion held by many men today that they are less powerful, that their authority has been diminished, and that their position of power has been invaded by the woman. Post Freudian analysts such as Klein, Mahler, Winnicott, and other child analysts and developmentalists spent decades investigating the mother/child relationship. In their eyes the father is dead. At least he had gone missing in the theory. I think that was one of the original reasons for the selection of the topic of this volume's study.

I believe that this view of men is quite unrealistic. On the contrary, the man's role in the family has become more powerful, more real, and more meaningful. The previous cultural or social distance established between the man and his family was not a sign of greater strength, but the result of both external arrangements as well as probably a number of internal conflicts and fears. But I have a feeling that we have not lost the authoritarian image of the father, that this loss is only a superficial impression. Tayler, in this volume, writes of the former perception of the authoritarian teacher who has now become a "friend," of whom the student is not afraid. However, I think that this is not really so. Candidates in psychoanalytic schools, for example, are just as afraid to speak up to their instructors as they had been in the past, leading to all the same problems as in earlier years. This may, however, be only my impression and probably can be disputed; but it is a very firm impression. This volume has examined both external cultural and social changes, as well as the internal psychodynamic aspects of these changes. All of the chapters have addressed the subject from various points of view. As I see it, the more gratifying experience of family life for the father may lead to a changing internal paternal representation. I find it intriguing that many people think of this as a loss of paternal power and authority – a "helpless, dead" father – when really it seems to me to be a sign of the greater strength, authority, and aliveness of the paternal function. What I mean is that the real father has more of a real impact on his children and his family. In clinical work, this is often demonstrated by the patients' revelations of their unconscious awareness of their views of their own fathers at the same time as their fears of the demands put on them in the role of father, as demonstrated in dreams and fantasies.

How has this change in the father image and paternal function, if there be one, come about? It has been suggested that it is due to external cultural phenomena such as women working outside the home. However, that appears to me too superficial an explanation. Green has suggested that this change is more related to the internal work of the negative. That would imply that more attention needs to be paid to the work of the negative instincts, the destructive, angry, rageful feelings, rather than only to the impact of the positive instincts such as life, love, and sex as Freud postulated. Work on the negative feelings appears to have been neglected somewhat in the development of analytic theory like Freud's classic libido theory. Since then there has been much more emphasis on the impact and strength of negative instincts such as hate and rage and aggression, as in the work of Parens and Mahler. The independent development of the negative instincts, starting with Freud's elucidation of the "death instinct" around World War I, has been put to the forefront as motivating drives only more recently. This relates to Green's discussion of the "work of the negative" which he believes to be very influential. Melanie Klein does too in that she accepts Freud's notion of the death instinct. The death instinct and the work of the negative have been less emphasized by North American ego psychologists, who do not believe in an inborn death instinct, but rather think of hostility and aggression as reactive emotions, not primary ones. Thus, while for Green the killing or elimination of the father image, the work of the negative, is primary, this difficult concept has not achieved wide acceptance in North American psychoanalytic thinking in which aggression and hostility are taken predominantly to be a result of frustration, deprivation, etc., rather than primary (Meyers). The idea that an impetus for change can emerge from negative instincts such as destruction and rage, while dominant in French and British psychoanalytic theory, is less present in North American analytic theory.

All this brings us to the concept of the "third," so prominent among this volume's theorists: the "third" – as an agent, the "third" as a balance to the dyadic structure. Let me back up for a minute. The original notion of analytic treatment in Freud suggested work with a single person, that is, the patient who needed to be understood, analyzed and helped. As time went by, we analysts internalized our intellectual surround of democracy and realized that the analytic interchange was not work on a single person but was the input of two people in relation to each other. Psychoanalysis came to be understood as the exchange of input from the two people involved, the analyst and the patient, their two subjective views contributing to the process. This has been conceptualized as "intersubjectivity." In other words, it involves both transference and countertransference as active agents that have to be understood and taken into consideration. Currently analysts have added the concept of the "third," the third contributor to the interchange, the presence of the third agent in the process. This third is said to be present from the beginning. It is present in the mind of the mother as an image of the father, and in the mind of the child as an image of the father; the third is present in the analytic endeavor in the mind of patient or analyst as an image of husband or wife or parent or child, not physically there, but very influential in the unconscious or preconscious of the patient or the analyst. Different authors have attributed different roles and different timing to this third contributor. Melanie Klein saw it as the presence of the father as a balance to the early dyadic mother/child combination appearing at approximately nine months of age. Abelin saw the third as the father balancing the intensity of the mother/child relationship at the age of three. Kanzer wrote about the presence of the analyst in the patient's dreams at all times. Ogden took this concept of the third and intersubjectivity to an even more abstract level in that he argued that we did not analyze the patient's subjectivity or the analyst's subjectivity, but a third process created in the interaction of the two subjectivities. He called this the "analytic third." This analytic third then was the subject of our analytic effort. Many theorists do not subscribe to this conceptualization, but did see some merit in thinking about analyzing a process rather than a person's subjectivity. Green saw this "third" as existing from the beginning as a distant, observing other; the role of the father. This role can also by played by a supervisor or the analyst's analyst. The timing of the presence of this "third" varies from author to author. The "third" assumes increasing importance in theories that involve cultural and societal input, the interpersonal theories which deal with the present rather than the past. The "dead father" thus is ever present as a "third" from the beginning of life. James Herzog, in his excellent contribution, gives a convincing and detailed description of this "third," i.e. the father's presence from the beginning from an ego psychological point of view.

I have found the contributions in this to be most stimulating. Much of what I have put together, of course, does not arise only from these actual chapters, but rather from my knowledge of the previous work of the authors, the basis for much of my thinking. This epilogue, then, is a sample of my attempt to integrate the different psychoanalytic theories currently on the scene, all of which are in need of further discussion and critical thinking.

This book has brought out some fascinating, different and yet useful new conceptualizations, some imported from foreign lands while others are home-grown. It promises to enrich psychoanalytic thinking, both enlarging and deepening the analytic field.

References

Abelin, E. L. (1975) "Some Further Observations and Comments on the Earliest Role of the Father", *International Journal of Psychoanalysis* 56: 293–302.

Kanzer, M. (1957) "Panel Reports – Acting out and its Relation to Impulse Disorders", *Journal of the American Psychoanalytic Association* 5: 136–45.

Klein, M. (1948) "A Contribution to the Theory of Anxiety and Guilt", *International Journal of Psychoanalysis* 29: 114–23.

Meyers, H. C. (unpublished) "On the Development of Aggression", a presentation given at the Philadelphia Psychoanalytic Society in the Fall of 1995.

Ogden, T. (1979) "On Projective Identification", *International Journal of Psychoanalysis* 60: 357–73.

Parens, H. (1973) "Aggression: A Reconsideration", *Journal of the American Psychoanalytic Association* 21: 34–60.

Index

Note: Page numbers in **bold** indicate entire chapters devoted to a subject, within which more specific references may be identified.

abandonment: by God/the father 41; maternal 33
Abelin, Ernst L. 108, 193
Abraham 66–7, 77, 78, 99; sacrifice of Isaac (*Akedah*) 62, 77, 78
absence 32; of awareness 41 *see also* (the) unconscious; bearing witness to 163; clinical material with an "absent father" 68–70, 124–7; fantasized and real loss of the father 41; lack *see* lack; the missing object 114; mother's absence as indication of her desire for the father 113 *see also* name of the father: Lacanian theory; play and 114, 116; reaching the father through 29–30, 44; symbolization and the representation of an object that is absent 114; as a threat 33; torture of absence, in the unknown but imagined 171
admiration 126
Aeschylus: *Eumenides* 94
affect 51
aggression 43; aggressive availability 140–1; aggressive fantasies 42, 43, 138; fixations and 43; and the gaze of the Other 60; identification with the aggressor 29; paternal toleration of 35; pregenital 43; as a reactive emotion 192; regulation with help of external object 113, 138; representation of 112; sadomasochistic 182 *see also* sadomasochism; *see also* hostility
Akedah 62, 77, 78
alliance 183

alpha function 38–9
ambivalence 37, 38, 41, 118; resulting from hostility 43, 44
anal phase 43
anality, primary 43
analytic father 38
analytic filiation 48, 53–4, 55
analytic object 31, 53
analytic practice: clinical material with "an absent father" 68–70, 124–7; clinical material showing symbolization process of the dead father 112–19; countertransference in *see* countertransference; creation of space for thirdness 118; dimensions of 69; Green's theoretical model of functioning 53–4; process of binding representations and affects 114; self-disclosure of the analyst in 108; transference in *see* transference; *see also* psychoanalysis
analytic setting 39–40, 51, 53–4, 114, 118, 142
analytic space (Spielraum) 133, 139, 140, 142
analytic third 39–40, 53–4, 119, 193
anorexia nervosa 59
anxiety: in oral phase 26; structural theory of 53
Anzieu, D. 9, 48, 50, 104
aphasia 10
archaic heritage 24–5
art: depiction of the Dead Father 12–13; Oedipus conflict and 10
Arthur legend 13, 17n8

artists 12
Ascham, Roger 154
Association for Psychoanalytic Medicine 3
atheism 81–2
attachment: to the mother 107 *see also* mother–child dyad; "straightforward" (Freud) 28; theory 4, 107
Aubrey, John 157–8
Auden, W. H. 91
Aufhebung (sublation) 79, 87–8n11
Augustine of Hippo 59, 157
Aulagnier, P. 48, 50, 51, 54–5
authority: killing the author/authority/ father 11–12; paternal *see* paternal authority
authors/ the author 12
"auto-haunting" the father **91–101**
awareness: absence of 41; *see also* (the) unconscious; in criminals 32

Bacchofen, J. J. 122–3
bastardy 40
ben Elizer, David (ancestor of Thomas Laqueur) 99
Bergman, Martin 47
Berkeley Free Speech movement 104
Berri, Claude 103
bijection 83, 89n26
Bilgrami, A. 7
Bin Laden, Osama 1
Bion, W. R. 30, 36, 45, 51; on knowledge 38–9
birth control 2, 27
bisexuality: bisexual identification with absent parental couple making love 113; psychic 115
Bleger, J. 51
Bloom, Harold 14
body: capacities 15; corporal punishment 146, 157, 178; dysmorphic disorder 59; effects of failure of paternal function on subject's body **65–73**; as a field of battle 1; the ideal body 60; identity transformations of 33–4; the imaginary body 5, 59–60; "imaginative elaboration" of bodily functions 30; and *jouissance* 61, 72; lack of possession of 33–4; the masculine body 138, 139, 140; of the mother 126; mutilation 78; physical contact *see* physical contact; and regression to

pre-genital stages 178; self confused with 32; sense of bodily unity 116; the sexual body 1, 2; transformation (piercing and tattooing) 71–3; *see also* embodiment
Bonaparte, Marie 106
Bonneval Colloquium 49, 50, 54
books: Freud on good books 11; stealing of 11–12
boundaries: between internal and external worlds 31, 36; self's loss of 34, 36
Braunschweig, D. and Fain, M. 113, 129n6
breasts: breastfeeding 42, 112, 113; infant's hallucination of the pleasure of the breast 72; movement from having to being the breast 114; playing with the breast 42
British Psychoanalytic Society 123
Browne, Sir Thomas 155
Butler, Judith 83, 84

Camden, William 154
Castoriadis, C. 50
castration 52, 61, 67, 78, 93; complex 26, 52, 78; of the father 114; father as agent of 77, 79; fear of 42, 94; Freudian, v. symbolic 51; mother as messenger of castration threat 114; passage from totem to the castrating father 78; "red anxiety" and 53; threat 3, 77, 114
cathexis: decathexis 49, 127; libidinal 113; of the mother 113, 114; object-cathexis 27, 73, 114
Catholicism 184
Cecil, William 157
Chabrol, Claude 103
Chasseguet-Smirgel, Janine 117
children: "a child is beaten" fantasy 176–9; child rearing 27; child rights 84; clinical material showing symbolization process of the dead father 112–18; dyad with mother *see* mother–child dyad; formation of abstract representation 111; Freud on paternal and maternal ties of 27–8; and the passage of a wound 165–72; sleeplessness 112
Christianity: Catholicism 184; effect on art and language as the resurrection of

the murdered sign 150, 184–5; and the "father beaten to death" 147–50, 175–6, 178, 180–6
Cinémathèque, Paris 103
civilization 28
Clark, D. L. 155, 156
Clinton, Bill 1
Cohn-Bendit, Daniel (Danny the Red) 103, 104
com-passion 181, 183
communal living experiments 76
communication 114; affective 116; ritual of 115; *see also* language
complexes: castration complex 26, 52, 78; father (*Vaterkomplex*) 23–5, 48, 176; *see also* Oedipus conflict/complex; Oedipus complex *see* Oedipus conflict/complex
condensation 9, 26
Confrontation (journal) 50
conglomerate 141, 142; constructing and deconstructing the conglomerate **133–42**
consciousness: conscious manifestation of unconscious repressed desires 41–2
contraception 2, 27
conversion hysterias 59
Copernicus, Nicolaus 154
corporal punishment 146, 157, 178
countertransference 118, 136–7, 139–40, 175, 185, 186, 193
Crapanzano, Vincent 2
creativity: creative universe of cultural experience 31; the father as a God-like creator 41; father-like feeling of the creative artist 12; Freud and 14; of language 153; paternal transmission of capacity for 114–15; reflection and 31; and the transmission of the tradition of innovation 118; as way to face the unlimited maternal space 113–14; women's symbolic creativity 179
criminals 32; criminal activity of a patient 68; the criminal pact 175
Kronos 23, 93
culture: birth of civilization 28; Christianity's effect on art and language as the resurrection of the murdered sign 150, 184–5; creative universe of cultural experience 31; cultural clash of the 1960s 2; cultural transformations and changes in

paternal function 3; erasure of the Law of the Father 103–4; Freud and 10, 65, 94, 104, 145; *Geistigkeit* 94–5, 99; and the ideal body 60; invention of paternity as great step forward for 94; *Kulturfortschritt* 94; language and the transcendence of cultural limits 9; linguistic foundation 10; and the living-dead father **163–72**; and the narrative of the symbolic father 9; origins in consequences of killing the father 3, 111; "paternal cultural" 65; patriarchal *see* patriarchal culture; relational culture in psychoanalysis 108; and the repression of incest 178; sacrifice of sexuality and the passage from nature to 121; of the spirit (*geistige Kultur*) 99; as the symbolic father 61, 104

Damasio, A. 141
de Mijolla, A. 111
death: "a father beaten to death" **175–86**; children's ideas of 23; dreams of death of parents 23; of fathers *see under* fathers; killing the author/authority/father 11–12; link of fatherhood with sexuality and 118; murder of the father *see* murder of the father; Oedipus conflict and *see* Oedipus conflict/complex
death drive/instinct 42, 49–50, 60, 192; "a father beaten to death" and 182–5; confrontation with regression 186
death wish, towards the father 42, 92–3; *see also* Oedipus conflict/complex
decathexis 49, 127
deconstruction of fatherhood 51, 75; constructing and deconstructing the conglomerate **133–42**; Lacanian 77–80, 88n15
defenses: arising from pleasurable physical contact with the father 42; conflict with drives 49; defensive fantasies 177–9; oral phase 26; primary 49
Deleuze, G. 50, 54–5, 182
denial 33
Derrida, Jacques 16, 50, 54–5
desire: to be the father 76; body of 1; destruction and 82; dialectic interplay between satisfaction and 114; and

encounter with an Other 61; and the existence of the child 34; expression in the analytic situation 38; forbidden 121; incestuous 178, 179 *see also* incest; infant 36, 113; kept alive by castration 61; masochism and investment in 72; mother's desire of the father 10, 43, 113; objects of 34, 63, 68, 79–80; obstruction of the child's desire 49; "original fantasies" and 176; of the Other 81, 82; of the *père-version* 63, 177; phallus as the mother's desire 26; regulation of 121; religion and 122; renunciation of *see* renunciation; representation of frustrated desires 181; repressed desires and their conscious manifestation 41–2; and repression of incest 178; for revenge 40; reversed delegation of 177; silenced 37; society and control over 124; subject and 117; sublimation of 181 *see also* sublimation; unsatisfied desire and the transference 38

despair 125, 165, 169

destructiveness 29, 33, 82; and the work of the negative 56

Deutsch, Helene 106

Diamond, Jared 16

differentiation 39, 124; dialectical, between inside and outside 114–15; of genders and generations through the incest taboo 124, 128; through an idealized figure 111; during the mirror stage 117

discharge 56, 72

disguise 15

disillusionment 38

disintegration 36; of filial and community ties 63, 73

displacement 9, 26, 114; of arousal 178

dissociation 32

distance: allowing room for a third 113; keeping the mother at a distance 33; paternal 41, 82–3; between patient and analyst 32; *see also* space

distributive justice 83

Donne, John 154

dreams: about dead fathers 93; dream work 26; Freud and 9, 23, 92–3; of impenetrability 125–6; linguistic structure 9; navel of the dream 15; not dependent on sleep 30; patient dream

about Heidegger 70; and self-continuity 30; space for 113; status compared to reality 69; violent 69; wishes and 23

dress code 1

drives 49–50; aggressive 138; conflict with defenses 49; death drive *see* death drive/instinct; masochism and 72; prehistoric guilt and 178; sadomasochistic 181–2, 185–6; theory of 60–1; towards *jouissance* 83; and the work of the negative 56

drugs 2

dyads: the deceitfulness of the dyad 139–41; dyadic motivation for speech 10; dyadic relation to the murdered father 149–50; and frustration at the intrusive third 112; mother–child dyad *see* mother–child dyad; shift from the dyad to the triad 38

Eckhart, Meister 183

education: grammar schools 155, 158; as mitigation of the effects of the Fall 157; modern secondary 158–9; pedagogy and the verbal authority of the dead father **153–60**; *studia humanitatis* 154

ego: a "double", ideal ego 149, 180; imaginary status of 60; sublimatory performance of the Ego 185

ego ideal 27, 28; the father's support of 119; symbolic identification as nucleus of 116–17

Ego Psychology 47

embodiment: of the Dead Father in the word 9; dissociation and 32; effects of failure of paternal function on subject's body **65–73**; father's embodiment of the Law 49, 67; *see also* law

empathy: the unempathic mother 106

emptiness 29, 118; *see also* lack

Erasmus, Desiderius 154

Eros 60

eroticism: erotic impulses 15; eroticization of suffering 184; protection of the mother from her own erotic feelings 113

ethics, and the war against terror 2

Études Freudiennes (journal) 50

exchange 26, 118, 124, 128

existence: distance between actual existence and the "for all" 82; etymology of "exist" 88n14; in opposition to the essence of the function 78–9; symbolic prenatal existence 10

exogamy 122, 124

experience, structured by the symbolic 13

Fairburn, W. R. D. 108

faith 184; belief 149, 183, 184, 186; in a woman 81–2

families: attempts to eliminate the family 76; changing nature and roles in society 25, 43; Gide on 75–6; man's role in the family 191; narrative and 10–11

family values 2

fantasies: "a father beaten to death" fantasy 180–6; aggressive 42, 43, 138; defensive 177–9; Freud's "a child is beaten" fantasy 176–9; incestuous 113; and the maintenance of the mother–child dyad 36; Oedipal 180–1 see also Oedipus conflict/complex; original 178; of the primal scene 53; space for 113; that accompany narrative 171–2

Father Tongue (Latin) 154–5, 156, 158–9

fatherhood (*Vaterschaft*) 93–4; deconstruction of see deconstruction of fatherhood; link with sexuality and death 118; lost aspects of 28, 29; voice of 100–1

fathers/the symbolic father: as agent of castration 77, 79; ambivalent feelings to 37, 38; the analytic father 38; as anti-sexual observer 28; approached through femininity 80–3; artificial presence of the father 36; authority see paternal authority; "auto-haunting" of the father **91–101**; childrens' relationship with 11, 43–5; Christianity and the death of the father/son 147–50, 175–6, 178, 180–6; clinical material showing symbolization process of the dead father 112–19; clinical material with an "absent father" 68–70, 124–7; construction of the lost father **23–45**, 36, 45; cultural transformations and changes in paternal function 3; culture and the narrative of the symbolic father 9; death of an already dead figure (the father) 42; deconstruction of fatherhood see deconstruction of fatherhood; distance of 41; division into the real, the symbolic and the imaginary 77–8; early aspects of paternity in Freud 27–8; as embodiment of the Law 49, 67 see also law; in the era of the global market 75–6; facing the communities of *jouissance* 83–5; the father captured by the function 78–9; father complex (*Vaterkomplex*) 23–5, 48, 176 see also Oedipus conflict/complex; father-like feeling of the creative artist 12; fatherhood see fatherhood (*Vaterschaft*); the father's look 28; as a figure of passion 181; fixations to the father 37; functions of see paternal function; as God-like creators 41; the Idealized Father 26, 56, 117; the imaginary father see imaginary father; importance of dead fathers in the psychic life 15; the incestuous father 121; increased power of the dead father 12, 24, 40–1, 93–4, 122–3, 145; invisibility of the father 123; killing the author/authority/father 11–12; the Lacanian father and the spoken word 77–8; the living-dead father **163–72**; love and see love; mediation role 35, 43–4; as the mother's incestuous object 114; movement from mother to father in the mirror stage 117; multiple fathers in an infant's life 117; murder of see murder of the father; name of the father see name of the father; the narcissistic father 124; narrative and 10–11; negation of the dead father 127; "new fathers"/the new paternity 29, 75; non-integration of the father into the internal world 36–7; object "*a*" formulation of 79–80; the Oedipal father 3–4, 180 see also Oedipus conflict/complex; the Other as Sovereign Father 180; paternal figure as a source of the work of the negative 56; paternal function see paternal function; paternal identification 27, 42–3, 49, 67; paternal metaphor 48–9, 51; paternal perversion 79, 80, 83, 84, 85, 121; *père-version* 63, 79, 80, 177,

182, 185, 186; physical contact by 42;
presence *see* presence; primal father
see primal father; as a ram 78; reaching
the father through absence 29–30, 44;
relation between the dead father and
the death drive 49–50; as a remnant
incommensurable with norms 86–7;
representations in the analytic space
133–42; represented by the analytic
frame 39–40 *see also* analytic father;
roles *see* paternal function; secret
preservation of external father 37; shift
from the murdered father to the dead
father 121; space created by 33; as
sperm 76; the superman father 149,
180; symbolization process of the dead
father **111–19**; "the real father" 62, 76,
85, 86–7, 117; as the "third" 15, 28, 35,
172; the totem/totemic father 62–3, 77;
in triangular relationship with mother
and child 27–8, 29, 43–5; turn from
mother to father as victory of
intellectuality over sensuality 28, 65,
111, 123, 145–6; *Urvater* (originary
father) 66–7; the violent and
incestuous father 121; witnessing by
28, 35, 166; the "would be" father 37
fear: of castration 42, 94; of close
contact 32–3; father's generation of
tenderness and 24; and the internal
mother 34, 126; and love of the father
41–2; phallus as signifier of universal
fears 123; phobias 24, 36; and the
rejection of an interposing third 35–6;
of retaliation 35, 42; of the unlimited
maternal space 115
Fedida, P. 50
feelings: unconscious 41–2; work on the
negative feelings 192; *see also* work of
the negative
feminism 2
fetishism 80
fighting: the father figure 45;
play-fighting 42
filiation: analytic 48, 53–4, 55; attempts
to nullify 67, 71; bearing mourning 61,
69; contemporary 86
fishing 11, 17n5
fixations 26; aggression and 43; to the
father 37; homosexual 43; masochistic
29; pregenital 43; refraction of violent
psychotic fixations through the mother

figure 44–5; transitions from negative
Oedipus complex to earlier fixations 45
Flaubert, Gustave 171
Fleming, Thomas 1
FLN (Front de Libération Nationale)
164, 168
Florio, John 154
Fonagy, Peter 35
foreclosure 36
Forrester, J. 9
"Fort-Da" game 114
frames: analytic setting 39–40, 51, 53–4,
114, 118; boundaries *see* boundaries;
"language apparatus" 53
fraternal pact 54
Frazer, James: *Totemism and Exogamy*
24
freedom: expansion of subject's liberty in
relation to drives and the object 56;
liberation from guilt 176, 181
Freud, Anna 106
Freud, Ernst (Sigmund's grandson) 114
Freud, Jakob 93, 111
Freud, Sigmund 111; "A Child is Being
Beaten" 176–9; on the analytic frame
40; *On Aphasia* 9; aphasia 10; burning
of his books in Berlin 14; centrality of
the Father in 104–6; Christianity 184;
complicity in the common crime 175;
creativity 14; culture 10, 65, 94, 104,
145; dreams 9, 23, 92–3; drive theory
60, 72 *see also* drives; early aspects of
paternity 27–8; *Female Sexuality* 105;
on good books 11; guilt 24, 118, 122,
145, 177–8; *The Interpretation of
Dreams* 23, 66, 93, 128; invisibility of
the father 123; and language 9–10;
Lévi-Strauss and 25; on the loss of a
father 41, 66, 105, 128; and love 186;
memories of his father 93, 104, 105;
Moses and Monotheism 3, 14, 24, 28,
40, 65, 66, 94, 105, 123–4, 145–6;
mother's death 105; Oedipus conflict
3, 13–14, 23–5, 41, 124, 190;
organizational function of the father
3; originary masochism 72; paternal
identification 42; patriarchal order 28;
post-Freudian filiation 48; pre-
psychoanalytic work 16n1; quest to
assimilate into a patriarchal culture
104; and the real or mythical nature of
the killing of the father 121; Schreber

case 67, 104; self-analysis 104; sublimation 176; *Totem and Taboo* myth 3, 12, 13, 25, 66, 77–8, 93–4, 122, 141, 145, 185; turn from mother to father as victory of intellectuality over sensuality 28, 65, 111, 123, 145–6; the unconscious 14; *Urvater* 66–7; *Vaterkomplex* 23–5, 48; *Vaterschaft* (fatherhood) 93–4; on writing 16
Fromm, Erich 108
Front de Libération Nationale (FLN) 164, 168
Frost, Robert 153, 159–60
frozen discourse 163, 165–72, 191
Fuller, Thomas 157
function: bijective 83, 89n26; existence in opposition to the essense of the function 78–9; father as model of the function 80; at the level of the "for all" 83; paternal *see* paternal function
fundamentalism 2, 7
funerary rituals 122–3

Galbraith, David 103
Galileo 154
gay rights 2
Geist 94, 96; *geistige Kultur* (culture of the spirit) 99; Spirit *see* Spirit
Geistigkeit 94–5, 99
"gender trouble" 83–4
Gerstner, Louis, Jr. 159
Gide, André 75
Gil, Alexander, the Elder 157
Gilbert, William 154
Glater, Jonathan D. 159
God: abandonment by God/the father 41; death of 182; divine name 77; divine transmission of phallic power 66–7; effectiveness of God's word 77; every father as 78; imaginary father as foundation for the providential image of 62, 78; interventions of 81; space between man and 34; the suffering God 147–9, 182–5; the Trinity 147–8, 150, 180; as *Vatershaft* 93
Godard, Jean-Luc 103
Godelier, M. 128n2, 129n8
Goethe, Johann W. von 11, 24, 48, 142
Goldberg, Arnold 108
Grail quest 13, 15
grammar schools 155, 158

grandfathers 97, 98, 104, 111, 116, 166; the idealized/mythic grandfather 111, 117
Graves, Robert 80, 81, 88n17
Green, André 10, 13, **47–55**; on the ancestral identity of the father 11; and the father, after Lacan 50–5; and the father, beyond Lacan 55–7; and the father, with Lacan 48–50; *Key Ideas for a Contemporary Psychoanalysis* 47, 56; *Language of Psychoanalysis* 53–5; *Nouvelle Revue de Psychanalyse* 50; "On Thirdness" 56; *Propaedeutics: Metapsychology Revisited* 56; *Psychic Causality* 55, 56; question-raising function of the father 15; "The Dead Mother" 4, 52–3, 113, 190, 191; *The Work of the Negative* 56, 183
Greenberg, J. R. and Mitchell, S. A. 108
Greenberg, V. 9
Grubrich-Simitis, I. 9
guilt: Christianity and 176, 180–1, 184; Freud's explanation of 24, 118, 122, 145, 177–8; liberation from 176, 181; from physical contact with the father 42; sublimation and 176, 178; unconscious guilt feelings and 40–2; underlying murder of the father as other side of desire for him 176–8, 180–1, 184

Harkis **163–72**, 190–1
Harry Potter stories (J. K. Rowling) 15
Hartmann, H. 108
Harvey, William 154
Hassoun, Jacques 121
hatred: of the father 41, 78, 122; imaginary father as father of hatred 78; mother's expression of regressed hatred through the child 45; of oneself 78; of the symbolic father 118
hedonism 83
Hegelianism 78–9
Heidegger, Martin 153; dream about 70
heredity 66–7; phylogenetic inheritance/transmission 11, 25
Herzog, James 108
Hesiod: *Theogony* 93
heterosexual utopia 83
Hippolytus 148
historicizing 69

Holt, Robert 107
homosexuality: defensive fantasies against 179; fantasies of homosexual father/son love 184–5; homosexual fixations 43
hopelessness 125
Horney, Karen 106, 108
hostility: ambivalence resulting from 43; confusion of hostile feelings with their unconscious effects 40–1; infantile sexuality and 44; as a reactive emotion 192; violence aroused by 68; see also aggression
humiliation 61, 68, 93, 179
Huntington, S. 1
hysteria 66, 179; conversion 59

idealization: differentiation through an idealized figure 111; a "double", ideal ego 149, 180; function of the ideal 56; the ideal body 60; the Idealized Father 26, 56, 117; idealized objects and tri-bi-angularity 51; of mourning 41; resexualization of the ideal father 181
identification: with the aggressor 29; bisexual 113; incest taboo and 124; paternal 27, 42–3, 49, 67, 73, 114, 119; with paternal superego 178, 179; with the patient 45; primal/primary 67, 184; process 116–17; symbolic 116–17; totemic 78; and the way to otherness 73
identity: individuation and a speaking identity 177; narrative and 10–11; paradoxical 186; the presence of the self 30; the search for self 31–2; self-definition based on sexual practice 84; "Self's identity DIY" 71; sexual 117; and transformations of the body 33–4
imaginary body 5, 59–60
imaginary father 16, 78; "auto-haunting" of the father **91–101**; disappearance of the totemic father behind 62–3, 77–8; as foundation for the providential image of God 62, 78; imaginary regained power of the murdered father 93–4
impenetrability 125–6, 127
impotence 49
incest: Christian renunciation of 184; incestuous fantasies 113; the incestuous father 121; incestuous guilt 180 see also guilt; incestuous love of/ for the father 176, 177, 179; incestuous objects 53, 114; preconscious 184; repression 178; suspension of the taboo 181, 182; taboo 111, 122, 124, 128, 181, 182
individuation 177
infantile sexuality 44
infants: coping with emptiness with help of the father figure 118; mirror stage 59–60, 115–17; mother–infant dyad see mother–child dyad; multiple fathers in an infant's life 117
inheritance 66–7; phylogenetic transmission and 11, 25
innovation 118
instinctual renunciation 111
integration 116, 117, 123; integrative satisfaction 141
interpretation 9, 39–40, 185; not absolute 14; representing the father 39–40; universal unconscious capacity for 24
intersubjectivity 193
introjection 31, 177, 183, 184
intrusion 112, 126
Isaac, Bondage of (*Akedah*) 62, 77, 78

John Paul II 14
Johnson, Samuel (Dr Johnson) 153
Jonson, Ben 153, 154, 158, 160–1n1
jouissance 60–1, 72, 80–2; the father facing the communities of 83–5; sublimatory 178, 181; suffering-*jouissance* 60, 181
Judas 176

K function 39
Kanzer, M. 193
kenosis 182–3
Kernberg, O. 108
Kessler, Michael 159
Khan, M. 50
kibbutzim 76
King Arthur legend 13, 17n8
kinship 81–2; incest see incest; Oedipal 177
Klein, Florence 134–5
Klein, George 107
Klein, Melanie 4, 26, 30, 106, 108, 191; and the "third" 193
Kleinism 47

knowledge: and the gap between conception and perception 38; not knowing 39; as something in the process of being known 38–9; *see also* (the) unknowable; (the) unknown
Kohon, G. 10, 34
Kohut, H. 106, 107–8
Kripke, S. 84
Kristeva, J. 10, 15

Lacan, Jacques 3, 4, 25–6, 30, 34, 55–7; André Green and the father, with 48–50; anti-Hegelianism 78–9; concept of exchange 26; on the creativity of language 153; deconstruction of fatherhood 77–80, 88n15; development of symbolic capacity 116; *The Ethics of Psychoanalysis* 62, 77–8; and femininity 80; God's being in the Real 150; identification process 116–17; *jouissance* 60–1, 72, 80, 82, 85; on the language-like structure of the unconscious 10, 50–1, 53; Name of the Father 77–8, 79, 80–1, 113, 146; object "*a*" 79–80; on the Oedipus conflict 16; *père-version* 63, 79, 80; primordial father 121; symbolic aspects of speech 10; "The Mirror Stage" 59–60; "the real father" 85, 86
Lacanism 47, 48–54
lack 52, 67; communication of 114; emptiness 29; and the image of the body 60; of masochistic investment of a painful expectation 72–3; metaphysics of 51; of possession of one's body 33–4; *see also* emptiness
Langlois, Henri 103
language: Christianity's effect on art and language as the resurrection of the murdered sign 184–5; creativity of 153; embodiment of the Dead Father in the word 9; the father and the development of 160; father as source of child's capacity for 119; Father Tongue (Latin) 154–5, 156, 158–9; Freud and 9–10; frozen discourse 163, 165–72, 191; influence of the unconscious on everyday speech 10; "language apparatus" 53; linguistic foundation of culture 10; Mother Tongue (English) 154, 157, 158, 159; and the movement towards symbolism 114; "other language" 15; pedagogy and the verbal authority of the dead father **153–60**; psychoanalysis and the study of 10; and repression of incest 178; rooting of psychoanalysis in 9; speech *see* speech; spoken language of the (m)Other 60; structuring the subject 10; tertiary processes as bridge between language and psychic apparatus 54; and the transcendence of cultural limits 9; as vector in the structuring of experience 13; Wittgenstein and 84
Laplanche, J. 48, 51, 54–5; and Leclaire, S. 48–9; *New Foundations for Psychoanalysis* 55; and Pontalis, J. B. 50; *Psychanalyse à l'Université* 50
Laqueur, Ernst 94–5, 97–8, 99
Laqueur, Moritz (ancestor of Thomas Laqueur) 99
Laqueur, Siegfried (great grandfather of Thomas Laqueur) 98
Laqueur, Thomas 11; *Making Sex: Body and Gender from the Greeks to Freud* 71
Laqueur, Walter A. (grandfather of Thomas Laqueur) 96–8
Laqueur, Werner 96
Latin 154–5, 156, 158–9
Laugier, S. 84–5
law 145; death of the father as law 103–4; embodiment by the father 49, 67; Law of the Father 103–4, 107, 124, 145, 185–6; Mosaic 14; recurrence through the ages of the dead father and 15
Le Breton, David 71
Leclaire, S. 54–5
LePin, Jacques 134
Lessing, G. E.: *Nathan the Wise* 95
Lévi-Strauss, Claude 13, 25, 124, 129n5
Lévinas, Emmanuel 73
libido 60
Lily, William 156
listening 38, 68, 135, 136, 137
loneliness 118
loss 52; of boundaries 34, 36; of castration *see* castration; construction of the lost father **23–45**, 36, 45, 137, 139–41, 142; Freud on the loss of a father 41, 66, 105; object loss and "*blanc* anxiety" 53; separation as 33; terror at losing parental bond 116

love: analytic frame standing for
    mother's love 118; "censorship of the
    lover" 113; and encounter with an
    Other 61; fantasies of homosexual
    father/son love 184–5; and the father
    44, 122; Freud and 186; frozen 53;
    incestuous love of/for the father 176,
    177, 179; intellectual 176, 183, 185;
    masochism and 181; of and for the
    mother 44; between mother and father
    44; and rejection 100; the third in the
    love triangle 114
Lucas, George: *Star Wars* 12–13
Lyotard, J. F. 50

McDougall, J. 48
madness: maternal 44; need to be part of
    a common madness 35; understanding
    and 33
Mahl, George 104
Mahler, M. S. 108, 191, 192
Mahoney, Patrick 9
Major, R. 50
Makarenko, Anton 76, 87n5
Makari, G. and Shapiro, T. 10
Malory, Sir Thomas 13, 15
Malraux, André 103
Mannomi, O. 54–5
marriage 76
Martial 86–7
Marxism 25
masochism 71–3; female masochistic
    fantasy 178–9, 180; male masochistic
    fantasy 179; masochistic fixations 29;
    masochistic passion 177; and the
    repression of incest 178;
    sadomasochism 51, 175, 178–9, 181–2,
    185–6; sublimation and 181
masturbation 178
maturity morality 107
mediation 39; language as a mediator 53;
    paternal role of separation 35, 43–4,
    80; symbolization and 114
mentalization 69
mère-versions 186
merger 113
Merleau-Ponty, M. 54–5
metaphors 114
metaphysics of "lack" (*manque*) 51
Michelangelo: *Creation of Adam* 34
Miller, J.-A. 60, 76, 80–1, 85
Mills, J. 108

Milton, John 12, 154, 157, 158
mimetism 179
mirror relationships 35, 115, 116; in the
    analytic setting 39; automatic 36;
    see also reflection
mirror stage 59–60, 115–17
modernity 83
Monarchianism 148
monotheism 123
Montaigne, M. 155, 156
"moral majority" 2
morality, and the Oedipus conflict 10
Moses 111
mother–child dyad 26, 28, 34, 35, 43–4;
    in attachment theory 107; and the
    interposition of the father 35;
    maintained through fantasies 36;
    merger 113; rejected by Green as
    theoretical/clinical model 51–2
Mother Tongue (English) 154, 157, 158,
    159
mothers/the mother: absence as
    indication of her desire for the father
    113 *see also* name of the father:
    Lacanian theory; the day and the night
    mother 129n6; and the "dead father
    syndrome" in psychoanalytic theory
    106; the dead mother 4, 52–3, 190;
    dyad with child *see* mother–child dyad;
    as earth-like seed bed for a son 94;
    Freud and the death of his mother 105;
    keeping the mother at a distance 33;
    maternal abandonment 33; "maternal
    function" 52–3; "maternal madness"
    44; maternal perversion 80, 124–7; the
    maternal space 114; *mère-version* 186;
    as messenger of castration threat 114;
    mother-centred perspective on psychic
    life 26; *Mutterschaft* (motherhood) 94;
    object-cathexis towards 27;
    omnipotent internal mother 36, 44–5;
    and originary masochism 72; as the
    Other 26; pathogenic developmental
    effects of disturbed mothers 107–8;
    possession by the mother 33, 34–5, 45;
    the pre-Oedipal mother 34; repression
    of the mother 179; restoration to their
    place in psychoanalysis 106;
    unconscious aggressive fantasies
    towards 42; violence and the internal
    mother 33, 124–7; voice of the internal
    mother 33; the "voracious" mother 45

mourning 41, 42, 53, 69; and hatred of
the symbolic father 118; incest taboo
and 124; of narcissistic infantile
omnipotence 118
Mulcaster, Richard 157
murder of the father 3, 23, 24, 111;
Christianity and "the father beaten to
death" 147–50, 175–6, 178, 180–6;
followed by remorse and guilt 122,
145; Freud and the real or mythical
nature of 121; impossibility of early
father murder 37; murder of the sign
150; Oedipal see Oedipus conflict/
complex; and the origin of culture 3,
111; primal parricide 24, 121, 122;
repression of 25; shift from the
murdered father to the dead father
121; unceasing attacks on the father
37; unconscious nature of parricide 40;
Urvater and 66–7; the violent and
incestuous father 121; violent rejection
of intervening third (the father) 35–6
murderous feelings/impulses 33, 36,
141–2; religion as antidote to 122
music 135–6
mutilation 78

name changing 118–19
name of the father 15, 26, 48–9, 51, 62,
76, 86; deceptive semblance of 83;
Lacanian theory 77–8, 79, 80–1, 113,
146; the totem father 62–3, 77
naming the son 104, 111, 116, 117
narcissism 43, 49; as defense against "in-
security" 60; mirror stage as basis for
60; movement to object-cathexis from
114; narcissistic availability 140–1; the
narcissistic father 124; narcissistic
omnipotence 117, 118; narcissistic
trauma 53; phallic narcissistic pleasure
116; primary 49, 53
narratives: distortion/mutilation of 14;
human development and 10–11;
identity and 10–11; of men and women
of the Harki children's generation
166–70; phylogenetic inheritance and
11; shared narratives in analytic work
69; transgenerational transmission 11
National Socialism 25
negative therapeutic reaction 72
the negative, work of 56, 183, 192
neurosis 82

Newton, Sir Isaac 154
Nietzsche, Friedrich Wilhelm 182–3, 184
nostalgia: of the father 28; and fixations
to the father 37
not knowing 39
nothingness 182–3
Nouvelle Revue de Psychanalyse (journal)
50
NYU Post Doctoral Program 108

objectalization/re-objectalization 69
objects: the analytic object 31, 53; of
desire 34, 63, 68, 79–80 see also desire;
expulsion of mental contents in
engulfing objects 36; expulsion of the
object from the body 78; idealized 51;
incestuous 53, 114; the missing object
114 see also absence; name of the
father as object of belief 146 see also
name of the father; object "a" 79–80;
object-cathexis 27, 73, 114; object loss
and "blanc anxiety" 53; open
triangularity and the object's other
52–3, 56–7; the primary object 127;
regulation of aggression with help of
external object 113; renunciation of
see renunciation; subjective 30;
symbolization and the representation
of an object that is absent 114;
symbolization as mediation between
object and subject 114; the "third",
and mental permutations of 31;
transitional 38, 116
Oedipus conflict/complex 3, 4; and
desexualization in paternal ties 27–8;
foundational convergence of religion,
morals, society and art on 10; Freud
and 3, 13–14, 23–5, 41, 124, 190;
Oedipal fantasy 180–1; the Oedipal
father 3–4, 180; as an open triangle
with a substitutable third 52–3, 56–7;
post-Lacanian thinking 51; pregenital
fixations and the negative Oedipus
complex 43; primal scene and
castration complex in 52; and the seam
between beaten-to-death and
resurrection 185; and society's sense of
tragedy 16; the story and the complex
121; thirdness and 52–3, 56–7;
transitions from negative complex to
earlier fixations 45; tri-bi-angularity in
51; in western culture 12–13; and the

Wolf Man 26; and the work of the negative 56
Oedipus legend 66
Oedipus Rex 40
omnipotence: death of the father as limitation of 111; fantasies of omnipotent control 30; limited by death of father 111; narcissistic 117, 118; not knowing as form of 39; omnipotent internal mother 36, 37, 44–5; relinquishing of 38; of thoughts 28; tri-by-angularity and the omnipotent bad 51
Ong, Walter J. 158
oral phase 26
order 15
originary functioning 51
originary masochism 72–3
the Other 26, 60; encounter with and Other 61, 116; the father as the figure of otherness 117–18; *jouissance* and 80–1; a mirror's representation of 116 *see also* mirror relationships; mirror stage; as Sovereign Father 180; yearning for 183; *see also* (the) unconscious
Ovid: *Narcissus* 117

pain 71–3, 170; the passage of a wound **163–72**
paranoia 67
parapraxes 10
Paris Cinémathèque 103
Paris psychosomatic school 68, 73n1
parricide *see* murder of the father
passion 139, 149; child's protection against 177; com-passion 181, 183; divine Passion 148–9, 181–3; immersion in paternal 180–1; Passion of Man 184; passion-suffering 176, 181
paternal authority 75, 191–2; death of the father as law 103–4; pedagogy and the verbal authority of the dead father **153–60**; undermining of father's authority by women in the workplace 2
paternal function: analytic work with new version of 186; as central to structuring and functioning of the mind 60; cultural changes in 3; and the dead father 189–92; death of God and

the suspension of 182–5; decline of 62, 63; in the development of identity 117; effects of failure on subject's body **65–73**; as embodiment of the Law 49, 67 *see also* law; the father captured by the function 78–9; of helping infant cope with emptiness 118; of the idealized father 117; involving the real mother as well as father 65; Lacanian models of 79; of mediation 35, 43–4, 80; narrative 9–11; organizational 3; as the organizer/regulator 115, 138, 141; in play 42, 138; of protection 43; question-raising 15; of recognition 85; of separation 35, 43–4, 80; socializing function of the dead father 145; as superego 119; transcultural 73; of verticality 115, 116
paternal identification 27, 42–3, 49, 73, 114, 119; with the dead and the idealized father 67
paternal metaphor 48–9, 51
paternal perversion 79, 80, 83, 84, 85, 121
paternal virtue 82–3
paternity *see* fatherhood (*Vaterschaft*)
pathogenesis 106, 107
patriarchal culture: the Dead Father in western cultural tradition 12–13; Freud and 65, 94, 104; pedagogy and the verbal authority of the dead father **153–60**
patriarchal order 26–7, 28, 41; Orestes' defense against charge of matricide as founding myth of patriarchy 94
patriarchal utopia 83
Paul, Saint 148, 180
pedagogy **153–60**
Peirce, Charles Sanders 56, 150
Pelikan, J. 147, 148
penetration 69, 126, 135–6, 140
père-versions 63, 79, 80, 177, 182, 185, 186
Perelberg, R. J. 27, 39–40
Perrier, F. 48, 50
perversion 66, 82; making *one* woman the cause of the father's 83; masochistic perversity 178 *see also* masochism; maternal 80, 124–7; paternal 79, 80, 83, 84, 85, 121; *père-version* and 80; sexual 67; sublimation and 178, 182
pervert games 45

phallic *jouissance* 61
phallic narcissistic pleasure 116
phallic power, transmission of 66–7
phallus 122–3; baby's identification with
    father's 113; decline in psychoanalytic
    theory 106; fetishist's attachment to
    80; and funerary rituals 122–3,
    128–9n3; and the Idealized Father 26;
    as paternal metaphor 49; post-death
    transformation into a phallic ancestor
    122
phobias 24, 36
phylogenetic inheritance/transmission
    11, 25
physical contact: by fathers 42; fear of
    close contact 32–3; with the mother 41,
    42
pictograms 51
play 30–1, 114; absence and 114, 116;
    with the breast 42; internal 114;
    play-fighting 42; play space 139;
    playfulness as internal mobility 142;
    representation of aggression in 112;
    rough and tumble, with fathers 138;
    trauma and 141
pleasure principle 72; phallic narcissistic
    pleasure 116
Pollock, Jackson 186
Pontalis, J. B. 48, 54–5; *Nouvelle Revue de
    Psychanalyse* 50
possession: of the mother 29; by the
    mother 33, 34–5, 45; taking possession
    of one's creations 30
preconscious incest 184
predominance of the signifier 25–6
prenatal constitution 10, 11
presence: artificial presence of the father
    36; of the dead father 42; of the father
    as a return of the repressed 41; forms
    of 30–1; of the real in the symbolic
    86
Pride Parade 84
primal deed 24, 121, 122
primal father 3, 93–4, 121, 145, 149;
    father of the primal horde 62, 145,
    149, 189–90; *Urvater* 66–7
primal scene 52, 53, 126, 127
primary anality 43
primary narcissism 49, 53
projection 116; transference *see*
    transference
Psychanalyse à l'Université (journal) 50

psyche: infantile 118; murderous tensions
    within the psyche 141–2; pre-Oedipal
    triangular matrix 52; tertiary matrix of
    the psyche 57; tertiary processes as
    bridge between language and psychic
    apparatus 54
psychic bisexuality 115
psychic space 41, 113, 127, 135–6
psychoanalysis: attack of science on 25;
    changes brought about by self-
    psychology 108; "classical" 25; clinical
    material showing symbolization
    process of the dead father 112–19;
    clinical material with an "absent
    father" 68–70, 124–7; clinical material
    with representations of the father in
    the analytic space 134–42;
    contemporary, beyond Lacan 55–7;
    dimensions of analytic work 69;
    Green's theoretical model of
    functioning of analytic practice 53–4;
    Lacanian period 48–50; language
    and 9, 10; "normalizing" enterprise
    of 25; post-Lacanian 50–5; practice
    of the symbolic function 14;
    relationalists 108; restoration of
    importance of mother/mothering
    106; study of pregenital stages 26
psychoanalytic listening 38, 68, 135, 136,
    137
psychoanalytic setting 39–40, 51, 53–4,
    114, 118, 142
psychodrama 69
psychosis 29, 72, 82, 124–6; duality and
    thirdness 34; refraction of violent
    psychotic fixations through the mother
    figure 44–5; treatments with psychotics
    32
punishment 149–50, 176, 177–8, 179,
    180; corporal 146, 157, 178;
    humiliating 61, 68
Putman, Hilary 84

Rachi (Solomon Ben Isaac) 77, 78, 87n7
rage 33; conversion into outrage 170
Rahmani, Zahia 165, 171, 172
ram 77, 78
Rangell, L. 107
Rappaport, David 107
rebirth 185
reciprocity 122
recognition 85

reconciliation 183
reflection 31, 116; absence and 32; in
    analytic interpretation 39; mirror
    relationships *see* mirror relationships;
    mirror stage 59–60, 115–17; of a
    reflection 35
regression 178; confrontation with the
    death drives 186
regulation 113, 121, 138, 141; parental
    co-regulation 141
relationalism 108
relationships: aggressive fantasies in
    negative relationships 42; giving up of
    the fusional relationship 35; mediation
    and 43–4; mirror 35, 36 *see also*
    reflection; mirror stage and the basis
    for 60; mother–child *see* mother–child
    dyad; therapeutic relationship *see*
    therapeutic relationship; triangular *see*
    triangular relationships; without
    threat to partners 34
religion: Freud and the role of god in
    monotheistic religions 123;
    fundamentalism 2; *homo religiosis* 186;
    and the Oedipus conflict 10; and the
    "parental complex" 122; *see also*
    Christianity; God
remorse 122, 145
renunciation 49–50, 56, 124, 128; and
    taboo of incest 111, 122, 124, 128, 181,
    182, 184
repatriation 101
repetition 32; compulsion 72; of frozen
    discourse 163, 165–72, 191
representation 15, 30; of aggression 112;
    analytical process of binding
    representations and affects 114;
    asymmetric 141; "ceilinged"
    representational mobility and motility
    141; changes in social and imaginary
    representations of fathers 65; child's
    formation of abstract representation
    111; development of capacity of 113;
    father as source of child's capacity for
    119; of the father by the analytic
    setting 39–40; of the father in the
    analytic space **133–42**; of frustrated
    desires 181; post-Lacanian thinking
    51; and repression of incest 178;
    resexualization of 181; the subject and
    30, 32; symbolization and the
    representation of an object that is

absent 114; thirdness in Green's
    general theory of 56–7; as a threat 33
repression 15, 28, 43; and "a child is
    beaten" fantasy 177–8; assimilation
    into paternal metaphor 48; of the
    father's murder 25; impotence and 49;
    of incest 178 *see also* incest: taboo; of
    the mother 179; structuring role of 49;
    sublimation and 185
resurrection 182, 183, 185
retranscription 9
revision 9
Richards, A. K. 106
Ricoeur, P. 54–5
rivalry: with the father 37–8 *see also*
    Oedipus conflict/complex; and the
    gaze of the Other 60
Rizzuto, A. 9
rock and roll 2
Rosenberg, B. 72
Rosenfeld, H. 39
Rosolato, G. 26, 48, 50, 51, 54–5, 66, 124
Ross, J. M. 4, 108
Roudinesco, E. 48
Rousseau, Jean Jacques 157
Rowling, J. K.: *Harry Potter* stories 15
rules, no absolute interpretation of 14
Rumsfeld, Donald 86

the sacred 2, 15, 41, 183
sacrifice: of Isaac (*Akedah*) 62, 77, 78; of
    sexuality **121–8**, 129n8
sadomasochism 51, 175, 178–9, 181–2,
    185–6
Saint-Pierre, J.-B. Bernardin de 75–6
Salome, Lou Andreas 106
Sandburg, Carl 160
Savio, Mario 104
Schafer, Roy 107
Schlomo, Rabbi 111
Scholem, Gershom 95
schoolmaster 158, 159
Schreber, D. P. 67, 104, 172
self: confused with the body 32; the
    conglomerate self 141, 142; imaginary
    status of the ego 60; loss of boundaries
    34, 36; the presence of the self 30; as a
    relatively recent concept 59; search for
    31–2; "Self's identity DIY" 71; sense
    of 32
self-analysis 107–8; Freud's 104
self-continuity 30

self-hatred 78
self-image 59–60
self-observation 28, 179
self-psychology 4, 106, 107, 108
semblance 83
semiotics: semiotic functioning 51; and
the Trinity 150
separation 33; expulsion of the object
from the body 78; funerary rituals and
123; paternal role of 35, 43–4, 80;
through violence 127
September 11 terrorist attacks 1, 112
sexuality: backlash to the sexual
revolution 2; bisexual identification
with absent parental couple making
love 113; the dead father and the
sacrifice of **121–8**, 129n8; demand for
recognition 85; desexualization 27–8,
49, 113–14; disjunction of desire and
reproduction 129n8; eroticism see
eroticism; funerals and 122–3,
128–9n3; "gender trouble" 83–4;
homosexuality see homosexuality;
infantile 44; link of fatherhood with
death and 118; masturbation 178; pain
and 72; parental renunciation of their
children's sexuality 128; between
parents, and their availability to the
child 140–1; penetration 69, 126,
135–6, 140; phallus see phallus;
promiscuity 126, 127; psychic
bisexuality 115; resexualization of the
ideal father and representation 181;
self-definition based on sexual practice
84; the sexual body 1, 2; sexual
perversions 67; society and control
over 124; violence and 69; and the
work of the negative 56; see also desire
Shakespeare, William 14–15, 26, 154;
bastardy theme in 40; Edward de Vere
as 40; *Henry VI Part 2* 154; importance
of dead fathers in the psychic life 15;
Troilus and Cressida 156
Sidney, Sir Philip 157
signifiers: affect and 51; of demarcation
51; heterogeneity of the
psychoanalytic signifier 50; and the
imaginary body 60; of the Other 60;
predominance of 25–6, 53
"silent majority" 2
sleeplessness 112
slips of the tongue 10

Smith, William Robertson 24
society: and complicity in the common
crime 175; Freud and the origins of
social institutions 24; incest taboo as
basis of social contract 111, 122; and
the Oedipus conflict 10; sense of
tragedy 16; social events and theory
25; social role/condition of women 4,
27; social unrest of the 1960s 2;
socializing function of the dead father
145; the Third as a regulatory function
in social encounter 172; see also
culture
sociological deconstruction of
fatherhood 75
somatization 73n1, 186, 190
somnambulism 38
Sorbonne 103
space: of abandonment 33; absence and
32; analytic (Spielraum) 133, 139, 140,
142; created by the father's existence
33; for fantasies and dreams 113;
between God and man 34;
intermediate space of experience 114;
maternal 114; and the mother's
internal world 113; play space 139;
psychic 41, 113, 127, 135–6; for
symbolization 114; for thirdness 118;
see also distance
spanking 178
speech: dyadic and triangular elements
10; Freud and 10; frozen discourse
163, 165–72, 191; influence of the
unconscious on 10; Lacanian father's
transmission of effectiveness of the
spoken word 77–8; and the
"omnipotence of thoughts" 28
Speilrein, Sabina 106
Spense, Donald 107
Spenser, Edmund 154
sperm 76, 77, 137; banks 76, 137; donors
137
Sphinx 66, 67
Spielraum (analytic space) 133, 139, 140,
142
Spinoza, Benedict de 141, 176, 183
Spirit 150; see also *Geist*
Stanford University 159
Star Wars (George Lucas) 12–13
Stein, C. 48, 50
Stoller, R. 72
Stow, John 155

structuralism 25
student protests (1968) 103
subject 31; acting as such 84; coexisting
    functions and the subject 31;
    expansion of subject's liberty in
    relation to drives and the object 56;
    individuation of the subject 177;
    linguistic structuring of the subject 10;
    representation and the subject 30, 32;
    self-construction as a subject 117;
    symbolization as mediation between
    object and 114; tertiary constitution
    and functioning 57
subjective experience 31
subjective objects 30
subjectivity 116
sublation (*Aufhebung*) 79, 87–8n11
sublimation 27, 28, 150, 175, 182;
    capacity fostered through
    symbolization 114; Christianity and
    176, 181, 183–4; of *homo religiosis* 186;
    masochism and 181; of physical pain
    72; repression and 185; sublimatory
    jouissance 178, 181; sublimatory
    performance of the Ego 185
suffering: eroticization of 184; of the
    Harkis **163–72**; passion-suffering 176,
    181; the suffering God 147–9, 182–5;
    suffering-*jouissance* 60, 181 *see also*
    jouissance; together (com-passion)
    181, 183
suicide 125, 134, 164, 171
superego: "a child is beaten" fantasy and
    178–9; birth of 28; father as superego
    figure 119; feminine 178–9; paternal
    178, 179; personification of 13; as
    Vaterschaft 93
superman 149, 180, 185
the symbolic: as a closed system referring
    to a "beyond" 7; destruction of 14,
    185; development of symbolic capacity
    116; division of fathers into the real,
    the symbolic and the imaginary 77–8;
    function of the symbolic father *see*
    paternal function; the narcissistic and
    the symbolic father 124; and the
    predominance of the signifier 25–6;
    psychoanalysts as practitioners of the
    symbolic function 14; rigidity in 2; and
    the structuring of experience 13;
    symbolic and drive activity 49, 181; the
    symbolic father *see* fathers/the

symbolic father; symbolic
    identification 116–17; symbolic order
    26, 51, 54; symbolism of the phallus
    122–3 *see also* phallus; symbolization
    process of the symbolic father **111–19**;
    "the real father" as the presence of the
    real in 86; traversing of the imaginary
    by 60
symbolization 51, 146; analytic object as
    matrix of transitional and tertiary
    53–4; the dead father and the
    symbolization process **111–19**; non-
    "phallocentric theory of" 52; and the
    representation of an object that is
    absent 114; sublimation and 114;
    triadic matrix of meaning and 56–7
symptoms: linguistic structure 9; role of
    fantasies in 36

Target, Mary 35
tattooing 71–3
teaching/pedagogy **153–60**
terrorism: destruction of the symbolic
    14; and the disappearance of the father
    2; September 11 terrorist attacks 1, 112
tertiary processes 51, 54
Thanatos 60
theft 11–12
therapeutic relationship: and the internal
    mother 33; search for self as motive for
    31
thirdness/the "third" 4, 192–3; analytic
    third 39–40, 53–4, 119, 193;
    "configurations of thirdness" 56–7;
    and the development of identity 117;
    dual relationships and thirdness 34, 35;
    father as 15, 28, 35, 172; the intrusive
    third 112; living-dead father as 172; in
    the love triangle 114; of multiple
    fathers in an infant's life 117; Oedipus
    complex and 52–3, 56–7; open triangle
    with a substitutable third 52–3, 56–7;
    as promoter of psychic activity 31;
    reflective role 35; as a regulatory
    function in social encounter 172; as a
    requirement for meaning and
    understanding 39–40, 117, 118, 128;
    role in symbolization 114; space for
    118; the Spirit as 150; transition from
    potential to effective thirdness 52; as a
    triadic matrix of meaning and
    symbolization 56–7; triadic reality and

the analytic space 141–2; the word as 53; *see also* triads; triangular relationships

thought: alternative worlds in 31; "complex thought" 56; expulsion of mental contents 36–7; the father and the development of 160; father as source of child's capacity for 119; formation of abstract representation 111; linguistic structure 9; "omnipotence of thoughts" 28; and repression of incest 178

thumb sucking 115, 116

Ticho, E. 9

time 118

toilet training 68

Topique (journal) 50

totemism 24, 77; the totem/totemic father 62–3, 77; totemic ancestors 123; totemic identification 78

transfer: emotional 171; of libido 178; reversed delegation of desire 177; to sublimation 185 *see also* sublimation

transference 139, 193; and the analytic father 38, 139–40; exchange through 118; function of 38; lost father found in 45, 139–40; love relationship of 185, 186; secret preservation of external father 37

transitional objects 38, 116

transitions 118

translation 32, 100, 150

transmission: of archaic heritage 25; of effectiveness of the spoken word 77–8; frozen discourse and the passage of a wound **163–72**, 191; of narrative 11; of the tradition of innovation 118

trauma 10, 141; frozen discourse and the passage of a wound **163–72**, 191; narcissistic 53; of a terrorist attack 112, 113

triads: of the intra-psychic vertex 57; originary triadic scheme 52; shift from the dyad to the triad 38, 142; triadic matrix of meaning and symbolization 56–7; *see also* thirdness/the "third"; triangular relationships

triangular relationships 27–8, 29, 43–5; foreclosure of triangulation 36; open triangularity and the object's other 52–3, 56–7; ternary structure of oedipal kinship 177; transition from

potential to effective thirdness 52; *see also* thirdness/the "third"; triads

Trinity of God 147–8, 150, 180

Truffaut, François 103

the unconscious: discovery of 14; expression in wishful dreams 23; influence on everyday speech 10; Lacan on the structure of 10; as the Other 60; reduction to language 48; repressed desires and their conscious manifestation 41–2; structured "like a language" 10, 50–1, 53

understanding, madness and 33

universal/eternal–particular opposition 78–9, 80–1

the unknowable 15

the unknown 15; but imagined 171–2; *see also* not knowing

unpleasure 28, 49, 72

Urvater 66–7

utopias 83; communal 76

Valabrega, J. P. 50

Vaterschaft see fatherhood

veils 1

Vere, Edward de, 17th Earl of Oxford 40

verticality 115, 116

Viderman, S. 54–5

Vietnam War protests 2

violence: arousal by a hostile world 68; in dreams 69; identification with the aggressor 29; the internal mother and 33, 124–7; maternal 124–5; as a means of separation 127; society and control over 124; the violent and incestuous father 121; violent impulses 15; violent rejection of intervening third (the father) 35–6

Virgil 156, 157

Weber, Max 7, 92

welfare state 83

White Goddess 80–1, 88n17

Widlocher, D. 48

William Alanson White Institute 108

Winnicott, Donald 4, 30, 31, 38, 51, 108, 191; father's role 36, 117; and the "good enough mother" 106; intermediate space of experience 114

Winter, Sara 105

wishes: relationship to a primal deed 24;
   wishful dreams 23
witnesses: bearing witness to absence
   163; fathers as 28, 35, 166; of ourselves
   38
Wittgenstein, Ludwig 84
Wolf Man 26
women's dress code 1
women's social role/condition 4, 27

Wordsworth, William 157
work of the negative 56, 183, 192
World Trade Center attack 1, 112
writing: as an element of speech 10; and
   the transmission of narrative 11

Yerushalmi, Josef 24

Zeus 93